# We Chose Alaska

## -1-

Henry Milette

**We Chose Alaska -1-**
Copyright © 2017 Henry Milette

# We Chose Alaska

**All rights reserved.** No part of this book may be reproduced, stored in a retrieval system, or transmitted in any form or by any means—electronic, mechanical, photocopying, recording, or otherwise—without prior permission in writing from the copyright holder except as provided by USA copyright law.

Printed in the United States of America

## Acknowledgements

I'd like to express my heartfelt thank you to my wife for loving and understanding me, all these years. She did a magnificent job proofing my work. We are a real team. I wish to thank my author friend, Chuck Dean, who provided me with the technical help so necessary to start this endeavor. I also want to express my thanks to Google Map for having such a wonderful media that brings life into the stories.

# We Chose Alaska

## CONTENTS

| | | |
|---|---|---|
| chapter 1 | ....... | How I Met Marcia |
| chapter 2 | ........ | La Danse Apache |
| chapter 3 | ........ | Our First Date |
| chapter 4 | ........ | Sleeping Under Stars |
| chapter 5 | ........ | The Beginning |
| chapter 6 | ........ | Going Hunting |
| chapter 7 | ........ | Scuba Diving |
| chapter 8 | ........ | Wrapping it up |
| chapter 9 | ........ | South of the Border |
| chapter 10 | ........ | The Wedding |
| chapter 11 | ........ | The Honeymoon |
| chapter 12 | ......... | The Preparation |
| chapter 13 | ......... | Northward to Alaska |
| chapter 14 | .......... | Alaska-Canada Hwy. |
| chapter 15 | ......... | Our Beginning |
| chapter 16 | ........ | Anchorage Life |
| chapter 17 | ......... | Graduation |
| chapter 18 | ......... | New Career |
| chapter 19 | ......... | The Carrot |
| chapter 20 | ......... | Liquidating |
| chapter 21 | ......... | Bush Teacher |
| chapter 22 | ......... | Jackie Gibson |
| chapter 23 | ......... | The Goat Hunt |
| chapter 24 | ......... | Brown Bear Hunt |
| chapter 25 | ......... | Time to Move On |
| chapter 26 | ......... | The Transition |

## We Chose Alaska

chapter 27 ........ **First Year**
chapter 28 ................**The Holidays**
chapter 29 ......... **The Christmas Letter**
chapter 30 .......... **Orthodox Christmas**
chapter 31 ......... **Life Goes On**
chapter 32 .......... **The Allusion**
chapter 33 ......... **Spring's a Coming!**
chapter 34 ......... **Summer's a Coming!**
chapter 35 ............ **2nd Year Ahead**
chapter 36 ............ **2nd Year part-1**
chapter 37 .......... **2nd Year part-2**
chapter 38 .......... **3rd Year**
chapter 39 .......... **The Goodbye**

# We Chose Alaska

**1.**

## How I Met Marcia

I have no idea where I got the bug to be a hair stylist. The very first day that I walked into the cosmetology school to fill out my application, was also the first time that I had ever gotten a whiff of permanent wave solution! "YUK!" I think of it as something like smelling salts or some sort of sinus clearing vapor! It's on the opposite end of the scale from perfume.

It doesn't bother me anymore. In fact, it was a very lucrative part of my business. However, before I go any further, I will lay out the events that wound up to the first meeting with my wife, Marcia. So, please be patient.

I have to go way back to my early 20's and set the scene. This would be circa late 1950. I had two aspirations for what I wanted to do in those days.

The first was to be a jet pilot. This proved to be the more difficult. I needed a college education and a learn-to-fly program. Then if I had those, I would be competing with those

# We Chose Alaska

pilots coming out of the military who had many hours of flight time.

I enrolled in a flight program under my GI bill program. As time went on, I learned to fly and accumulated about 40+ hours of flight time and passed my written exam. I never took the time to take my test after my cross-country solo flight. The test was the last step to a pilot's license.

I also enrolled at Long Beach Junior College and was taking night classes. As time went on, I felt that I was way behind the curve of this ever being a success—so I turned to my second choice which was to be a hair stylist. I transferred my GI Bill to cover my cosmetology school.

Talk about radically different career goals! I got a few raised eyebrows when I mentioned what I wanted to do. In those days the cosmetology business was viewed the same as a man becoming an airline steward. You've got to be kidding me—get real! I'd never wanted to be an airline steward; it is a great opportunity—but not mine. Although if I wanted to, I suppose I could do it. I never had any qualms about my sexuality. I know who I am. I'm happy, but I'm not gay!

However, I'd like to make three points on the subject. #1. There are more straight people

# We Chose Alaska

in this world than those that are gay. #2. Neither being straight nor gay is synonymous with pervert. #3. One would conclude that since we outnumber them—our group has more perverts. It would be quite possible for any family to have a pervert or two in its family tree! If so, I'll bet that person could be gay, or not!

I enrolled in the cosmetology class for a fourteen-month course that would prepare me to take my California State Cosmetology Board exam. The student body was composed of about 155 girls ranging in all ages from the late teens to somewhere past fifty. There were also only three guys.

The surprising part of that statistic is that in an industry composed largely of females and quite a few of the 'also want to be' guys. The three of us were all straight! The instructor, Mr. Ted, definitely would not be called one of the boys!

Three guys (all straight) in a school and approximately 155 girls—talk about a paradise! However, I was focused and remained so. I enjoyed the course and did rather well. I took to it like a duck to water. Soon, it was graduation time and then the taking of the state board. They only held the board exams a

# We Chose Alaska

few months out of the year. My time gave me almost a two month wait before the exam.

I had learned that the Clairol Co. (world's leading hair color company) had a free clinic at its Hollywood, CA office. The building served as the west coast operations headquarters as well as the clinic. This clinic allowed cosmetologists to bring any of their customers who had difficult hair coloring problems. Clairol furnished all the supplies and the supervision by their color technicians. All free!

What attracted me was that they also trained and encouraged all cosmetologists who came to work with the technicians. What a great opportunity. I went every day; I would commute almost an hour from Long Beach to Hollywood. The clinic was open from 9 am until 9 pm. It made for very long days.

While I was there, the western states manager asked to see me. I went to his office and he asked if I'd be willing to come to work for Clairol! DUH! That was a no-brainer. I said yes! I found myself heading for New York City—their main office—to attend classes for a few weeks to be trained as a color technician.

My duties were three-fold. I would work the clinic with the other technicians until I was needed for traveling. My travels were that I'd

# We Chose Alaska

be flown to a western city, where I would hook up with a beauty supply house. I'd go with one of their salesmen on his regular route and visit the beauty salons that were his clients. My job was mainly to offer help if they had any hair coloring questions. It was a huge PR gesture on the part of Clairol. The real reason...I was there to push their products. I felt that they were the best.

I would also fly to wherever there was a 'hair show'. That was like a trade show or a convention. Cosmetologists would come to see the latest products and some of the leading and famous hairstylists perform hair styling techniques. The big draw was a judged hair styling contest. Any hairstylist that wanted to compete needed to register and bring his own model.

My job at these was to assist the featured stylists with their hair coloring needs in preparing the models appearing for the platform demonstrations.

While I was working behind the scenes, a leading stylist mentioned to my general manager, who also attended these events—that I be given a spot in the program! That was a huge step up for me.

They also set me up for a photo shoot with a famous photographer to the stars! It is

## We Chose Alaska

Hollywood and his place of work. He took great pride in stressing, to me, that he had put the stars in my eyes! He was a true professional.

These pictures were used at the entrance to the ballrooms to display the featured presenters in the program. The company ordered fifty of these for me.

When Marcia and I moved to Alaska, about seven years later, they suffered with the winter in our trailer. They all stuck together and mildewed. I put them in the trash. Anyway, no need for them anymore. We just found this one with some of my mother's picture collection that Marcia had stored away in California. That gave me the idea to develop this journal on the events that led to our meeting.

# We Chose Alaska

I would walk out onto the stage with a model and do her hair coloring application. What was surprising and unique about that, was the fact that I made the complete application to only the roots in about three minutes! Most of these applications usually take around ten minutes. I just zipped through it. It stemmed from my work as a technician.

At the clinic, I had to learn to speed up the process because I had a class of at least fifty operators who would need help. There were only three technicians per shift. I couldn't afford to take my time. That was my job.

A year or so later my job got a little bit too demanding and I was straying further and further away from my goal of being a hairstylist. I began to get dissatisfied with it. I had those long commutes to work and spent a lot of time away from home, flying around the western states in a DC 8. How ironic, I had worked for Douglas Aircraft before going to cosmetology school, as a data processor.

After I tended my resignation, I asked one of the stylists, a presenter, whom I befriended at the many hair-shows if I could work for him. He owned a large salon in Hollywood. He said that he would hire me if I had more training in the styling of hair. He was

## We Chose Alaska

absolutely right. I had zilch in that area. I only had my school training to offer as experience. This was a top-notch salon and he couldn't afford a trainee!

I set out to get my styling experience. I got a job at the Disney Land Hotel Salon. It was a small shop with just three of us working. It proved to be quite slow and wasn't giving me the experience that I wanted. I left them after about a month.

I then found a job closer to home in one of the leading dept. stores, the May Co. I worked there for over three years. It was all that I thought it would be. They did a huge business.

I progressed rapidly; I merely needed practice and I got it—lots of it! A month later, they moved me to the first styling chair near the front desk at the entrance to the salon—anybody passing by would be able to see me working. Talk about feeling used!

At that time, I had two good friends. Al Hatten, Norman Dunn and I were hunting buddies. Al was a neighbor and a salesman for a parts supplier. Norman was a hairstylist who worked in the salon with me.

Later when Marcia and I were married, you might say that they were my 'Best Men'. It was a difficult choice so I said they were both our best men. You're probably thinking, "At last

# We Chose Alaska

he's going to tell us how he met Marcia." You're absolutely correct, we are close. But no cigar!

Norman was a rugged looking, semi balding guy who smoked cigarillos (a small cigar with a plastic mouthpiece). When asked what he did for a living, he'd take a puff off that cigar and say, "I work construction. I drive a truck." He was straight but would rather not talk about being a hairdresser! Al and I would roll in the aisles when he'd pull that one.

Al, a heavy smoker, is gone now and I don't know about Norman. He's not on Facebook. I guess nowadays that's as good as being dead!

Now, I felt ready to go out on my own. I bought space, set up for a beauty salon, in a small strip mall on Artesia Blvd. in No. Long Beach, CA.

It was a new building and I had to design and build the interior decorating. I knew what I wanted and I couldn't afford to have it done. So, I did it myself. It turned out well—I opened for business. I even designed my own business cards. It was a script written font, *Mr. Henri Coiffures,* printed on a red velvet covered card—it was eye-catching.

My salon had room for four styling stations. Soon after opening for business, a young Hispanic man called Caesar asked if he could

# We Chose Alaska

work for me. I hired him—it was a good choice. He also wasn't one of the boys, however that didn't matter. In fact, I didn't realize the situation until he introduced me to his partner.

I'll interrupt here to smell the roses and tell a story about Caesar. He worked for me for over three years and then opened his own salon. I was supposed to work for him for a short time after I sold my salon and before Marcia and I moved to Alaska.

Caesar and I were good work friends. Fridays were very hectic long twelve-hour days. We closed at 9 pm., which meant that we would go home before ten pm. This one evening after work, I decided to introduce him to a small local bar called Club 85. They had excellent steak dinners with salad and potatoes for eighty-five cents to promote their name! Well worth it.

A month or so later Caesar's partner came to pick him up after work. He hadn't made it a habit to do this. In fact, I only saw his partner probably three times in the three years. They pretty much kept to themselves.

I happened to mention what a great time Caesar and I had after work on that Friday. Me and my big mouth! I could cut the descending tension with a knife! His partner turned to

# We Chose Alaska

Caesar and said in a chillingly crisp voice, "YOU DIDN'T TELL ME ABOUT THAT!" Caesar responded that it had slipped his mind. I could see that Caesar was in deep poo-poo! I quickly said that it was no big deal. We were both worn to a frazzle and hungry.

I made myself scarce and headed for home, leaving the two to settle the matter. That little scene still gives my heart a little chuckle. So, I'm sharing it.

It was a couple of years later that I was going to hire another operator. A young lady right out of beauty school asked me for a job. I was training her on how I wanted her to drape the customers when they sat in the chair for service. This was a system that I had learned from Clairol that ensured a customer's comfort during shampooing, hair coloring or permanent waving.

I was playing the role of the client—Marcia walked into the salon. The salon was an open concept arrangement. This meant that I had full vision of anybody in the waiting area. I acknowledged her presence and told her that I'd be right with her.

I asked her how she found out about me. She said that her friend Pat, a customer, recommended me. She made a weekly appointment and became a steady customer. ~We fell in love. ~

That was it! The rest is history. One little side note...later after we had started dating, she confided in me, "That day when I walked into your salon and saw you sitting in that chair with that getup, I thought, oh, oh, he's gay!"

I've spent the rest of my life trying to prove to her that I'm not. I'm LOVING it, and I see no end in sight! If I hadn't gone to beauty school to be a hairstylist and she hadn't gone to college to be a schoolteacher and hadn't moved to California from New York, our paths would never have crossed. This journal would then be the saddest story never written!

~ I'm flying high and I have a wonderful co-pilot. ~

**2.**

**La Danse Apache**

Marcia told me that I shouldn't have mentioned the 'being gay' thing in my last chapter. She said that it made her look as

# We Chose Alaska

though she had jumped to conclusions. Valid point, so let me explain what probably made Marcia think the way she did.

I have two outfits that I like to wear. Each has a national theme. The first is Spanish and consists of a rather loose, full white shirt with a ruffled collar that opens halfway down my chest. This is accented by two gaudy, brilliant gold chains that I loosely wear around my neck—complimented with two gold buttons about six inches above the waist. I wear a tight-fitting pair of narrow legged black leather pants that come over the top of my flamenco boots. It just oozes "stunningticity"!

The other outfit is similar to the one worn in the French cafe dance called, Apache (hence the title). I wear a tight, bold striped crew neck T-shirt, a black pair of pants (not as tight) and black patent leather shoes. Topping this all off is my beret. This is more dressed down than my salsa outfit. The Apache outfit provides more freedom to move around!

My dilemma is that I started keeping track of my tips. Even though salsa was very restrictive, the days that I wore it my tips eclipsed the days that I didn't.

I was wearing my salsa outfit when Marcia walked in. I still couldn't figure out how in the

## We Chose Alaska

world she would arrive to that 'gay' opinion of me? Then, I happened to look in the full-length mirror to my left.

Oh! Drats! My purse! There it hung—over my arm!

~ This story is all just a spoof anyway...hope that gives you some relief. ~

You can see how my mind works. Evenings are a time for some creative thoughts. One recent night, I had a restless moment and found myself alert to the silence.

The only sounds that interrupted were Marcia's soft and gentle breathing accompanied by an occasional snorting—which caused me to smile. Along with this was an ever present and incessant ringing in my ears. (God, I love old age!)

I felt overwhelmingly in love with her. I decided to write a few words to sum up just how much I sensed the urge to shout this from the rooftops! Living in Alaska this would only result in my words becoming lost in the rustle of the trees. So, I began to write her a letter.

>My heart is my compass.
>My mind is its needle.
>You are my North.
>We travel through life together.
> I thank God for a wonderful voyage.

# We Chose Alaska

**3.**

## Our First Date

If it hadn't been for Mary Ellen the following would never have happened...God bless her soul. I received an email from Mary Ellen Kestel. She was instrumental in enabling our first date. It was dated 11/9/2011 10:38: 10 A.M. Pacific Standard Time and went like this: *"Well, I was there in Long Beach at the time and Marcia was my roommate. I suspect that is how I started coming to your salon—through Marcia. Of course, you did great cuts, and finally my hair, for our wedding in 1964. I love the story and the photo!"*

If I left you with the idea in the previous chapter that I met Marcia and we started dating right away, that's not what happened. At the time, I was dating someone else and Marcia had broken off the engagement to her boyfriend, Perry, who was a dentist in a small beachside community south of Long Beach, California. However, they were still dating when we first met.

## We Chose Alaska

I had been divorced just a year and a half. My wife, Charlotte, was and is a wonderful lady. I was a scoundrel. I behaved like the fox that was in charge of the chicken coop.

She finally grew tired of it and did the right thing. She divorced me. There was never any animosity that developed between us. To this very day, we are all good friends. We even take cruises together and have a ball during the holiday season. In fact, she and her husband, Will, hosted a Thanksgiving feast.

Later on, when I asked Marcia if she'd like to go on a motorcycle ride with me on a Sunday, she said that she'd let me know. She went home and asked Mary Ellen whether or not she should go on a date with me! She had a lot to be apprehensive about. I was a divorced man, had two children and we would be going on a MOTORCYCLE ride! Mary Ellen said, "Sure, why not." (Thank you, Mary Ellen).

I borrowed Norman's Honda 160 motorcycle for the event rather than use my small Honda 55 Trail Bike. His was a real motorcycle. It's what you'd expect a cigar smoking hairstylist to have for transportation. It was much faster and more comfortable on the highway.

# We Chose Alaska

I arrived at her apartment complex early in the morning. We were going south of Long Beach into the woods of Orange County. (In those days it was mostly forested, now it's all homes, sad!)

I pulled up to the curb, in front of her apartment house, revved the engine loudly and yelled at the top of my voice, "HEY STELLA!" I'm sure that brought back all the apprehension she might have originally had. I was mimicking the scene from one of Marlin Brando's hit movies. I don't recall the name of it now. It's not important.

It was a gorgeous day. The sun was shining and the temperature was moderate by California standards (about 80 deg.). It took us about an hour of paved driving to get to our destination. The unpaved part of the trip was mainly a large trail which was used by off-road vehicles—mainly motorcycles with large balloon tires.

The pace slowed dramatically, because of the terrain. Best part of the trip! We were going over a mountain trail to get to the next valley, when in front of us we saw a snake! It was a coral snake; it had the right coloring. Highly poisonous! Being young, foolish and wanting to show how "macho" I was and not wanting to run over it—I stopped the bike. I got off and proceeded to move the snake from the road, to prevent someone else from running over it.

I had my leather driving gloves on when I bent over and reached for its tail—it was a little more than a foot in length. My idea was to grab his tail and in one swift swoop fling it into the brush off the trail. (Yeah right!)

I reached down, and before I knew what had happened—the little sucker had put his own plot into action. He recoiled so fast that I didn't even see it coming! Next thing I knew, I was in the flinging part of my swoop and he had struck at my hand!

I imagine that my face must have exhibited a look of sheer terror! Believe me, I wasn't angry. Although, if I'd had a 'soiling accident— I'd have been more than capable of using some rather nasty expressions! He had luckily not pierced the glove when he struck! He had embedded one of his fangs along the edge of my gloved index finger!

The whole scene resembled a sport fisherman making a perfect cast with his fishing rod. I saw him being jerked smoothly and swiftly off the ground—moving through the air still connected to my glove. It was suddenly released and freed by my equally swift and not as smooth recoiling action. He disappeared into the brush. The whole scene took only seconds—yet I viewed it in slow motion. Little did he know; he won the battle.

We continued onward. It was gorgeous country. We soon left the tranquility behind and entered the road system. We stopped for lunch at a small roadside stand. We looked up at the mountains that we had just left and thought that it was really a fun trip.

It was a perfect first date.

### 4.

**Sleeping Under the Stars**

Yesterday, I was working on my journal about 'Dating Part 1'. I made a remark about it being 'awesome'. That bothered me. Nowadays, it's used so frivolously as a superlative for 'great'. I felt awkward about using it. It caused me enough concern that I had a restless moment during the night and my mind gravitated to what really sleeping under the stars means to me. I came up with two words. Heavenly and Celestial are synonymous. I'm using a different scenario depicting each word and what it means to me.

Picture yourself lying on your back looking up at the sky. The moon is full and bright and its light allows your peripheral vision to see the outline of all the trees that surround you, against the sky.

You are in the center of this cone-like funnel. The moon's brightness obscures all that is behind it and reflects directly upon YOU—reinforcing the illusion—YOU are the center of the Universe! This is what a perfect warm fuzzy must be all about. The stuff that oozes romance and passion. Love stories are full of it. Or they should be.

It is all about the heart. It is all about YOU—it is self-indulgence on a grand scale. There's no doubt about it. No need to question it. No reason to question it. It's a wonderful heartfelt experience which allows you to grow emotionally—an essential step in being human. There's absolutely nothing wrong with it. God put it there for your enjoyment. He knows how we humans are. We thrive on such stimuli. I'll be the first to admit it. I'm a romantic. I love to look at the moon—especially its reflection on water. That's the greatest. It's just heavenly!

# We Chose Alaska

Let's bring on the new moon. Same situation on the ground. It is pitch black and you have no reference point. You are forced to look for available light. If you've just put out your lantern it may take a moment or so for your eyes to adjust.

You focus on the little diamond-like sparkly dots in front of you. The whole sky is filled with them. They appear to go on forever. There seems to be no rhyme nor reason to their pattern. You marvel in the beauty. It is a wondrous sight. But wait, something is wrong! Drastically wrong—you are not the center of the Universe, anymore!

You are, what appears to be, sitting somewhere along the edge of the Universe. You are merely an observer. You aren't even one of those little diamonds. You're insignificant! Hmmm, you think, "What is it all about?"

Your brain is now in command and wants answers. How? Why? When? Who brought all this beauty into existence? You'd like to know so that you can grow intellectually. It's a matter of the mind. Enquiring minds want to know! All you can do is enjoy the awesome beauty. You find peace in the fact that nobody else knows the answers. You are merely enjoying the moment! Pure and Simple.

# We Chose Alaska

This is how I describe my thoughts about sleeping under the stars. As for the answers to the big questions.

I have an idea! ~ As we travel through life, our body is our vehicle. The parts that make it work are the mind—the heart—and the soul. Maybe, just maybe, we have the answers already. We have to merely look into our souls! ~

## 5.

## DATING PART I (The Beginning)

My only mode of transportation when Marcia and I started dating was my Honda motorcycle. She sure as heck wasn't after my money! Later, I used to tease her that the only reason she had dumped her dentist boyfriend and started dating me was that once she had all her dental needs met—she saw the lifelong potential of dating a hairstylist!

The following week after our first date, I went to Marcia's apartment on a Saturday

## We Chose Alaska

afternoon after work to visit. I had a date that evening with my girlfriend. I asked Marcia if I could borrow her car! She said, "Sure". We were just friends and it was that simple. OR— I must have been one arrogant ------! (Multiple choice) I prefer the first. My thought was— WOW!—the gal that I was going to see would have handled that—way differently!

My reason for beginning to distance myself from her was that she was insanely jealous! I'd never dated a girl who was. It's not a pleasant existence, especially in my line of work.

Later, I bought a beautiful 56 Buick Roadmaster sedan. It was eight years old and had belonged to an elderly couple. It was pristine, (and very reasonable). I had a history of buying big older cars. I loved them! They were not in favor with the younger people, very comfortable and inexpensive. It was all that I could afford.

Mary Ellen had married her husband John. Marcia had moved in with, Barbara Beggs, ("B") another schoolteacher friend who taught in a parochial school. B was gorgeous, friendly and bubbly. She was a joy to be around. We double dated and became good friends. On our first double date—on our way back home from wherever we had gone—we got into an accident.

## We Chose Alaska

We were in the country (dairy farmland) traveling on a long stretch of road with another road entering from the left—it had a stop sign at the end. The oncoming car had only two choices when it reached the intersection, a right or a left.

We were slowing down to make a left turn onto that road. I glanced left and could see his car approaching along the fence. I slowed down and concentrated on making the turn—I thought that he was also doing the same. I was wrong—he had a third choice!

As the left front of the Buick entered the path of the intersecting road, I heard the screeching of tires! (Not a good sign)!

Suddenly, we were jolted and spun around. We wound up facing the fence that was along the right side of our road. It was all a blur. He had never seen the stop sign until it was too late to stop! He was going too fast!

He had stopped by plowing into the side of the ditch between the road and the fence. He'd been drinking and had three female passengers with him! The only injury that we had was a bruised knee on Marcia.

Another couple of seconds later would have put the impact squarely in the car's midsection. That would have been another story—and possibly told in the obituaries! The other

## We Chose Alaska

car proceeded across the intersection—after smashing our forward driver's side at the wheel! The car came to a halt—nose first—into the ditch—I was 'carless' again! ~ Drat! ~

I had the car towed to a parking spot behind the salon. Later, I had it picked up by a junk dealer who paid me $35 and towed it away! C'est la vie! That was the last time that B double dated with us. We did, however go on several camping trips and to the beach together, using Marcia's Volvo.

Most of our dates centered about hunting, camping, spending many days practicing archery and going to the beach. Marcia became quite proficient with the bow and arrow. Marcia, Norman and I spent many weekends bow hunting in the hills behind the Mulholland Drive area—it runs adjacent to I-405 in California. There were plenty of deer there and only bow hunting was legal due to the proximity of 'large estates' in the area.

This new lifestyle for her was a radical departure from her previous dating experiences. She was used to fine dining and fancy restaurants. I, on the other hand, had the "Club 85" and the 'Mustang Bar'. The Mustang was a local bar that served excellent meals, most about a dollar. A few high-end dishes were available for about a dollar fifty!

## We Chose Alaska

It was just a couple of blocks from my salon. However, it was a BAR! The first time that I took Marcia there—we ordered their fish fry special. The place was jammed.

As the waitress reached in front of me from my left to put down Marcia's plate to my right, she had to stretch so far that the Kleenex that was tucked under her blouse's short sleeve—fell into my plate!

At last, I felt as though I'd finally taken her to a restaurant that would be memorable—and had a high level of personal service!

Our dates also included the kids, Corine and Henry ll. We would take them swimming at the beach and at Marcia's apartment pool. These are pictures taken in front of her apartment

# We Chose Alaska

# We Chose Alaska

# We Chose Alaska

## 6.

## DATING PART II (Going Hunting)

We also went on several hunting trips. The Mulholland Drive area is located in the foothills of the San Gabriel Mts., in southern California. It was our favorite close hunt. The area was heavily populated with deer. It was a short trip from where we lived in Long Beach. The weather is some of the best for outdoor activities.

Another trip was to the eastern slopes of the Sierra Nevada Range. The nights are cold in the fall and the days are warm. Camping is a necessity due to the distance from home.

We set up camp and Marcia started to prepare our late breakfast. The first ordeal was to handle the bravado POOF! the stove did when first turned on. The Coleman stove was in the habit of giving a healthy burst of energy as the fumes met the match.

# We Chose Alaska

Now, SUCCESS! Back to cooking.

## We Chose Alaska

Another bow hunting trip was to the China Lake area. It has a desert climate; there's a beautiful huge dam that is wonderful for thirsty animals. This time of year, it's cold and dry.

I'm up on an adjacent hill looking down at Marcia sitting on a rooftop that we're using as a stand. There were deer trails all around that area. Here's a close up. Doesn't she look fierce?

## We Chose Alaska

We spent most of our dates doing outdoor activities. We loved hunting and worked at perfecting our skills to be successful. The main activities were using a bow and arrow. We practiced frequently. We could set up our targets in any park and not bother anybody. When it came to the rifles and the pistol, we would do those in the forested foothills of the nearby mountains.

I have a wonderful story about Marcia's first try to shoot—a 44 magnum revolver—a very formidable weapon! It is NOT by any means a ~girly~ thing. Guess who wanted to give it a whirl?

My Marcia was eager. We set up a paper target on a huge evergreen tree. Marcia was standing about fifty feet from it. She assumed the firing position beautifully—cocked the hammer and aimed.

I was filming this on an 8mm video camera. I was at the ready—any time now—NOTHING! She was very reluctant to squeeze the trigger! This scenario went on many times. She was genuinely anxious. I was never sure when she'd fire, so I got more lax as the scenes progressed—unchanged—again and again.

Each time, I would start to film her, in order not to miss anything. I was at the ready—she started—FIRED!

# We Chose Alaska

It caught me completely off-guard—the blast startled the heck out of me! I jumped—so did the camera! When I finally got the camera back on subject, Marcia was eagerly running toward the target to see how she had done.

She was very excited. She had hit the target! I didn't say the bull's eye. It didn't matter—she had done it! I was very proud of her. It showed that she had the necessary guts.

The rifle was a different ball of wax, she handled that very well and is still an excellent shot. The revolver was just a, "I want to do It." thing. The beauty about this whole life sharing adventure is that it's exciting—comforting—and dynamically rejuvenating. We are one, as you'll find out.

Before we leave California in our 'North to Alaska' chapters, there are two episodes that have come to mind. The first was a deer hunting trip with Norm Dunn into the Mammoth Mountains in California. The second was a subsequent trip with Marcia to the same area.

Norm and I headed for the Mammoth area on a deer hunt. When we arrived, we set up our tent and fixed something to eat before going to bed. We noticed that the air had gotten colder during the night. When the

# We Chose Alaska

morning nature call summoned—it had snowed about six inches of the big flaky stuff.

We ate breakfast and headed out to hunt. We were traveling the back roads. The sun was shining warmly and things were beginning to melt rapidly. This was a freak early storm that had passed through.

As we traveled along—we noticed some tracks leading across the road and into the woods to our left. We parked the car and headed out to follow the tracks. We entered a brushy area with clearings among the trees. We were gingerly moving along and the snow cover helped to muffle our noise.

Suddenly the clearing ahead of us erupted with deer—fleeing our arrival. They must have been bedded down and didn't know we were there. It caught both of us somewhat off guard. We didn't even have a chance to get off a shot. Man, those little suckers can move!

We headed in the direction that they had taken, out of the clearing and into the brush. We got to a double wired fence—probably a cattle fence. I spread the wires so that Norm could scoot between them and he did the same for me. As he was holding the wires on my left, he happened to notice something on the ground to my right—"Henry, there's a deer

## We Chose Alaska

lying on the ground just beyond you!" We were astonished!

There was this beautiful animal with not a scratch on him. He evidently had not seen the fence and in his fleeing attempt—had hit the top wire and snapped his neck! We dressed it out and took it back to Long Beach to hang before butchering. Not a shot had been fired!

This caused Marcia and me to plan another trip to the same area. We left Long Beach in Marcia's car, very early in the morning, and headed for CA-395. I couldn't find the location where we had hunted and decided to push further north.

The hunting trip had turned into a sightseeing venture. We were heading for Reno Nevada, and planned to head west to Long Beach, on I-5. The whole trip would encompass about eleven hundred miles—easily done in a weekend.

As we approached Reno, we headed west to avoid the city. We were probably on what is now I-80. Just before entering the mountains, I noticed that the temperature gauge was spiking! The venture had just become an adventure!

Luckily, just in the distance was a bridge over a small river. There was a small dirt road on the right that led to the water's edge. We

# We Chose Alaska

stopped and I opened the hood. There was a loud hissing sound coming from between the water pump and the engine block! This was a Volvo and I had never seen a set up like that before.

The two components were connected by an adapter, a short piece of stiff rubber tubing through which the water flowed. It had developed a leak and caused the hissing—hence, the culprit!

I asked Marcia if she had any tools. She said, "There's a small pouch in the trunk that came with the car—it has tools in it." So far, so good.

We now had to wait for the engine to cool before being able to touch anything. We ate lunch and sunbathed. It was a gorgeous day. Bright and sunny, no wind and no bugs—almost too nice. We could find refuge from the sun, under the bridge, when we needed to cool off.

I disconnected the pump and removed the adapter. I found that if I had a small cylindrical piece of tubing, I might be able to fix it. We ram sacked the car, but to no avail. Then Marcia opened her purse and said, "The only thing that's in here that's round is my lipstick."

She handed it to me and it looked as though it might work. Everything seemed to

## We Chose Alaska

be made to order, except the cap was solid on one end. I used my hunting knife to puncture the lid and turn it into an open cylinder. I slipped the cap inside the rubber adapter. It looked like a perfect fit in length and diameter! It was one of those—Divine Intervention moments!

I bolted the pieces down, filled the radiator and started the engine. It's one of those moments that the anticipation is pumping more anxiety into your system—while waiting for a result. The engine had been running and no sign of a leak even after it had reached its running temperature—AMEN!

I then filled every container that we had that would hold water. I figured if it sprang another leak—we could limp all the way back to Long Beach (about 500 miles), from service station to service station—and refill the containers.

We were now on a mission—back to Long Beach—as fast as possible! We found ourselves on I-5 late at night and really needing coffee. Marcia was driving and I made coffee while riding in the passenger's seat.

I held the small Coleman single burner stove in front of me on the floor and steadied it between my feet. On the stove I held the coffee pot while it perked—foolish youth!

## We Chose Alaska

We arrived home at daybreak, exhausted, but very, very thankful. The trip was almost a twenty-four-hour endurance test!

The Volvo was sold a year later before our leaving for Alaska. The leak never happened again. In fact, it had completely slipped from memory. I hope the Volvo dealer was able to find another lipstick lid that fit!

### 7.
### DATING PART III (Scuba Diving)

Timewise, I really don't really know when we changed from a dating couple to an engaged couple. It was in the latter stages of our relationship. As time passed—we became engaged.

Norman had started seeing a young lady that he later married and settled in Bellflower, CA. Al had his family and was in the process of changing jobs. They later moved to Indiana.

We had also become interested in scuba diving and snorkeling. Scuba is with the use of an air tank for underwater breathing—while snorkeling is with the use of a 3/4" rubber breathing tube that looks like a big 'J'. It has a

# We Chose Alaska

mouthpiece at one end and the other is the straight part that sticks out from the water's surface, through which the air is drawn.

We both had neoprene diving wetsuits made for ourselves. We had complete outfits for snorkeling. Scuba is a whole different ball of wax. It's very expensive to buy, as well as maintain the equipment and get the air tanks refilled.

Marcia had taken swimming lessons but was very uncomfortable in the water. She didn't feel confident enough to enroll in a scuba diving class. She was right.

Now, with her wetsuit, she could snorkel all that she wanted to do without worrying about drowning. You just can't sink in one of those wetsuits.

You have to be weighted down with a weight belt in order to go below the surface.

I enrolled in a diving school for classes and passed the tests necessary to obtain a scuba diving certificate from L.A. County. We had to do a series of dives as part of the final testing toward certification. Included was a trip to Catalina Island off the California coast.

The ship was a twin mast schooner which made the whole trip enjoyable. Since Marcia had come with me to all of the pool classes,

## We Chose Alaska

they asked if she wanted to come along. DUH! Heck yes! ☺

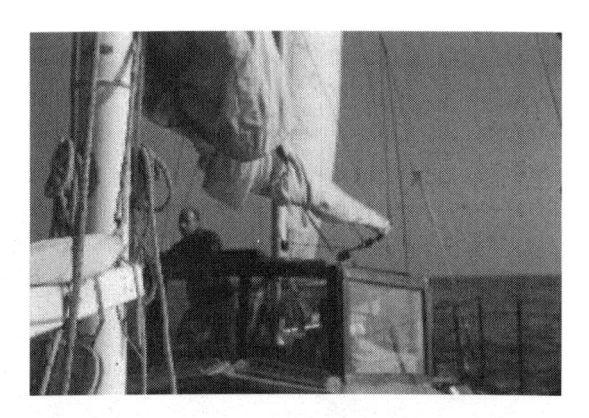

We anchored to the left of town in a small cove. It was a picture-perfect island marine area that seemed to be mystical by its

# We Chose Alaska

isolation—although we were just a short distance around the bend from town. I'm sure that it was chosen because it had all the elements necessary for a thorough hidden test of our problem performance skills—the 'final' test.

After one of the deep dives, Marcia was on the bow watching as I surfaced. I was surfacing along the anchor chain to slow my ascent, (I'd already done the damage without realizing it.)

When I broke the surface, I hung on to the anchor chain and pulled off the mask. She said in a loud, concerned shocking tone, "You're bleeding!" I had no idea. I felt nothing. It was news to me. I was told that I had waited too long before starting to 'equalize' when I started my ascent.

That's a common mistake with newbies! You equalize by slowly exhaling the air from your lungs as you ascend. That relieves the pressure on your lungs, sinuses and prevents the formation of air bubbles in your blood.

Nose bleeds are indicative of inexperience. Problems can be compounded when diving to a depth of more than thirty feet. That cove had a depth of a bit less than the thirty-foot limit. Therefore, it prevented any bad results from happening.

## We Chose Alaska

This is the picture that Marcia took as I climbed aboard after finishing all the tests. It looks like a picture from an old-time silent film! And NO, I'm not wearing black leather nor am I wearing ballet slippers! I survived that one! What's next?

Next, was for me to swim under the surface from the boat toward a specific point near shore. Sounds easy enough. Piece of cake! You know something is coming, don't you? After all, if it weren't memorable—I sure as heck wouldn't have remembered it.

Scuba divers have a cute way for entering the water. You sit on the edge of the boat with your back facing the water, you look down and around to make sure all is clear, no obstructions nor debris. Then you grab your face mask, firmly push it into your face, and just roll yourself back. You fall straight into the water and the tank on your back clears your way. No impact felt!

## We Chose Alaska

I was enjoying the trip. Scuba diving is a real adventure. It's a whole new world. I'd already experienced flying solo during my flight training—however this was a completely different sensation. I felt as though I were really on my own and apprehensive!

There is a hard fast rule that you should never dive solo. You should always have a buddy. If a problem occurs, you can protect each other.

As I did my dives, (solo, mind you) I gained an appreciation of that rule. I noticed that as I got further from the ship and closer to the shore that I had swum directly into a monster of a kelp bed that I hadn't noticed from the deck. The instructor was sending me directly through it. It was overlooked by my inexperienced eyes. Swimming through a heavy kelp bed was stressed in class. It's a common situation.

The most important thing is to never panic. (In life, also a very good point to remember.) Kelp beds are common and occur within a depth of thirty feet. They need the photosynthesis from the sun, and the ground or rocky bottom, in order to cling to and grow.

Traveling through a kelp bed is like no other sensation. You aren't in any danger, if

## We Chose Alaska

you just handle yourself properly. The kelp rises from the bottom and seems to be reaching out to you.

Visibility is rather limited except when looking downward. You can't see much going forward because of all the leaves at the top. That's why moving through is best done from the surface.

Then of course what is downward visibility worth? Nothing unless you want to dive! Foolish as that would be, you would wind up in trouble due to the physical effort that is necessary to propel yourself downward.

I did exactly as they had instructed. Simply EASE yourself through, with very SLOW movements—GENTLY move (not push) the kelp from your path and swim SOFTLY by it. It worked!

The idea being that any swift or panicky moves would cause you to become entangled with the kelp. I eased myself along the water's surface into a snorkeling position just above the kelp in order to have a full view from the top.

After a while of being highly successful, I relaxed and started to enjoy the whole experience. If need be, we all carry a large knife strapped to our leg to be used as a tool.

## We Chose Alaska

Here I thought, all the time, that it was to fight the sharks!

We now were fully outfitted for snorkeling. We spent many days at the beach going through the breakers with our yellow raft—snorkeling around off-shore.

We had found a nice little cove south of Long Beach with rock outcroppings, a reef and a nice little sandy beach. It was a perfect spot. Barbara Beggs, B, Marcia's roommate and friend would also go there with us.

The first time we went, Marcia and I pulled the raft to the water's edge and prepared to enter. We were both dressed in our wetsuits and flippers. Since this was mainly for snorkeling, Marcia did not wear a weight belt (much safer that way). This was to be her maiden voyage!

Previously, we had practiced underwater safety rules in a pool. As we slid the raft forward, until we were knee high into the water, and were about ready to board—Marcia asked, "Are we going to be safe in this raft?" I replied, "Marcia, this is a four-man raft! You couldn't tip it—even if you wanted."

In my inexperience, I made it past the breakers and easily paddled out, to the left, to the reef—and had a ball! The day was bright and sunny. Visibility was excellent and the fish

## We Chose Alaska

life was abundant. All in all, it was FANTASTIC!

We had spent all our time in the water snorkeling. I would make occasional dives to the bottom and then return to her side. This was also good practice on holding my breath—so necessary for someone who wants better snorkeling skills. So went the time.

It was now time to return to shore. We paddled in. As we hit the breaker area, we were greeted from behind by a fairly good-sized wave. It started to roll under us—picked up the raft from the rear—and started to turn it lengthwise! Both Marcia and I were thrown off balance and cast to the same lower side of the raft. We were responding to good old gravity.

We had slipped down to a sitting position on the right side of the raft between the floor and the flotation bladder. This all happened quite rapidly. We had drastically changed the raft's center of gravity!

The raft flipped over on top of us and we were submerged in a huge swirling mass of churning water. The three of us, Marcia and I—plus the raft, being rushed toward the shore! Luckily, we were heading, not for the rocky shore, but toward the sandy beach. We floated to a stop and were in shallow water

## We Chose Alaska

trying to regain a footing. When Marcia, suddenly and loudly, in all seriousness says, "Henry,—we'll both be killed!" We were in less than a foot of water!

We stood up, grabbed the raft and started to drag it to shore. All of a sudden it felt as if something had jammed on the brakes! We then dumped the water out of it and pulled it more easily up on the beach.

Now whenever we are in a touchy situation and she asks for my advice. If she has any doubt about my reply—she always throws it in my face. "Yeah, just like, ~ this raft will never flip!" ~

I'm glad that she wasn't with me the time that I was by myself, in that same spot. She and our friend B were sunbathing on the beach. I was snorkeling, solo, by the same reef, when all of a sudden, the yellow sand on the bottom, that was visible through my facemask—started to turn black!

A humongous ray fish swam right under me just a foot or so below me! It completely blanked my view of the bottom for an instant. I first saw a sandy yellow bottom, turn into a huge black form, then the black form's tail petered out into that sandy yellow bottom!

I didn't panic. If you lose control, you are in trouble. However, it did startle the heck out

## We Chose Alaska

of me! Had Marcia been there, she'd have never entered the water, ever again!

I thought I'd write about what happened some 20 years after we were married because it is relevant to the previous 'Scuba Diving' chapter. After we retired from teaching school in Alaska, we would spend a month or so in Hawaii. Maui was our favorite. We visited several short times with Mary Lou's parents and fell in love with it. Eventually we rented a B & B from the many available.

Kihei had the most places for us. Our usual day would start after breakfast (at home). We'd pack a snack and all our beach stuff into the rental car and head to an EXCELLENT snorkeling beach about six miles from Lahaina.

We'd pick a spot under one of the many low hung trees, spread our towels out on the sand and sunbathe for a while. When we wanted to cool off, we'd grab our snorkeling gear and head into the water.

We would then dry off and head for Lahaina, catch lunch and walk around. It's a tourist hot spot. We'd head back for the beach for our afternoon session which was an exact duplicate of the morning.

The beach (sandy part) was in a large wide crescent shape several miles long. After you

# We Chose Alaska

entered the water, you could walk out a long distance and still not be above your head. It was teeming with colorful sea life. If you wanted to venture further out, you'd have many rocky areas just above and below the surface on which to stop and rest.

That side of Maui faces Molokai and is sheltered from very heavy wave action. This is definitely not surfing water. It's rather placid and wave less. That's what makes it an ideal snorkeling spot.

Marcia still, (even more so after 20+ years in Alaska) was reluctant to venture out without some sort of protection. We had everything except the life vest. A vest isn't a necessity if you're a good swimmer. So, we bought one of those small inflatable plastic donuts. It had the usual warning about not using it as a life preserver!

As I said this wasn't a Jacques Cousteau episode. If all else failed, I could hold her in my arms, while I played in the sand with my toes! She got comfortable with the whole situation and the enjoyment level increased accordingly.

I said, "Do you want to dive and get a closer look at the fish?" She said that she'd try. I assured her that when she resurfaced—I'd be there with the donut. We spotted some

## We Chose Alaska

colorful fish feeding on the reef's side near the bottom.

I reviewed and demonstrated for her, the diving procedure which entails pushing the upper part of your body under the surface by bending at the waist and plunging your arms towards the bottom. At the same time, you raise your legs out of the water and into the air. This shifts the center of gravity of your body. Basically, you go from a prone position to a slanted vertical one. Hopefully, heading for the bottom.

Sooo, she executes the maneuver to a tee—she did great! I watched her go below the surface and could see that she was having a rough time getting the fins to penetrate the water. She flailed them and was losing the momentum of the dive. Up bobbed her butt!

I made the suggestion that when she gets that far she should use her arms to help the dive. Armed with this new information, she tried again. Same result! She tried several more times, each being more hilarious.

Of course, I joked about it and told her, "You're so afraid of drowning—you can't even keep your butt below the surface!" I still have happy visions of that day, when someone gives a toast and says—"BOTTOMS UP!"

# We Chose Alaska

8.

## DATING PART IV (Wrapping it up)

Sometime in the dark early morning, all three of us bolted to a sitting position, as we heard the sound of a locomotive barreling down on us! WHOA! What the heck was that? It came—passed on by—and went with great bravado! The ground shook and rumbled—we were startled and rattled! I have to mention this was the time that B went up the coast from LA with us to do some overnight camping.

## We Chose Alaska

We found our way to the beach in very poor light conditions via some old dirt road that wound up there. We set up camp shortly after arriving and went to bed.

In the morning we went up above where we had camped and noticed the railroad tracks. It evidently didn't register with us when we had crossed them the night before when we arrived. This was also Marcia's first experience with the dreaded 'MONSTER POOFING' Coleman stove!

I have three memorable motorcycle trips to mention. One was on a twenty-six-mile evening trip to Redondo Beach, CA. Marcia had fallen asleep as she was riding behind me on the way back home! It was dark and noisy as we rode. I never realized it until she told me. All the time, I thought she was enjoying the trip. Wrong!

Another time we were out riding and I made a left turn on a green arrow. There were no cars waiting to make the turn. I was going fairly fast and didn't notice that the intersection was somehow wet! As I leaned the bike into the turn, it started to slip out from under us—it had lost traction! I regained control after much swerving and jerking. The bike finally stopped a few feet from the curb. I

# We Chose Alaska

looked back to see what had happened to Marcia.

She was no longer with me! She had slipped off of the carrier and was sitting in the middle of the intersection! Thankfully—she was fine. She picked herself up and ran to get back on the bike. None of the traffic had moved. I think everyone was watching the show.

The third, was on a deer hunting trip into the mountains north of LA. We had setup camp in a very nice public campground. We made our preparation to head out on the trail. In those days, they didn't have three or four wheelers for off-road travel. They had motorcycle-looking rigs with huge balloon-like tires.

We had our Honda 55 trail bike! This was going to be very interesting. The word trail must have several meanings. We were going to find out if it would fit the bill.

The trail went up and down hills interspersed with valleys. The valleys were a piece of cake—the hills posed more of a challenge. The trails on most of hills were cut into the sides and were no wider than a couple of feet. A few had scree slopes. Going in went rather well. When a hill was too steep or too rough, Marcia would get off and walk.

# We Chose Alaska

We found a lush looking spot with birch-like trees. We had traveled better than an hour when we decided to stop and make camp. We hadn't taken a lantern—big mistake! We found ourselves in the dark very quickly. Two reasons why we hadn't built a fire were because we were camped in a dry grassy spot and didn't have anything to cut firewood.

We had figured if we ever shot a deer—we would have a real problem. As it was, we felt lucky to have gotten ourselves this far. Put a deer into the equation and the trip would darn near be an impossibility! Wisdom set in—the hunting trip became just a camping trip.

We had a great spot for a tent. The setup was fast—the sleep was faster. We had been pushed and were dog tired. After a very good night's sleep, and after a fast breakfast we—headed back for the campground. We packed up all the gear and tied it to the rack that was mounted over the rear wheel. This was Marcia's seat and from there she carried the rifle, perched over her shoulder.

We were heading up a scree slope full bore, to make it to the top—the slope got too steep—the bike lost its momentum! You guessed it! Up went the front wheel and a sudden shift of gravity took effect! It all shifted to the rear of the bike since I was straddling

## We Chose Alaska

the bike in an attempt to control it. My weight was no longer being used to balance the bike!

It ended with the bike standing on its rear wheel and Marcia lying on her back with the rifle under her! She got herself up and decided to walk the rest of the way to the top. I returned to the bottom of the hill and made another run for the top. No problem this time. I no longer had a heavy load behind me.

On one of the trails which led down the hill—Marcia was in her place—straddling me with her knees sticking out to each side. The trail narrowed down to just wide enough for the bike. My main concentration was on the downhill edge. It was quite sheer beyond it.

There was a root sticking out from the bank on the right. When I saw it from the corner of my right eye—I jammed on the brakes and we started slipping down on the sandy gravel (gravity again).

There was a sudden jolt. Oh yes—accompanied by a painful yell! Marcia's knee had hit the root squarely and stopped the bike! Yes, it was the same knee that suffered in the car accident! She was severely bruised. We got to the bottom of the hill, she sat down and bawled from the pain. We rested and when she felt better; we headed for camp once more.

## We Chose Alaska

Beneath that sweet and almost princess-like appearance is a very strong, gentle and loving lady. Thankfully—still in one piece—bruised but not battered!

We are very thankful that we were unsuccessful in our deer hunting adventure. We both feel that the hunting stops being fun and turns to work after you shoot! An unsuccessful hunt is not bad. It's, for us, about twenty-five percent of the total experience. A successful one is preferred and priceless! C'est la vie!

I had decided to ask her to marry me! One evening we had gone to party at Judy and Joe's apartment. When we decided to head home—we wished everybody a good-bye. They lived on the second floor of an apartment house.

*Just as we had shut the door—I took hold of her and asked, "Will you marry me?" "YES", was the answer!*

# We Chose Alaska

9.

## South of the Border

Going camping in Mexico was a favorite spot for us. We camped in an area about sixty miles south from Tijuana along the coast. Rosarito Beach is a very small stretch of shoreline several miles long. At that time, it was uninhabited except for a very small beachside hotel, named after the town.

This was our first trip together. I had been there a couple of times before. I knew how rustic it was going to be. We brought snorkeling equipment just in case the opportunity arose. It was not a snorkel situation unless you're a daredevil! It turned out to be rather windy and very cool after our first day. Great for the increased swells—but not for us.

The shore was mainly rocky outcrops with small inlets and caverns. The caverns gave birth to the blow holes—caused by the persistent ocean's advances. Blow holes aren't indicative of a safe snorkeling area. Its beauty could surely be missed by passersby, since the

# We Chose Alaska

rocky cavernous beach was a good ten feet lower than the top of the mile's long cliff.

We camped in a section that had a blow hole. That's where the waves wash ashore and are stopped abruptly by the caverns. Over time this eroding action usually develops deep caves. As the wave fills the cave, it builds up pressure and eventually the pressure is greater in the cave than in the oncoming wave—it jettisons a fountain of water and spray out of the upper portion of the cave with a gigantic SWOOSH! It's a beautiful scene! The sound and the fury are truly spectacular!

The place was completely deserted. We were a mile or so down from the hotel. The only structure was a functional old, weathered gray one-seater plank outhouse. The remnants of an old piece of torn weather-beaten canvas framed the door—it hung down about a foot from the top of the entrance. A six-inch-wide piece barely stretched down the right side—it was only a decoration. You had the full view of the Pacific as you sat on the throne. It was truly majestic—yet so simple—very private and functional.

The terrain is flat on the top of the bluffs. It's very difficult to find a good, rock and gravel debris free area. We cleared a small area to make it suitable. It's amazing how small

# We Chose Alaska

sized pieces of rock can cause discomfort problems.

We set up camp and inflated the raft. It was a gorgeous day. (Again, this is during the winter and the nights get quite cold. The heat drops with the sunset and rises with the sun. It seems to be the norm for the upper portions of Mexico. Elevation is also a key factor that set the temperature extremes.) Because the ground was rocky, the raft served as a ground cover for sunbathing purposes.

Later on, we used them as a shelter against the wind, in our camp. During the sunny part of the day, the weather was usually hot. Which made for some nice sun tanning moments. It was quite similar to conditions in Southern California.

## We Chose Alaska

We spent the night and decided the next day to take a trip to Ensenada, a half hour away

# We Chose Alaska

We savored the whole experience. A boat had just brought in a huge pregnant female shark.

We made our way down to the dock, to see what all the commotion was about. They had just finished gutting it and were waiting for a truck to come and get it, for processing in town. She had several small sharks inside of her. It was

# We Chose Alaska

all very interesting. I was amazed at what we saw.

They had gutted her and pulled out about five or six small sharks.

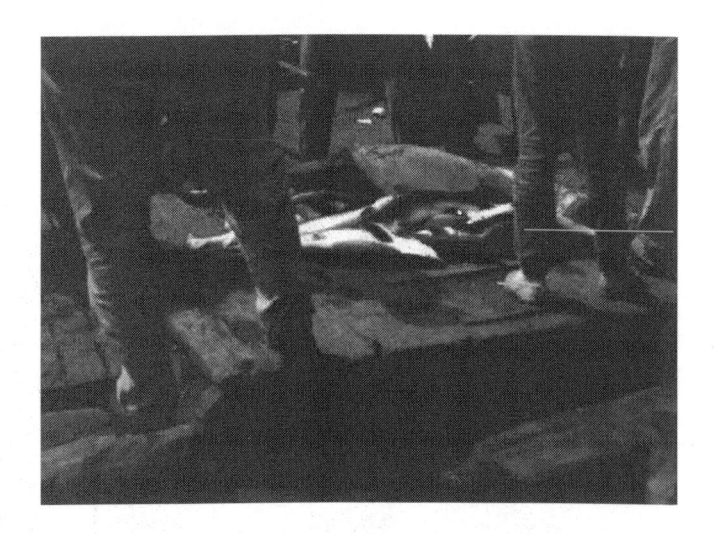

They were all dead and lying beside the mother and were being fascinatingly watched by a small crowd of local fisherman and spectators—which included us. To our left was a huge metal warehouse. From the left front of the roof's peak to its right front—sat—in full observance of the happenings—a full complement of majestic white seagulls—more than likely focusing on that gourmet pile of entrails. I even took a picture of the entrails!

## We Chose Alaska

They were also a big part of the process. It was quite an event for us to be there and witness this very basic and essential part of the food chain at the Ensenada dock.

We bought some clams at the dock (I think, Pismo clams?) and had them for supper when we returned to our camp. We gave our maxillaries a real workout on that meal. The seagulls enjoyed it more than we did.

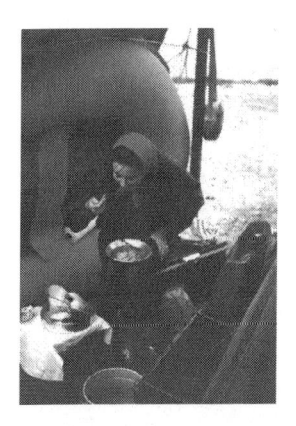

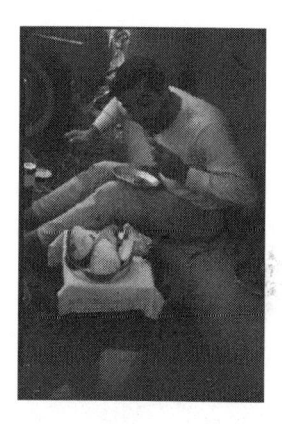

We had to use the raft as a windbreak. We never did use it for exploring. It was way too dangerous of an environment. It would have been suicide! We washed the dishes by rubbing sand on them and then rinsing them in the surf—a highly efficient energy-saving system. We had a good time trying to keep our feet dry, on the lower bluff level.

# We Chose Alaska

## 10.
## The Wedding

The day to finish what I started by proposing to Marcia had arrived. This is the first day of the rest of our lives (not an original statement but definitely true).

There is one picture that stood out among the wedding pictures. For me—it seemed to give a seal of approval for what was about to happen. It was my totem pole of that particular event.

I think that day, HE really did shine his light on us. Hindsight is certainly a wonderful thing.

# We Chose Alaska

I'm writing this almost forty-seven years later! At the time this was a huge step for me.

I knew full well what this ceremony would do. It could lead to unhappiness and the resulting pain to both of us—or it could lead to happiness and all the splendid things that accompany a happy marriage.

This was—A BIG HUGE STEP—so much so that I found myself playing host to tears when the vows were exchanged! What brought that on? I certainly wasn't in charge. All I know is that I was looking into her eyes and I became overwhelmed. I was marrying my soul mate and some ONE knew; He made me feel it!

Marcia's mother and cousin came from Western New York to attend the wedding. The weather was perfect, warm and sunny—just like my Marcia

These are some of the few pictures that survived our disastrous house fire in Alaska on the third week of September 1999.

# We Chose Alaska

I mentioned before about having my two best men at the wedding. This picture also includes our friend Norman. But for the record—Al Hatten was it! Here's one with Norman Dunn (w/o boutonniere), matron of honor, Tammy McVicker, and on the left is Dorothy Dunham, Marcia's mother.

## We Chose Alaska

We took a few formal pictures (formal is loosely used) before the festivities kicked in. Now that the formalities were out of the way, things loosened up! I got with the program. Just look at that teamwork. We were kind to each other when it came to 'sharing' the first piece of cake!

The reception was held at Tammy and Ben's house. It was a small gathering of our friends and Marcia's family (her mother and cousin).

The gift opening was the last actual formality before the partying! I think I'm right in not counting it as a formality. It's more of a ritual that leads to the closing of such a wonderful day.

## We Chose Alaska

Some might ask, "How did you ever get her to say yes?"

I say, "Just look at the cake-cutting knife.

I made her an offer she couldn't refuse!

# We Chose Alaska

All great things come to pass and so did this day. We left it full of good cheer and a very carefree spirit. I'm happy to say that we still have the same joy in our hearts. That was so long ago.

I'd do it again at the drop of a hat! (If you didn't have one—I'd lend you one of Marcia's!)

Little did I know—how long it would last.

I couldn't tell the future. Now, I have the benefit of hindsight, and it appears that it will be a great love story.

She was my 'best friend'—and still is!

# We Chose Alaska

11.

## The Honeymoon

We went to Las Vegas for our honeymoon. We stayed at the Hacienda Hotel, which was situated on the outskirts of the strip (at that time). It was not in the same league as those in town such as the Mint nor the Sands (e.g., these pictures are now heirlooms)! Even the Sands has bitten the dust. (No pun intended)

Las Vegas is about 300+ miles from Long Beach, CA, our home at the time. These

## We Chose Alaska

pictures are real classics! Everything was low key in those early days. (So, to speak!) We just relaxed, ate, stayed by the pool and walked around town. You can see how the hustle and bustle of nowadays was absent in these pictures.

The first day that we arrived was a hot and sunny, as it usually is in the desert; after the long trip—I took a shower. You don't mess with the desert heat in mid-afternoon you stay where it's cool—La Hacienda Hotel!

As I raised my right arm to wash under it, my hand hit the top part of the shower and I felt a sharp bite on my finger. I recoiled it and noticed that I had cut the top side of my middle finger! The ceiling had a half inch wide

## We Chose Alaska

crack that crossed the top of the stall! My finger was bleeding profusely!

This little accident set off a series of hustle and bustle of a different kind! I informed the desk of the incident. In short order, we had several visitors (staff personnel) at the door. They made arrangements to get me stitched up and obtained a brief history of the situation. I was told that their attorney would be contacting me. Fine with me.

~ Back to the ~ honeymooners. ~

You'll notice the bandaged finger. That was not the most memorable highlight of our honeymoon, however it did cramp our happiness—a bit. Neither one of us remembers much about it. I guess it pales in comparison to the rest of our lives!

## We Chose Alaska

The situation had put me out of operation as a hairstylist. I settled with the attorneys for what would be about two months of my earnings. I felt that to be fair. That was also the catalyst that put an end to my hair styling in California.

I had just sold my salon and was scheduled to go to work in Caesar's salon about two miles away. This was within the limit of the sales agreement, not to practice near my salon. I notified Caesar about my accident and told him that I wouldn't be working in his salon and to please handle my clientele. He was a very friendly and loyal worker.

Marcia and I had talked about going to Australia. I had researched and was intrigued with the hunting and wanted to move there to hunt crocodiles—out of Darwin—in northern Australia.

I had already contacted the Australian embassy in San Francisco and asked about doing such a thing. They responded that they were very sorry; they were more interested in professional people. Darn it! They had just torpedoed my chance to become the first Crocodile Dundee! Thanks, Australia, for doing me a VERY BIG FAVOR! Hindsight is always so nice!

# We Chose Alaska

We said, "So be it. Now what?" We thought about it and decided to go to Alaska! Marcia applied for a teaching position in Anchorage. I decided that I'd like to go to school full-time and get a degree. I thought it would be beneficial for me to better communicate with my clientele. I also applied for a cosmetology license from Alaska and was accepted, on the basis of my California experience. We were all set.

About two months before we were to leave—Marcia got a letter stating that at that time there was no position open! We were stunned! What to do? What to do? Another shot across the bow!

I think we were already in possession of some of the daring that you need to make it in Alaska. We decided that we'd proceed as planned and deal with it when we got there. I used daring as a quality. Now that I'm much older, I feel it's the positive naivety of youthful energy—which more closely resembles stupidity! But, the good Lord, willing it seems to work! Thank God!

About a week before heading north—we heard from Anchorage. They were sending along a contract for the 1965 school year. YEAH! ~ Divine Intervention ~

# We Chose Alaska

So here we were with nothing to do but prepare for our trip. The naivety comes into play again when I called it 'nothing' to do!

12.

## The Preparation

"Yup, I got me a bride and I'm heading north! Heard there was a woman shortage in that 'thar' country. Something like three to one or worse! Didn't like the odds, so I 'brung' me own!"

We had already bought a brand-new Chevrolet half ton pickup. We talked about buying a trailer or a pickup camper for our trip. We were undecided so we went looking around the sales lots.

They hadn't coined the term RV yet, so there were just trailer and camper sales dealerships. My trailer knowledge was zilch. I had never pulled anything behind any of my vehicles.

We were traveling along the Pacific Coast Hwy. in Long Beach one evening at about ten and decided to look over the inventory of this

## We Chose Alaska

closed dealership. We could browse at our leisure, to see all the styles available, and not be bothered by any sale hungry salesman. Traffic at that time of the evening during the week on the Pacific Coast Hwy. was very light.

In fact, in those days it was possible to cruise around on a warm balmy evening with the top down and enjoy a ride.

The picture is of my 1953 Buick Skylark convertible taken on Irene & Craik Murray's wedding day.

I enjoyed driving in the evenings with the top down. They now fetch a whopping $225,000. Should have hung onto it. Buick only made a few of these. They had chrome wheels

## We Chose Alaska

and a continental kit with another chromed wheel hanging off the rear. I loved it!

Whoops! Henry, focus!

At the time I was carless. We were using Marcia's Volvo. (Remember our accident?) We started looking at an old used teardrop styled trailer that looked as if it wouldn't make it off the lot—much less up to Alaska. It was unlocked.

I opened the door and shined my flashlight inside. Whoa! The whole wall on the opposite side exploded into a moving panorama of cockroaches escaping the area of the sink! We were taken aback and quickly shut the door.

Marcia stunned, and bewildered asked, "Just exactly what do you have in mind?" I really didn't have anything in mind except curiosity. "I just wanted to see."

We quickly upgraded my expectations and started to look at some new models. Turned out they were locked. However, we did find a beautiful ten-foot pickup camper that was unlocked!

'Benri desu ne'! Japanese for 'how fortunate'! We entered and looked around and made ourselves at home! I had never been inside of a camper before. I was really impressed with all the comfort that was

## We Chose Alaska

available. We just enjoyed sitting there and talking. It was like a secret hideaway.

We noticed an ad on a grocery store bulletin board that had a thirty-five-foot Traveleze trailer for sale nearby.

We went to see it and were impressed by the quality of the living accommodations. It had a bedroom in the back, with two bunk beds. They were on each side with a small aisle between them. Commuter style living! Between the bedroom and the living room was a bathroom with a tub and shower combo. The opposite side had a Coleman built-in gas furnace and a closet. Then the kitchen area, which faced the front door, was open to the living room. The front had a cab over section with a double bed.

## We Chose Alaska

So, we decided to buy it. It was setup in a mobile home park and owned by an older couple. It was immaculate. This is a picture of our new home, taken on the Alcan Hwy. on our trip north.

They moved out and we moved in. Basically, it was a fully functional and very comfortable home. "We 'dun' good!" I didn't like trailer park living. I enjoyed the pool and our neighbor. He and his wife were our ages—the youngsters in the park! The neighbor on the other side was just a grumpy individual.

The manager was always after me to mow the grass area adjacent to our spot. With what? The only thing that I owned that could be used—were my haircutting scissors! Besides, I didn't think it was that high. I really felt that they should have provided a mower for that purpose. It's ridiculous to expect a tenant to have a mower for a 4' x 45' patch of grass.

I guess I was way ahead of my time! We were short timers and before push came to shove we were hitched up and heading north to I-5. Already saddled with two payments and no clue of what to expect job wise, we pulled onto I-5 North—happy, excited and a bit petrified. What a gigantic load. We had stuffed everything that we owned, including a

# We Chose Alaska

large four foot plastic Santa Claus, into the trailer. I went by a weigh station sign that had a large intimidating sign which said, "Truck & Trailers Stop at Scales" So I did! That was my setup (truck and trailer). So I did as requested.

The gentleman at the window asked where I was going, etc. I told him and he listened intently with a slight smirk on his face and finally said, "You can go." He never even asked to see my papers—whatever they would have been! He was just curious about us. I looked at him and said, "I really didn't have to stop here, did I?" "No," was his answer. I thought to myself, "DUH!!" We drove back on to I-5 and continued with our trip north.

13.

## Northward to Alaska

One of the major realizations for those of us who answered 'the call of the wild', is the separation from family. (To quote a very dear friend, "Alaska is a very cold—cold place—far—far away." He had never been to Alaska. However, after having—reluctantly—agreed to

## We Chose Alaska

come here for a vacation by his wife, who loves and had previously lived in Alaska for ten years—he was completely smitten! They have since bought a piece of lake front property and built a beautiful house.)

You find out very quickly that all of a sudden—you are alone. Alaska either makes or breaks a marriage! You better have married your 'best friend'. You're all the family you've got here.

Communicating with the "Outside or "Lower 48" as America was referred to in those days, was costly. There was no Skype and long-distance calls were out of sight. In some of the places we lived, the mail either arrived by float plane or boat every two weeks. This meant that when you got a letter, your answer to it will catch the next flight or boat out in two weeks!

Now, back to the story. Let's hit the road or I-5 as it's called. The first part of the trip from Long Beach, CA to the Canadian border went very smoothly. It was freeway all the way, except for the last 25 or so miles. From I-5 to the border at Sumas, Washington the roads were very rural.

We were in no hurry and enjoyed a lot of beautiful sights along the way. We usually spent the nights parked right after an overpass, if it had a slight pull-off that looked safe from traffic. We

## We Chose Alaska

didn't sleep very soundly. Quite often we could hear the big sixteen wheelers coming in the distance. You'd hear a drone that increasingly got louder and louder until it was passing right by you.

This was accompanied by vibrant shaking of our trailer and a subsequent reduction in the Doppler Effect as the trucks sped away down the freeway! The Doppler Effect is exactly what a sonic boom does to the sound wave that is pushed ahead of the plane. In this instance it's a truck—the speeds aren't ultra-sonic.

The middle of the night is not the time to split hairs! Campgrounds were not as numerous as nowadays. We did use a campground with facilities just one time, in Washington State. It was right off of I-5 and had a marked exit. It was a bright sunny day and we stopped in mid-afternoon and just enjoyed that new experience. It was our first official rest stop.

I can remember sitting by a picnic table—in the dark—I could see Marcia fixing supper in our lit up new home! I said to myself, "This is great!" The whole ambiance thing just oozed! Warm fuzzy feelings abounded!

Our biggest drawback was that we only had a Standard Oil map by which we navigated. We were so unprepared in that area. It wasn't until after we got to Alaska—we found out that there is a publication written specifically

## We Chose Alaska

for traveling the Alaska Highway through Canada and Alaska. It's called "The Milepost" and it's updated periodically. It's been our must-have for all subsequent trips. The further north we went—the more magnificent the scenery.

The ocean has always been one of our favorites—however those snow crested mountains were just magnificent. We took tons of pictures—Sooo—click—click! We had no idea what lay ahead for us. Every mountain around the bend was even more spectacular than the last. This pattern continued all the way to Alaska.

That meant almost all the scenic pictures taken from then on, on this trip, would pale in their enormous beauty as they would be surpassed! It probably took us about four plus days to enter Canada. I must mention a method of telling where the location of something is, in both Western Canada (British Columbia, Yukon and Northwest Territories) and Alaska. There is a mileage sign marking almost every mile or kilometer of a highway or road, called the milepost.

In the old days traveling across the west, you might get directions from a local about where a certain place might be. It would probably go something like this. "Hello. How

## We Chose Alaska

do I get to the Tipton farm?" The reply, "Howdy, Stranger. I see you're from back east. The Tipton farm, eh? Well, let's see now. You head east out of town for, mmm, let's say fifteen miles 'til you get to the old Boos place. You'll know that by the big green mailbox along the road. Just a short distance on the left, you'll notice a big oak tree with a lightning scar up its behind! You take your next left ... etc., etc."

Translated: "Hi there. (Same question) You go east out of town to milepost 'xxx'. There'll be a farmhouse there with a large green mailbox. Take the next left to milepost xxx.... etc., etc. .... That'll be the Tipton's farm." So simple and so very effective. As you get further north, you'll find mileposts being used for locations, when you start leaving the cities.

We entered Canada without incident. Things were very relaxed in those days. We could even take our guns (rifles and revolvers) and several cases of Red Mountain Burgundy wine gallons ($1.25 retail in California). They asked what our purpose was for entering and wanted to know if we had insurance on our vehicle and at least $500 cash in case of problems. That was about it. The good old days!

## We Chose Alaska

We had purchased two spare tires for the trailer. It was common knowledge that the 1200-mile gravel stretch of highway, from Dawson Creek on the far eastern edge of British Columbia to the Alaskan border, would just chew up your tires. Our total distance for the trip would be almost 3600 miles. So, one third of our trip would be on a gravel road!

The Canadian roads (paved, that is) were good and didn't have the hectic pace we'd been traveling since leaving Long Beach, CA.

We didn't have a clue to what driving on gravel for 1200 miles would be like. In the meantime—ignorance was bliss! The whole atmosphere was one of relaxation and sightseeing. We even saw cowboys (real ones) working their cattle.

Our miles traveled during the day also decreased. That was much more evident when we reached the Alaska Hwy., the Alcan. We considered it a good day if we clicked off at least 300 miles.

Crossing into British Columbia, the mountains even got better and sometimes their tops were barely visible when looking out the car windows. You had to roll the window down to be able to look up. It was like driving down the cleavage of the Grands Tetons of Wyoming. I've never been there. The name is

## We Chose Alaska

fitting here, and has stuck with me, since the word Tetons was given to those mountains, by early French trappers who named them.

Tetons is French slang for boobs! I guess the early trappers weren't leg men! A little culture never hurt anyone!

We no longer had to hunt for overpasses for our sleeping accommodations. Anywhere there was a creek, river or lake with a pull-off—it would become home for the night.

One of the most memorable stops and a very valuable lesson learned was at the lake Lac La Hache (the hatchet) campground, at about milepost 114 on PH 97, the Cariboo Hwy (PH = Provincial Hwy.).

Marcia kept a diary of our trip, in fact she documented most of our goings-on for many

## We Chose Alaska

years and sort of still does. Those notes were all lost in our fire.

We are left with only recall as our source. Pray for us! We'll be relating just the highlights. It's funny the way the brain works. We spend hours, days, weeks and even months living. Do we remember all those fantastic moments? Heck, no! What reigns supreme are the moments when we were angered or scared out of our wits!

I guess the brain feeds on pleasant memories and stores the anxious ones for future reference. So, the first things that come up in recall are the leftovers from the brain's banquet.

We were traveling on the Cariboo Hwy. which started at Cache Creek - milepost 1 for that highway. We saw the entrance to a campground and pulled in. It was about mid-afternoon and the campground was quite full.

There was a road that forked right for entering and departing. It was basically a one-way road once we passed the fork. I made a few turns—all was fine. My next turn—which looked rather sharp—to the left, was to be another matter!

I couldn't maneuver around it and found the front right of the truck up against a tree. I turned my wheel to the right to pull away and

# We Chose Alaska

straighten out. When I tried to resume my left turn, I found that the left middle part of the trailer (a 35-footer) was about to nudge another fairly good-sized tree. I huffed and I puffed! All to no avail—I was stuck—but good!

The campers saw that I was in a bad fix and descended on us like a swarm of bees. They were just wonderful. They were mostly elderly travelers and for them—this was entertainment made to order! How many of us have some elderly traveler in the family that wouldn't consider this was a match made in heaven.

That was my first experience with the "law of the west" (northwest). You always render assistance to a stranded traveler. Next thing I knew they were directing me to turn the wheels this way and then that way... etc. etc.

Finally, it was decided that I should unhitch the trailer and reposition the truck at a better angle. Also, we cut that tree down! I imagine it quickly disappeared into their fire pits.

I made a hasty retreat to the highway—quite relieved and not wishing to be around to answer any questions about any trees being cut down! It was not a malicious intent!

We spent the night another fifty miles further at Williams Lake. Lesson learned:

## We Chose Alaska

Never enter a campground with a long trailer without first walking in to see the potential pitfalls. The next time I had to use that lesson was just south of Tok, Alaska—many more hundreds of miles and days away, on this trip.

Shortly the campgrounds gave way to gravel pits and pull-offs similar to this. In fact, this spot where we spent the night was about 375 miles from Dawson Creek. Very doable on a paved road. That meant one more day and no more paved roads! We felt as if it were our own private campground. We were the only ones who camped there that night.

~ Goodbye paved roads! I still couldn't fathom what all that meant! ~

14.

### THE ALCAN (Alaska-Canada Hwy.)

I'll start this journal with a short paragraph by Wikipedia about the ALCAN Hwy. in order to provide a bit of background information.

## We Chose Alaska

[The ALCAN Hwy (Alaska-Canada Hwy.) The official start of construction took place on March 8, 1942 after hundreds of pieces of construction equipment were moved, on priority trains, to the northeastern part of British Columbia, near Mile 0 at Dawson Creek. Construction accelerated through the spring as the winter weather faded away and crews were able to work from both the northern and southern ends; they were spurred on after reports of the Japanese invasion in the Aleutians. On September 24, 1942, crews from both directions met at Mile 588 at what became named Contact Creek, at the British Columbia-Yukon border. The entire route was completed October 28, 1942, with the northern linkup at Mile 1202, Beaver Creek, and the highway was dedicated on November 20, 1942, at Soldiers Summit.]

The highway has continuously undergone major reconstruction and in some cases by-passed areas of the old road. When we headed for Alaska in 1965 the road was still all gravel and pretty much the same as the original construction. It was an

## We Chose Alaska

adventure. Almost a rite of passage test. Those two Google pictures say much.

We finally arrived in Dawson Creek, the beginning of the ALCAN, and found a wonderful park right in town with a place to park our trailer. We spent the night, did some shopping and fueled up. While at the gas station, we met some tourists that were just exiting the hwy. and expressed great curiosity about us. We told them that we were on our way to Alaska to live.

They wanted to share their experiences with us and made a few suggestions about having spare tires (which we did). They also said to leave any windows or vents closed in the trailer while on the road. To leave the front vent open on the truck so that it would create an outward pressure inside the cab and keep the dust out.

They gave us their humongous protective screen that was bolted to their front bumper, and even

## We Chose Alaska

helped me install it on our truck. The screen went all the way across the front of the truck and extended outward about 6" on each side as well as about a foot over the front of the hood. This was to deflect the rocks that were kicked up by oncoming cars and especially the trucks! I was glad that we had four-wheel drive on our truck. They told us that there were a couple of sections under construction with very poor driving conditions. They said that the highway dept. had equipment stationed there to help travelers that might get stuck. We already had to use our four-wheel drive back in Seattle, of all places.

Let me introduce you to our ALCAN memory for the next 1200+ miles! There were basically no campgrounds as we now know them. It was fair game. Wherever you wanted to stop for the night, was your decision. The only thing you had to pay attention to was the fuel gauge. There were lodges with fuel within about a day's travel between them (+/- 300 miles). Garages (repair stations) and gas stations were stationed in between those stops at varied distances.

One of our memorable moments occurred when we had chosen a large gravel pit off the side of the road to spend the night. Gravel pits are a common site along the route since it was the source of gravel for the highway. We pulled in and did our usual 'dance' before entering the trailer.

# We Chose Alaska

Every morning after rising, we'd cover our bed with a sheet. It took us only one day of travel to figure out that if you didn't—you'd have a bunch of dust to clean up before you could go to sleep! We'd simply gently pick up the sheet, take it outside and shake it clean. We turned it into a daily humorous dance. The dance was done to make life more bearable.

There was so much dust that filtered into the trailer—even with all the vents closed. We had to lighten the mood. I would have to go in and bring out a beer that we'd share before Marcia could face entering our little home! We had unrolled toilet paper, cabinets popped open, and supplies strewn all over the floor. Dust covered every square inch of every surface area. After the beer had done its job—we went in—cleaned up as best we could and got ready to fix supper.

That night, while we were sleeping, we were awakened by the sound of a truck pulling in and stopping. In the cold night air it sounded as though it were right next to us. I wondered why he would park so close to us when this was an immensely large area. We felt tense and since I'd rather know what's going on than not know.

I got up. I got my rifle—cranked a round into the chamber and handed it to Marcia. "Here—take this and if someone comes in while I'm gone—use it!" I said as I headed for the door.

I went out and couldn't see anything except a truck in the distance with its motor running. I

## We Chose Alaska

figured that the driver was doing exactly the same as we were—stopping for the night.

I returned to the trailer. I opened the door and walked in. From the dark of the back bedroom, she asked "Henry—is that you?" "Yes," I answered—not even thinking about my parting message!

My poor little Marcia was petrified! I hadn't even thought that I should have announced myself before barging back in!

As I write this—I get a little emotional when I think about the enormity of that situation—she's a real trooper!

We decided to take advantage of a crystal-clear creek along the road for one of our bathing stops. I went down first and immediately felt the sting of very cold water coming from the mountains! It was almost paralyzing and kept us from enjoying the moment! We had all we could do to just keep our feet under water.

The bathing part was done in spurts and splashes of frigid torture. We'd wet down, lather up and wash all the necessary imperatives of a bath. The flat metal pieces are the edges of the grader blades that were replaced during the construction and maintenance of the highway.

# We Chose Alaska

Then the horrible thought of rinsing had to be endured. I'm standing by about a three-foot bank. The blades were our only salvation. They were heated by the sun's rays—nice and hot! Easily cooled by the splashing of the creek water. I guess we weren't the only ones who sought to cleanse ourselves in this far off little creek! I bet it was greatly appreciated—despite the chilling introduction! Bottom line, we were clean—refreshed and happy.

## We Chose Alaska

BRRRRrrrrrr! Now that's what I grudgingly call refreshing! The hot sun was soothing! The next time we would bathe—a few hundred miles ahead—was a complete reversal of conditions. Instead of a glacial creek, we stopped at a famous hot springs campground. The following is an excerpt by the Liard Hot Springs Provincial Park.

["Relaxation seeps into your body as you ease into the second largest hot spring in Canada. Liard River Hot Springs provides relief to Alaskan bound travelers after a long day on the road. The hot springs complex is of national ecological significance and is well known for its natural setting in a lush boreal spruce forest.

The park is such a popular stop over for tourists—the campground fills up early each

## We Chose Alaska

day during the summer months. Liard is also open year-round. There is a hot spring open to the public called Alpha pool with water temperatures ranging from 107.6° F to 125.6° F. Facilities include a change house and composting toilet.

A boardwalk, which leads to the hot spring pools, passes through a warm water swamp and boreal forest which supports rich and diverse plant communities as well as mammal and bird species. Visitors are asked to stay on the boardwalk at all times in this area so as not to disturb the sensitive habitat. Watch for moose feeding in the warm water swamps. Due to the lush plant life influenced by the warmth of the springs, the area was originally known as the Tropical Valley."]

Back in those days, there was a nice parking lot, possibly some tables. There was a nice wooden ramp leading quite a distance, several hundred yards, to the lower and then the upper springs. They had nice small dressing rooms adjacent to the springs for changing into your bathing suit. It was a very welcomed spot for that kind of relaxation.

Another pause that refreshed us was when we arrived in Whitehorse, Yukon Territory. There were real live PAVED streets! We even went shopping in a supermarket! We loaded

## We Chose Alaska

up on our dwindling supplies. It was such a pleasant time—no shake rattle and roll—no dust and no flying rocks. Just a small return to life as we knew it before Dawson Creek. You can see that we already were developing an appreciation of the simpler things in life. That's one of the effects of living in Alaska. It has a mind-altering effect on you. It's a great molder. It gives you a feeling of belonging. It becomes—MY STATE—not just another state! At the time, we didn't know how deeply our emotions would carry us. But, I'm jumping ahead.

The only flat tire that we had was when we headed north out of Whitehorse, about 30 miles. I guess the stress of the pavement was too much! As we were going along—I felt a lurching movement in our momentum. I had never felt that before. I pulled over and saw that one of the four rear tires (two on each side) had gone flat.

I jacked up the wheel and removed it. We unhitched the trailer and headed back to Whitehorse in the truck with the new spare that we had brought along. It was a no-brainer. I had the tires changed at the first garage we saw.

We were very happy to see this sign!

## We Chose Alaska

You can see what gorgeous days we had! No complaints. It was a very wonderful trip. This is a picture taken just before Alaska. The Yukon is the last Canadian territory—next to Alaska We had driven ourselves into a world where God went absolutely crazy with his creativity. We were in awe and the further north we traveled the more 'awe-full' it was.

The major concern with living and traveling in Alaska is that you might become immune to all the beauty that constantly surrounds you. Thank God that hasn't happened to us. We are still in awe and have ample scenic shots to show for it.

15.

## ALASKA LIFE (Our Beginning)

In this chapter, you'll find out what made me say these words. "I think we'll push for the campground and rendezvous with Jim. We'll get another chance to bag a moose!" I've regretted ever saying them.

We arrived in Anchorage around the first week of August 1965, the first place we headed for was where Marcia's school, Abbott Loop, was located. On our way down Lake Otis Road, we passed a small trailer park—Spruce Trailer Court. We found the school about a quarter mile away from it.

## We Chose Alaska

We returned to the park and luckily, they had an open space for rent. We started to set up the trailer. My first problem was the electrical connector from the trailer—it was a standard 110v outlet. I know these technical terms NOW because I attended the school of hard knocks! In California my expertise was limited to the standard knowledge of city dwellers. I could put a switch on and off. I could plug something into an outlet (they all looked the same). But here I faced a power base that had a different configuration that my brain couldn't compute.

Luckily (or NOT!), there was a lineman from the electric company working on the main meter board about 50 feet from our pad. I walked over and asked, "Do I plug the three-pronged cord from my trailer into that large three-pronged outlet on the power supply base?" "Yes," he replied as if he were being bothered.

I walked back and saw that I needed to buy a different plug. I went to an electrical store and bought a standard 220v. outlet. (Notice the fancy tech. talk!) Here's what I should have said, if I had known the proper lingo, "Do I plug my 110v. plug into the 220v. outlet, on the meter base?" DUH!

## We Chose Alaska

Regardless—that lineman should have known—by my question—that I didn't know anything about the electrical connection. He should have been a slight bit more attentive to the problem. Maybe he had his own quagmire?

I returned home and replaced my plug with the new one. I was a little confused at first—but then I figured out that I should put the black colored wire on one terminal and the white on the other. That left the ground to go to the third spot. It fit beautifully into the outlet box when I was finished. DUH!

Marcia was inside just waiting for the power to be turned on. She had her vacuum cleaner at the ready. Remember this was our first major cleaning, after driving the Alcan. The whole trailer was a dust bowl. I yelled to her, "Power's on". I headed in to check things out. Marcia had just turned on the cleaner and it started to jump and dance. She promptly shut it off and yelled that something must be wrong with it.

OK. I'd check that later. My interest was to see what kind of reception there was for television in the park! I went to our huge walnut cabinet combo Curtis Mathis TV/phonograph/radio set (about six feet long). I flicked from radio to TV and watched the screen enter a black hole in just a flash. I

## We Chose Alaska

started to suspect that something might be up. DUH!

I opened the refrigerator and it was almost as if someone from "Smile You Are on Candid Camera" had been hiding within—just waiting for someone to open the door. As soon as I opened the door the light bulb died in a brilliant flash! I noticed some smoke coming from our built-in gas furnace and I decided to cut my losses. Kill the power!

The final tally from that fiasco was first of all the lack of concern on the lineman's treatment and dismissal of my question and the resulting series of ruined equipment. The furnace had not suffered any damage. At least it worked well for three years as did the vacuum cleaner. The hot water heater (electric) had to be replaced. The refrigerator had vibrated so much on the Alcan that the copper tube to the compressor had broken. We had to buy a new free-standing 17cf refrigerator which took up an immense amount of space in our little trailer. The TV never worked again. At least the trailer didn't catch on fire! We settled in.

I decided to go back to school and finish the education that I had started in California. I had attended night school since I had stopped my flight training to take advantage of the

## We Chose Alaska

extra boost in income from the GI Bill's education provisions. I checked with Alaska Methodist University (the only university in Anchorage) and they would accept me as a sophomore for the coming semester.

I agreed and was told that if I chose a program that would lead to a teacher's certificate, there was funding available that would pay for my education and a write off 20% of it per year for five years upon graduation. "I'll do it!" That's how I decided to become a teacher. I've loved it. So, I guess someone was looking out for me.

I got my classes all figured out and also got a job working after school and weekends for Ree's Beauty Salon on Gamble St. in Anchorage. I worked from about three P.M. until nine P.M. daily. As time progressed—It turned out to be a strain on me. It was very tiring to be in school all day and then work in the salon well into the evening. I didn't have any problem with doing my job (hair styling)—however having to deal with people became stressful. I was tired—I needed to find something where I could turn off my brain and just work.

I got a job as a relief custodian for the school district. My job was to fill in whenever a custodian called in sick or for longer terms

## We Chose Alaska

such as vacations. It was perfect! I went to work and became quite efficient in completing my duties. I even found some time to study when all was done. I got off at midnight—dog tired. It was a different kind of tired—not mental.

I had never tackled a building project. I built a small 8'x12' leanto to be used as an entry way, as well as a living room. I put in a small pot-bellied stove (cast iron) that burned coal for heat. That was a wonderfully nostalgic way to heat the space and relieve some of the burden from the trailer's heater; it put out more heat. The following year I changed it to a 100,000btu oil pot burner furnace. Out went the nostalgia—kept the heat comfort!

Our first hunting trip was with one of Marcia's fellow teachers, Jim Hopkins and his wife. They had invited us for a moose hunt in the Swanson River area of the Kenai Peninsula, south of Anchorage about two hundred and fifty miles. We headed down in separate vehicles and camped in tents.

Just after turning off onto the Swanson River Road, we spotted a huge bull moose across a meadow. He was at about one hundred and fifty yards, standing broadside to me, perfect distance! My inexperience robbed me of getting my first truly magnificent

## We Chose Alaska

moose! ("I think we'll push for the campground and rendezvous with Jim. We'll get another chance to bag a moose!") Little did I know how naive that remark would turn out to be! After all we were Cheechakoes (term for newcomers to Alaska)! How did we know the difference between truth and fantasy? I had visions that the moose would be lined up waiting to be chosen! Needless to say—I was living in Fantasy Land. No moose on that trip!

Reality set in when we returned home to our little trailer and found that someone had driven by while we were gone and stolen our Honda 55 trail bike. It was just parked beside our trailer. We had no place else to put it. The insurance on it had expired two weeks earlier! Reality set in! Even in Alaska, there are thieves! There went another bubble.

Our space in the park was on the lower road. It ran along the fringe of a large bog area of small black spruce. There was a resident who had his dog chained to a small wooden shelter in the bog. The dog had just given birth to several puppies. We went to see the litter! We got Nanook—our new puppy! He was a Husky and German shepherd mix. He also took up residence in the bog, immediately in front of our trailer and about fifty feet in from the road. He was a good—well-behaved dog.

# We Chose Alaska

The only other hunting trip that year was with Bob (another teacher from Marcia's school). We left Anchorage around supper time on a Friday, and drove to the Paxson area, just about 350 miles away. We were back home on the following day with four caribou that we had shot that morning.

It was the fastest and the most successful hunt we'd ever been on. We ate caribou that whole winter until the following year when we shot a moose. Marcia still remembers those days. It wasn't the tastiest caribou. You might say, Yuk! That happens with caribou—some are delicious and then some aren't. It could very well have been in our handling of them during the field dressing.

The moose was a real treat. We had to let it age in our bedroom! It was more than we had the capacity to keep frozen, even though we shared with Bob and family.

We also decorated the outside of the lean-to with one of the dried caribou hides. I guess it's sort of like taking scalps!

## We Chose Alaska

The single pane windows, typical construction for California had to be covered with plastic sheeting, to keep the accumulation of frost on the windows from blocking our view and mainly to increase the insulation value.

Our two bunk bed frames were like solid rectangular boxes, with access doors from the room and from the outside.

We basically slept on two mini freezers, in which we had stored a lot of our stuff! By the time we got to look into those cabinets (February)—the things were frozen to the floor. We had to wait for warmer days before we could do anything about it. When we could get to handle the contents, we found Marcia's

## We Chose Alaska

beautiful wedding dress had mildewed! I also lost some pictures from my Clairol days.

We were settled in nice and cozy-like and ready for winter, along with our new refrigerator. We even frolicked in the snow. We were about to find out just how much more frolicking we would be given the opportunity to do as winter did its thing! We found that we needed to upgrade our winter clothing to Alaskan standards. That's a big change from what we called cold in California!
Spring finally arrived, we ventured south to the Kenai Peninsula for a weekend camping trip. The Kenai is a spectacularly scenic area.

## We Chose Alaska

We basically were shaking off the tail end of winter. It had been a rough winter, due to the fact that our cold weather clothing was in line with a southern California winter! NO COMPARISON, at all! We were learning and were going to make sure that the coming year would be different.

Nanook had really grown over the winter.

## We Chose Alaska

The trip took us to the town of Homer on the west side of the peninsula. On the way there shortly before Homer we overlooked the village of Ninilchik, a small native fishing village on Cook Inlet.

We took a weekend fishing trip to Tolsona Lake about 175 miles northeast of Anchorage with Ree and her husband. Ree owned the beauty salon where I had worked. Tolsona Lake is about twenty miles from Glennallen. We didn't know it then—but that's where we would finally settle to live, into 'old age'! Of course that's many years from the time of this event!

## We Chose Alaska

We also went on a camping trip with the Pansings to the Swanson River Area.

# We Chose Alaska

There were four of them: Dad and Mom, Pauline and David—Jane and Matthew.

It was their first time ever to go camping. Pauline also was one of Marcia's fellow teachers and a good friend. Her husband was an attorney.

They slept in the tent and we slept in the back of the truck.

## We Chose Alaska

The only one that caught a fish was Matt!
We had a great time!

☺

Marcia enrolled in an English Institute course for credit toward her certificate renewal. There was a requirement of six credits of extra course work for all teachers. It was necessary to renew required certification.

## We Chose Alaska

The kitchen was a very important and versatile piece in our home. It was one of the few flat surfaces that we had available. I even used it as a work bench when I overhauled the engine of the Volkswagen bus that we bought after selling our pickup truck.

That was quite a deal, we used the truck and sold it two years after driving to Alaska. We got about six hundred more for it than we paid when we bought it new!

We had to adapt other flat surfaces as needed. The following year when we shot a moose, we didn't have any place to put the meat during the curing time, as I mentioned earlier. (After you dress out the carcass, you need to let the enzymes in the meat work, in

## We Chose Alaska

order to have a better meat product.) Usually, it is hung in a cold space.

Since we didn't have anything that would suffice, we improvised. I think the term "permaculture way" (serve more than one purpose), would apply.

We had to give up our bedroom and remove the mattresses so that the moose could cure on plastic sheeting that covered the plywood tops of the bunks. We had to keep the room cold for about five days. Easy to do in Alaska.

We slept in the cab-over section of the trailer and kept the back bedroom door closed, and the window open slightly to keep it cold. When the moose meat was cured—we butchered and wrapped it on the table.

There were at least five hundred pounds of processed meat. We had to rent a frozen food locker from a local cold storage. It suffered a fire a few months later and we could only salvage a fraction of our stored meat. So we ate a lot of prepared canned tuna flakes. YUK! All in all after the first winter—we fared rather well—as these two pictures, taken on a bright, beautiful, sunny spring day, show.

## We Chose Alaska

# We Chose Alaska

16.

## ALASKA LIFE (Part 1- Anchorage Life)

# We Chose Alaska

Henry II had been a bit difficult to handle in California during our first year in Alaska. He became our little photographer. He had a natural knack for framing a picture. Soon we headed back for Alaska. Our first stop was at Fort Tejon, CA, on I-5 on the way to Bakersfield for a watermelon break. It was an old military outpost, where camels were used by the army to patrol the desert valley below.

The trip to the Canadian border was uneventful; we spent the nights in our camper. We would pull off after an overpass on the freeway and park as far as possible off to the side. The first few nights until we entered Canada were not the most restful. Needless to say, the first night was a repeat of last year's journey for Marcia and me.

This time we were in the back of a non-insulated camper shell! We were sound asleep and from the distance you could hear the hum of an approaching sixteen-wheeler. The hum would get progressively louder and louder until it passed with a rumble and a vibration shock to the camper. We knew the drill really well! Then back to sleep. Remember the freeways of yesteryear were not the insanely busy 24/7 of today.

We camped all the way northward. It was a very pleasant trip. We had a wonderful time. Soon we were back in Anchorage in our 'chateau' doing some of the projects that we couldn't do last fall

## We Chose Alaska

before winter hit. I involved Henry II in our front porch construction. It was wonderful having him home again.

# We Chose Alaska

Yep, you guessed it. School time!

Henry started third grade at Marcia's school and I continued at AMU and my custodial job with the school district

Henry II fit right in. There were many kids his age in the court where we lived. He was a very good student. He was a joy. Marcia and Henry II would come to wherever I'd be working and we'd share fish sticks together for our special supper.

By this time our dog's ears had straightened out. He was a nice friendly dog. A perfect friend for the whole family. His main residence was still the bog. We would let him come in and share the day with us. He and Henry Jr. became good buddies.

We had become very good friends with Bob Rood, a teacher at Marcia's school, and his wife Ruthanne, also a teacher. Every payday, we would alternate which house would host a supper for the six of us. We would share the cost of a king crab and make a humongous salad and top it off with a gallon jug of Red Mountain Burgundy wine, at about two dollars a gallon.

The boys, Henry Jr. and Robert Clark, didn't especially care for king crab. They wanted hot dogs. We 'reluctantly' fixed their choice for them! (Yeah right!) Bob took advantage of our couch when he'd visit since his living room only had a few pillows and was barren of any furniture. His kitchen had a card table, a three-legged stool and a folding chair. A man after my own heart! The kids (Henry II & Robert Clark) ate while sitting on the floor when we all got together, even at our home (trailer). This was handy for us and later we

## We Chose Alaska

found out also for the kids. Both places put the kids in the kitchen, slightly out of view, with easy access to the trash cans. We were sticklers that whatever food was put on their plates would be eaten. We found out later that any food that they weren't going to eat was conveniently and sneakily dropped into the trash! God love them!

Bob and Ruthanne also lived in a small trailer before they bought their house. They didn't furnish the house so that they could enjoy not feeling cramped, as they had been in their trailer, by all the furniture and limited space. Their furniture very sparingly decorated the house! They must really have suffered while living in the trailer! They achieved what they were after, a barren look—Wow!

A rather (sort of) comical event happened as a result of all the lack of furnishings. Someone had broken into their home and stolen some of Bob's hunting trophies that were hung on the walls. He was an avid hunter just like his dad.

He reported it to the police and when they came to investigate—he let them in at the front door which opened into the living room. One of the officers exclaimed after glancing around, "Boy! They really cleaned you out!"

# We Chose Alaska

We found that Marcia needed to get a warmer coat for playground duty when it's really cold. The teachers had to do playground duty during the recess periods. They stopped letting the kids go out, for recess when the temperature drops below twenty-five degrees below zero.

One of the teachers that taught at Marcia's school had purchased a wolf parka. It was gorgeous! I asked her where she bought it. She told me at David Green, the master furrier in Anchorage. He was the best at that time. It was a small family operation, run by the dad.

# We Chose Alaska

We went there to look over his selection of parkas. He had several beautiful styles from which to choose.

We chose the style we would like, then he took us to a room where all the available wolf pelts were stored. We got to pick out the pelts that we liked. They were silvery grey with black features. The ruff was wolverine fur—absolutely gorgeous!

We bought the parka for six hundred dollars! A lot of money in those days. We financed it on a two-year contract. It was a very special gift. She cherished it proudly. Even when we left Anchorage to go teach in the Bush—we had to store it at the furrier's location—for safe keeping.

The weather in Southeast Alaska was too mild for that much cold protection. We would have to wait until we returned to colder winters! We did six years later, when we got a teaching job in Glennallen, a place where the parka would be really needed.

My geology class went on a field trip to the Nabesna Mine in the Wrangell Mts. foothills. It was very interesting to travel back into the backside of the Wrangell Mts. and visit an old gold mine. You would think that your line of travel would be downward—much to the contrary, you climb very high! The scenery just

# We Chose Alaska

seems to explode in grandeur—the higher you climb! It wasn't a bad trip. The accommodations were perfect—a warm and dry miner's mess hall—with everything intact. None of this rough camping on the ground in a tent business. I was really impressed at what I saw—a lack of vandalism, everything was in perfect shape! I guess that sort of character isn't up to taking a trip that far back into the woods.

# We Chose Alaska

The class was taught by two excellent professors. Bill Long (on left) is credited with finding the tillite that is used as proof of Continental Drift. On the right (center) is Prof. Ross Schaff, head of the department, and another student.

# We Chose Alaska

# We Chose Alaska

These are the last shots taken as we descended toward the mine camp. This is one of our female classmates.

Here are some shots of our trip that show the spectacular beauty and heights that we operated in. We slept on the dining tables in the mess hall in the mine camp below.

The camp was an old mining company mess hall. It was gigantic. It had many long tables arranged in an orderly fashion. There were two large cast-iron cook stoves and various kitchen ware areas.

Each one of us chose his own table for sleeping quarters. Not having a sleeping pad was uncomfortable! However, we were nice

## We Chose Alaska

and warm and very tired from our climbing. Sleep was not difficult.

This was the big field trip of the fall semester. Needless to say, it was FANTASTIC! I really was enjoying my college experience. Life was getting more comfortable.

We had Henry II with us, the heating situation of our little home was comfortable and cozy—we were happy and better prepared for winter's arrival.

This is when I started making our own down clothing and buying rugged hiking boots, which were much needed and welcomed. Our first year, we suffered because of a lack of decent winter clothing. It drove me to change that.

The early dusting of snow was signaling the start of winter. We did a goat hunt in the Portage Glacier area. Bob, Ruthanne, Marcia and I walked to where they were.

## We Chose Alaska

## We Chose Alaska

Bob and I both were successful. He brought his goat out. I had to drag mine down the mountain side and leave it at the base until I came back with an akhio sled. It was too large to handle.

The following Wednesday, I drove down to the Portage area with the ahkio and our dog Nanook. He was almost two then and was a great help in pulling out the goat. I had a rope tied to the sled along with his harness. If he happened to stop and had trouble getting started, I also pulled until he was moving it by himself. He did a great job!

# We Chose Alaska

Henry Jr. wanted a photo with it.

We enjoyed the usual snowman building.

## We Chose Alaska

There were many restful moments of reading.

We also attended the sled dog races during Fur Rendezvous days.

# We Chose Alaska

We were planning to head for California to visit Corine and Henry II. He had gone there earlier, with the Roods. I still can see how sad Henry Jr. looked as he watched me from the front door window—load his belongings into the truck before heading to Bob's house. That really stuck with me! It was a very sad moment to see such a painful expression in my young son's face.

The plan was for me to drive down in the truck and Marcia would fly. We would rendezvous later and start our vacation. During that time, we took Corine and Henry back east to Massachusetts, New Hampshire and New York for a visit with our families.

I left and had no sooner started out of Anchorage when I picked up a hitchhiker with a sign saying that he was heading for Seattle. I usually didn't pick up hitchhikers, but I felt that this would be nice for me to have company for the four thousand plus mile trip.

He was a young man in his early twenties and seemed to be a nice person. We headed for the Canadian Border, a full day's drive away. On the way I started to feel sick and by the time evening arrived—I was almost a basket case. I had come down with some sort of bug that just knocked the pins out from under me.

## We Chose Alaska

I slept most of the way down through Canada. I was so thankful to have made that stop and helped him out by giving him a ride! We made it to Seattle and I stayed with him and his friends who shared a house. The friends knew of his arrival and had planned a big party for the arrival evening. His friends were a different story. They lived on the wild side. The party was going full bore and I decided to crawl into the camper shell and get some sleep.

I was planning to leave early before breakfast and eat something before heading out of Seattle. I told my travel buddy goodbye and thanked him for the great help he had been. We grew to be friends during the trip. I headed for the camper.

During the night I heard someone opening the camper door and trying to step up into it. It was one of his friends with a young lady in tow! I spooked the heck out of them and they apologized for waking me up. I guess they thought that I was still at the party and they were looking for a little privacy! The trip to Southern California went well.

First on our agenda was a visit with the kids. They were bronzed from all the swimming that they had been doing. They were very glad to see us, as we were to see

# We Chose Alaska

them. They looked wonderful. It had been a long year, for all. The purpose of making the trip was to start a sharing of custody—of the children. Our first year had too many unknowns to include them. We planned to start having one of them return with us and alternate every year, before we left for Alaska. Henry was to be first to accompany us on the return trip.

The four of us headed back east. We had a HUGE family gathering at my Uncle Henry's house. It was wonderful to all have a chance to spend some time together.

We are of French descent and are very affectionate. My proper English wife must have been terrified. They come on strong. One particular moment was when we were visiting my Uncle Henry (my mom's brother) and Aunt Florine. It was usually the gathering spot. They lived in the country and had ample accommodations for company. My brother Normand and his wife Joann were also visiting. Also included were my mother and two of her sisters.

Beware, when that crowd gets together. I love them. My family is very much a down to earth—loving—and hospitable family.

Normand and Joann were bunking in the room with the double bed. Marcia and I were

## We Chose Alaska

in the room with the two single beds. First thing in the morning as we were awakening, Marcia and I could hear a ruckus in the other room. We listened very quietly (protectively) to feign sleep. The sisters had gathered around Normand and Joann's bed and proceeded to yank the covers off of them, and said, "Come on, we want to see what you've got!"

The giggling was rampant. They were having a great time. They were more familiar with Joann because it wasn't her first visit with the family, so evidently, they showed her no mercy!

I could feel Marcia snuggling closer to me and whispering, "You don't think they're going to come here too?" I assured her, "I don't know!" I didn't—it wouldn't surprise me at all—if they had! We lucked out!

They evidently had seen enough, and had probably decided that Marcia was an unknown! They wouldn't have hurt her feelings for anything. They are very loving and caring. When the time to leave—Marcia had grown to appreciate and love them.

When you live on the other side of the country from your relatives, visits are few and far between. So consequently, it was a very much needed visit. Compound that with

Marcia and I moving to Alaska, and you have the ultimate in "fracturing" of family bonds.

## 17.

## ALASKA LIFE (Part 2- Graduation)

I finally graduated from AMU, Alaska Methodist University, in Anchorage—somewhat. I did finish all my needed credits but wasn't around for the actual graduation ceremony! It seems like history will verify that I have a natural affinity to not be present at my school graduations! For my high school senior year—if you joined the armed forces near the end of your final semester—they would graduate you early.

I joined the Navy and wasn't present for that one. My diploma was mailed to my home address. The college graduation followed the same pattern. Only instead of mailing me my diploma—Marcia was present to accept it. The reason for this is part of my following story. I

## We Chose Alaska

know that each of you is tingling with interest and anticipation—sitting on the edge of your seat! Here goes.

Marcia was left with an empty nest as school let out for the summer. Henry Jr. had gone back to California with the Roods who were driving back for their annual summer visits. I had been asked by Judy Moerlein, one of my college classmates, if I would like to cook for her husband's (George) exploration group. I was to stand in for his regular camp cook who wouldn't be available to be on site until later on in the season. He asked me, "Do you think you can do it?" I told him that I'd always liked to cook and I thought that I could!

Funny how doors open up when the person—who needs the help—has only one choice. This was my moment—I was it! (GULP!) This posed a slight problem. I still had some course work to do in a couple of my classes prior to graduation. I set out to get clearance to end the semester early. I was given the OK from my professors.

Hence, when graduation time arrived—my Marcia was there to receive my diploma. I think she was quite justified to do that. After all, she supported the home front while I

## We Chose Alaska

attended school. I wouldn't be where I am now if it weren't for her.

George was a geologist who had a contract with an exploration company to drill for molybdenum in Nunatak Cove—a small area in Glacier Bay National Park in Southeast Alaska, just north of Juneau. Little did I know in what a beautifully pristine and virgin area I was about to spend some time!

The glaciers had just retreated from that area recently and their front edges were in full view in the next cove up from Nunatak Cove. The vegetation was still sparse and game was also somewhat absent except for an occasional fox. I came to appreciate that part. No bears—to speak of!

Molybdenum is an element that is a critical additive to steel. The free element, which is a silvery metal with a gray cast, has the sixth-highest melting point of any element. It readily forms hard, stable carbides in alloys, and for this reason most of world production of the element (about 80%) is in making many types of steel alloys, including high strength alloys and super alloys. Thanks, Wikipedia.

George and I flew into Juneau ahead of the crew. He ordered supplies and building materials for the camp. Two days later—we flew into base camp. Our supplies that had left

## We Chose Alaska

Juneau by boat earlier, arrived on the same day.

Base camp was "very basic". It had the foundations and floors to several tent frames. The largest was to be the cook tent (mess hall) about 12'x12'. It was to contain a small gas range and a long table. The personal residences were slightly smaller (about 8'x8')—large enough to accommodate two bunk beds. Dimensions are usually dictated by plywood sizes in Alaska—less cutting.

The crew arrived and was a genuine representation of a hard-working drilling crew, an opinion that was reinforced, as I lived with and cooked for them—during my two month contract.

There were four drillers who worked two-man shifts every twelve hours. They were rough and unpolished; however, I would come to see through that visual armor. They were kind, friendly and emitted a kind of honesty about whom they were. I felt very comfortable around them. There was a comradery that developed among us and helped all to make the best of a situation of hard work and isolation.

The daily ration of two cans of beer and an occasional hell of a drunk (R&R)—in town—didn't hurt either! One of my pictures that

## We Chose Alaska

burned in our house fire was of me sitting on the front bench of our mess table and the four of them along the back bench. The dirty sunlit tan canvas of the wall tent and the dark dimly lit room was framing the picture of an exquisitely looking young lady posing prone in panties and an equally exquisite pair of breasts! I had found the picture in Juneau and thought it might add a little atmosphere in my mess hall. I think I really bought it because of her hairdo!

The four guys were grizzly looking and still in their drilling attire. I was sitting sideways on the front bench with my left leg raised and my foot resting on the bench. I was leaning forward resting on my knee. I was shirtless and looked very dark from all my days that I spent sunbathing. I was sporting my black beret that I wore for sun protection. In fact the whole exposure turned out to be a classic—typical of black and white pictures of the Klondike era. I loved it! I can still see that cute smile on that little sweetie pie. No, I'm not talking about myself!

I used a flash exposure on the camera and used color film and still got those fantastic black & white results! It was a perfect screw up and just meant to be.

# We Chose Alaska

The crew was allowed to go to Juneau by plane for a day every two weeks for a little R&R. Other than that, their schedule consisted solely of eating—working—and sleeping. This meant that after I cleaned up the breakfast mess, I was free until about five o'clock, in time to prepare for supper. I spent my idle time by doing some climbing, sunbathing and archery practice. That's how I got such a dark tan as was shown in the picture that I mentioned above.

I'm sure nowadays—I'd have been stopped at the airport as a possible terrorist. My hair was jet black then. Ahh—memories! I guess I was a sort of surrogate parent to them. Their feeding was my sole responsibility. I took that very seriously—they appreciated it.

My first breakfast was a major disappointment. They didn't say very much (hence kind). It was my first meal and I thought, "How can I feed these guys as efficiently as I can (easier for me)?" I decided to do hard boiled eggs, bacon, toast and coffee.

They no sooner walked into the mess tent that the silence was deafening! I'm great at catching body language. Needless to say, no accolades and no nasty remarks (hence both kind and friendly) were expressed. Even I had reservations as I served it. The only remark I

# We Chose Alaska

received was, "Is this the only type of eggs we have?" That remark could have very well been expressed in more colorful terms and tone.

They knew it was my first cooking job. I changed my attitude—the next day the breakfast menu consisted of eggs al gusto, hashed brown, toast or pancakes, bacon or sausage and coffee. Life thereafter was much happier! I had learned. I was there to serve and bring joy. Cooking was my method. I WAS going to be successful!

The plane would fly in with the grocery order that I gave them when they had dropped of the previous order—the week before. My suppers were mainly a roast of some kind or roasted chicken, chops, steaks and occasionally spaghetti and pizza. My famous mashed potatoes were created for those meals.

About a month into my job—I had one of the guys complain! "When the hell are we ever going to get to have just beans and hot dogs, around here?"

I took it as a wonderful compliment. I served them their beans—life continued to be perfect. My job at breakfast was to also have lunch material, such as cold cuts, peanut butter & jelly, candy bars, soda pop and jerky, to fix and pack for themselves. Those that were on the night shift would head for bed and the

# We Chose Alaska

day shift would hike up the mountain to start work.

Glacier Bay is a national park and in the cove to the south of us there were two park service rangers and their families that occupied some of the cabins there. The rangers would occasionally come over and in a sense inspect the goings-on. One time when they arrived, I was on the beach practicing target shooting with my bow and arrows.

Hunting equipment is forbidden in a national park. One of the rangers mentioned that he could prohibit my target practice because it was a weapon. I assured him that I only had target points and no hunting broad heads. I felt he was only yanking my chain. Things were fine. Nice guys. They were under the thumb of isolation and boredom just as we were.

During one of their many visits I had asked about their little community. I had been thinking that it might be possible to send for Marcia and set her up in one of their cabins. I had mentioned it to George and he couldn't see anything wrong with it. "It is 'our park', as such and a distinct possibility." I asked the rangers if it would be possible for her to stay there. They said, "No problem. We have a cabin, but it doesn't have a bunk bed!"

# We Chose Alaska

I set the plan into motion. I would put her up in one of the cabins and after my supper cleanup—I would hike the three miles up to the head of the cove—cross over the small mountainside to their cove and down into their camp.

But first I'd have to get a bunk over there for her. So, one morning after breakfast cleanup, I strapped one of the bunks from one of our wall tents on my backpack and headed to the park cabins. As I walked into camp and passed one of their cabins—the ranger's wife was looking out the window. She turned and asked her husband what that guy was doing there with a bed strapped to his back! He told her, "That's the cook from the drilling camp. He's bringing a bed down for his wife!"

Now for the travel plans. Once she flew into Juneau, I had arranged for her to fly out to the park camp on the next mail plane. OH! Joy! The mail plane also serviced the park service station. The day of arrival finally came. I was sunbathing on the rocks, when I heard the sound of a plane approaching and landing in the next cove.

I swelled with joy and anticipation! It had been over a month since we had said goodbye in Anchorage. I listened intently to hear that wonderful plane rev up and again take flight. It

# We Chose Alaska

was just a short time and it appeared at the Nunatak Cove's entrance. He was making his approach. He taxied up to the shore and handed me the mail and said, "MAN, you should see the gorgeous gal I just dropped off—over in the other cove. She's really beautiful!" In my thought, "I hear you, man!"

I really hadn't realized what an energy consuming schedule I had brought about. It meant after supper—I would hike over to the park camp—spend the night with Marcia and wake up at three thirty to hike back to camp. The actual distance took about an hour and a half—one way over some rough terrain—no trails here! I was probably the first Homo sapiens to walk there.

I was apprehensive about traveling through the wilderness on those trips—especially during those times of the day. I was aware of wild animal behavior. They sleep during the day—hunt and feed early in the morning and late in the evening! I attribute my behavior as foolish youth. The expression I like to use is, C'est la vie! It means—that's life.

Needless to say, I was wearing myself down to a frazzle. I decided after a few days of that schedule that I needed to make some changes before I started having hallucinations of something lurking behind every large tree or around the next bend of my path.

I had seen a gorgeous little tarn (a small depression left in the terrain by the scouring action of the glacier as it moves down the mountain side), filled with crystal blue water and ringed with alders, during one of my hikes. It was located directly above our camp.

It was from where we were piping our camp water through a piece of three-quarter inch plastic pipe. It was gravity fed. ~ Once you create enough suction to have it head downhill, gravity takes over. Voila, running water! ~ I would usually take my shower in the late afternoon when the water in the black pipe was nice and hot. Our shower was a three-sided elongated box facing the bay. It had a shower head and an on and off valve.

We decided that I'd move Marcia there during the daytime when no one would be aware of her arrival. I set up an Indian style teepee with a plastic sheeting skin spread over some alder trees that I had cut and trimmed to make poles. It was a fantastically scenic spot. It overlooked the camp and a hundred and eighty-degree view of the cove and its small mountains.

Every day, the cove would present a panorama of icebergs—which had calved off

## We Chose Alaska

the glacier feeding the main channel during the day and carried out with the outgoing tide during the night—to be captured by the shallow waters of the cove. The icebergs were like brilliant bluish-silvery sculptures, of many fancy and shapes and configurations—framed by a lush dark green wreath—rimmed occasionally with snow-capped mountains, that encircled this shallow pool of water—reflecting the blue sky. Some of them would have perfect tunnels in them which shown up in vivid varied depths of blue.

The view to the right of camp looked out at the main channel of Glacier Bay and occasionally you would see large chunks of ice the size of houses among this white dumpling-like stew. They would flip and turn in response to their ability to redistribute their weight as they lost some of their mass to the heat of the sun—isostatic adjustment. To the left were the mountains that were snuggling our little camp. It was a really majestic panorama! We were truly blessed.

Marcia settled into her new camp and really enjoyed the ambience. It didn't take long for the boys to wonder what was happening to me during the day. We could hear them yelling my name quite often. I told them that I was out hiking and exploring. However—I couldn't

## We Chose Alaska

keep this pre-tense up very long. The breaking point came for us to decide to let them know what was going on.

They had all gone to town for their R&R, in Juneau and came back full of spirit! They went to my tent to have me share in their celebrating. They yelled and screeched repeatedly. "Henry, where in the hell are you? HHEnnnrrrYYY, where are you?"

We decided to let them know after they woke up that Marcia was staying nearby; I would bring her down for the evening meal.

They took the news rather well. "So, that's what you've been up to all these past days!" They were eager to meet her. Marcia was sitting in the mess tent awaiting their arrival.

The boys must have waited on each other—they all marched in at once and introduced themselves. They also had spruced up and put on clean clothes. Cougar (nickname), the oldest of the four, walked in—and in turn shook Marcia's hand and welcomed her.

This next statement still brings wonderful tears to our eyes. Cougar had shaven for the first time in a month for the occasion and was sporting several blood dotted pieces of toilet paper where he had suffered razor cuts. You have no idea about the depth of that presentation! I think you probably do.

## We Chose Alaska

It was decided that it would be better for her to move in with me in my tent camp. That made it much safer for her. The only reason that we did the 'tarn' thing was because ecologically, wild animals were not an issue. Neither was it a sure thing—some might show up, in the area!

Now, I had my partner with me to do the sunbathing, hiking, and exploring. Life in camp was great. She filled a huge void in my life and theirs.

The time had come for her to return to Juneau—on the mail plane—with the very pilot that had dropped her off at the park's camp, in the neighboring cove. He was mouth-dropping surprised! We all had a good chuckle about it. Marcia is getting ready to board the plane with the mailbag.

# We Chose Alaska

I was about to begin my solitude—again. ☹

I showed up at home in Anchorage a couple of weeks later sporting a full beard that made me look like a rabbi. It took just a little time to shave it off. I grew very weary of all those stiff bristles.

18.

## Alaska Life (Part 3 - A New Career)

My contract with Alaska Methodist University was to work as a teacher for a period of five years after graduation. Each year 20% of the indebtedness that I had incurred while attending school would be forgiven.

I was fortunate that during my senior year—I did my student teaching in French at Dimond High School in Anchorage. My master teacher was excellent. She had been teaching for quite a long time and was due to retire. When I finished my student teaching—I was told that there would be a position opening up for the coming school year.

## We Chose Alaska

I guess the wheels were already set into motion about my applying for her job. A double whammy was that there was also going to be a position opening in the science dept. to teach a class in Geology and in Earth Science. I seemed to fit the bill. My major was in French and my minor was in Geology (e.g., Earth Science, etc.).

A rare combination of language arts and science in one package. I put in my application for the position and when the contracts were handed out—I was hired to teach three French classes, one Geology and one Earth Science. A full schedule in courses for which I was qualified. I was VERY fortunate.

Corine flew up from California (by herself)! She attended 6th grade at Marcia's school.

We made a climbing trip to a mountain northeast of Anchorage in the Knik River area. A couple of my fellow teachers and I had planned a mountain climbing day hike.

We left on a Saturday morning after breakfast and headed for the area. We had packed a lunch for when we reached our unspecified goal. When the terrain got a little too advanced for just a casual hike, we rested and ate our lunch.

We had a great time and Corine kept up very well. She was a real trooper. When we

## We Chose Alaska

reached the cars after our descent, we all expressed our concern that she might have pushed it a little too much.

We got home to the trailer and no sooner had we gotten in—she hustled out and started to play ball with Ricky and Kathy Hatten. We acknowledged that we might have been mistakenly concerned about her endurance.

(Recently, while reviewing the happenings of that year with Corine over the phone, I asked her to fill me in on a few details that were vague. Two of the stories that she recounted to us dealt with trips to the Kenai Peninsula during the spring.)

The first one was a trip that took us south around Turnagain Arm into the Portage Glacier area. On the way there we saw eagles swooping down on fresh hatchings of baby turtles.

Corine still vividly remembers those details. She told us about this trip when we hadn't remembered it. While she was telling us—both Marcia and I said that not only didn't we remember—but we were not even sure that we had turtles in Alaska—much less hatchings!

I Googled it and learned that she was absolutely right. Alaska has Leatherback

# We Chose Alaska

Turtles that migrate to the coastal waters in spring.

She also remembered seeing the devastation caused by the 1964 'Good Friday Earthquake'. That area had subsided about three feet which, accordingly, submerged the cabins and trees that were in the area. The trees had been subjected to a permanent salt-heavy diet since the tides of Turnagain Arm inundated the once fertile land.

It was a very eerie scene that was exposed to us whenever we would head south from Anchorage for many years to come. The tides were systematically choking and returning the land to its original state. Sort of like, "The dust to dust" from the Bible!

The next trip was on a Saturday, (most trips were on weekends, the plague of the working man!) to the Bird Creek area just south of Anchorage. It was on the same route taken to Portage Glacier.

I had scheduled an informal trip with some of my Geology students to do some hiking up one of the hills adjacent to Bird Creek and part of the local coastal mountains. It was basically a family climbing trip that also involved my students. We had a great time; we went high enough to have a fantastic view of the Arm and Cook Inlet.

## We Chose Alaska

Then came the time to rest up and head back down. The slopes were mainly dry with patches of snow about six or so inches deep. As we started our descent, I found out what Alaskan KIDS do with a slope that has a good amount of snowy patches on it.

All of a sudden—I was no longer in control. They exploded like a bunch of locusts in a wheat field. They were taking the easy way down—not on their feet—but their hind ends.

Everything turned out just fine. I had a few anxious moments when I had to reign them in from the abrupt edges that border the creek. Kids are fearless. I was so very glad to reach the base. As fate would have it—I never had the chance to see if I would ever have done such a field trip again. I know that I probably would not! Oh yes, Corine had a great time.

That same spring, two of my fellow teachers, the football coach, the band and choir director and I went on a bear hunting trip south to the Resurrection Creek area on the Kenai Peninsula. The purpose of this trip was to get a bear for the coach. He was a newcomer to the state from Florida.

We arrived at the trail's parking area around mid-morning. It was a gorgeous cool sunny day, perfect for hiking up a mountainous trail.

# We Chose Alaska

Marcia and I had learned a valuable lesson about camping gear during our nearly four years of hiking and camping in Alaska. Keep it light! You have to haul it all with you! We had revamped our complete camping gear setup to light, warm, down sleeping bags, a small lightweight white gas single burner cooking stove, and a hand-made nylon water-repellent tarp with a mosquito netting section, to be used as a tent. So, on this trip I was well equipped.

I strapped on my 44-magnum revolver and put on my Kelty titanium backpack and hoisted my eight-pound Winchester 338 magnum rifle upon my shoulder. I guess as the old saying goes "I was loaded for bear!" Once we were all geared up we headed up the trail. The plan was to hike up the trail to the top and hunt along the way. We had been climbing for about an hour and decided to pause for a rest.

We were sitting there for a while and from a distance we could hear the clinking and clanking of metal coming up the trail. As we listened—the clanking got louder and louder. Slowly the source appeared! There were three guys coming up the trail with the same intentions as ours. They were hunting, clinking and clanking. Hopefully, they'd run

# We Chose Alaska

into an old bear that was hard of hearing! The scene was all very comical.

We watched and restrained any show of emotion, just, "Hey, how's it going?" As they passed by, the last guy was wearing one of the old-fashioned oak board and canvas backpacks. He was dripping with perspiration and had stripped down to a tee shirt. From his pack hung a cast iron skillet on one side and a Coleman lantern on the other.

We saw the source of the noise and he was not doing very well. He still probably had another fifteen hundred feet or more of elevation to get to the lake at the end of the trail. The forest service had a cabin (maybe two?) there for hikers to use. We really felt sorry for him; however it was still funny. Almost a case of "déjà-vu" that we'd experienced when we first started camping. The skillet and lantern did reflect a lack of common sense.

There was quite a bit of traffic on the trail that weekend so we made a decision to avoid the trail and cross the saddle of one of the small mountains that would drop down to the creek below. We would then go up the creek to the lake and consequently the cabins.

We headed off the trail, as we passed the saddle, we found the going to be quite easy.

# We Chose Alaska

We had hiked high enough to be above timberline and were only encountering open grassy patches and small alder-like bushes. There was a nice trail that suggested that it was often used. It was lunchtime. We picked a nice spot along the trail to sit and eat our sandwiches. It was just magnificent. Way up and away in the wilderness and in a fantastically scenic spot.

If all you get out of a hunt is the game that you shoot—you're missing a lot! We were about to find out what we were going to be in... more than our share of what some people miss! We finished our lunch and harnessed our gear. I was in the lead; the coach was behind me and the choir director was bringing up the rear.

I forgot to mention these guys were both BIG TALL HUSKY GUYS. We hadn't gone more than five hundred yards when from the right—out of the bushes—at the beginning of a small clearing—rushed a bear! He was about one hundred feet or so away when he started his charge!

The first notice of the bear was from the director—who had spotted it to his right—charging toward us!

He yelled in a humongous choral voice, "BEAR! BACK ME UP!" We all started to

## We Chose Alaska

bellow as loudly as we could— "YAH—YAH". (Hoping that didn't mean kill in bear talk!) I can joke about it now; however, I can honestly say that I have no recollection of taking my rifle off of my shoulder and getting ready to shoot!

It was weird. All of sudden the director and I were facing the bear as it was making its charge! Almost at the instant that we were going to shoot—the bear made an abrupt stop—made a hundred- and eighty-degree turn—in what looked like one hop—and trotted calmly back into the bushes! It must have been all the yelling that spooked him—or just a bluff from the very beginning.

When the bear started his charge, the coach came around behind me—this put him directly to my left. I was now between the bear and him! I was surprised to see movement coming from my left. He had raised his rifle and that's what caught my eye.

For all I knew he was still supposed to have been on my right. I glanced at him and saw that he was taking aim at the bear! I grabbed the barrel of his rifle—raised it and yelled at him, "DON'T SHOOT! DON'T SHOOT!"

He pulled on his rifle but I wasn't about to let go! He yelled back at me—"God damn it! I

# We Chose Alaska

didn't come all the way up here for some son of a bitch to tell me—Don't Shoot!"

The danger to the bear had passed. My actions allowed him the time he needed to be out of sight into the brush.

The director and I explained to him that if he had shot that bear in the butt—it would have turned around and been very pissed at us—this time its charge would not have been a bluff—it would have torn 'US' a new butt!

No doubt about it, the Homo sapiens were definitely shaken! Needless to say, we were very much on the alert for the rest of the trip. We continued down to where we could hear the creek below.

We descended. It wasn't bad except the last hundred yards or so where we had to find a not so steep way to get down. We then followed up the creek. The water was shallow and provided us with some good walking spots. We would have to occasionally go under some alders that were drooping from the banks. Never mind thinking about walking along the creek's sides. It was the thickest of thickets. We stuck to the creek.

We had no sooner started our ascent up the creek when there was no choice but to cross under some low lying alders.

## We Chose Alaska

TADA! Snagged on the overhanging branches were patches of long brown coarse-looking hairs—the pressure was on again! It was really time for us to stop for the night and fix supper. We'd had a very full day of it and the last couple of hours weren't any picnic!

We chose a nice grassy spot in the middle of the creek. We tramped down a camp spot and even had a large log that provided us with plenty of seating room. It was another picture-perfect moment.

As we got our meal—I sat down on one end of the log and put my rifle down next to me, up against it. The director—who was sitting on the other end of the log—suddenly got up to get something from the fire. I felt the log drop down from under me and the jolt spurred me to action. I had no idea what was happening, it was all sheer reflex. I snatched my gun up and then quickly realized what the problem was.

The director who outweighed me by a fairly large amount, had caused a shift in the balance of the log. So, down I went! The two had quite a laugh at that little scene. I had to agree, it was quite comical once the adrenalin rush had subsided.

After we had eaten and taken care to burn or throw into the water any exposed source of

# We Chose Alaska

food, we proceeded to lay out our sleeping bags, for the night.

We had a small space that would be perfect. The director placed his bag down first. When I finished flailing mine around in order to fluff out the down feathers—I put it next to his and left about sixteen inches between them.

Next thing we knew—the coach had placed his bag between ours! I was getting to know much more about this guy. On second thought, I was getting some very good info about him. He was frightened—so were we!

It's funny. When you sleep in the wild, and circumstances aren't conducive to a restful night, the tiredness of the day usually takes over. Before you know it, morning is here—so are you!

We ate breakfast and prepared to head for our trek around the side of the lake to the cabin. The terrain (thicket) around the edge of the lake was an exact duplicate of the terrain along the creek. The only and very big difference was the creek supplied us with enough dry spots to navigate our travel. The lake offered us—only every now and then—a very small lens of rocky beach along the shore—not very often.

The rest of the travel was along the edges through the thicket. What made it more

# We Chose Alaska

challenging and exhausting was that dodging under and over the branches with a backpack was akin to having antlers. We finally arrived at a clearing with the cabin in the background. We didn't stay around there long. Our boots were soaked so we felt that we should make a bee line—down the mountain—for the parking lot.

As we reached the beginning of the trail we noticed—at the entrance—a large sign that we hadn't noticed upon our arrival. It said, "Blah, blah, blah, (and then this statement) Be aware there are bears on the trail." "YEAH, MAN! NOW, you tell us!"

That charge which turned out to be a bluff was my closest encounter with a grizzly. It is etched in my mind as if it were yesterday! I look back on it with a certain fondness. I guess if an adventure has taken us on a fine line— that separates between safety and tragedy—we appreciate the positive outcome more dearly. It's not an intended path that we choose. It is however all the elements that had to be present to feel the fondness of success.

I guess this is a time to talk about what kind of investments we made—a year or so after we arrived. I was greatly impressed by what Alaska was, and is still doing, pertaining to its plan of land distribution. While still at AMU

## We Chose Alaska

(Alaska Methodist University), I saw a notice about state land auctions. The state put up parcels, chosen by the Dept. of Natural Resources, available for sale at auction.

If the properties didn't sell at auction, they would be registered in the OTC (over the counter) bulletin. The OTC bulletins became my catalog of possible parcel acquisitions. We were excited to look over what was available. The terms were very reasonable.

The state wanted to get the land into the peoples' hands. They required a five percent down payment and carried the contract for ten years! Not a heavy burden—at all. I noticed in the Land Line, a monthly publication about available properties, that there was a hundred-and sixty-acre parcel—for sale—in the Matanuska Valley, across from Anchorage.

(In those days, 1965, that area was still quite unoccupied. The whole state had only about a two hundred and seventy thousand population. Anchorage had about one hundred thousand of that number, a little less than half! Remember, we had just been granted statehood in 1959, just six years before we arrived. This was called, "Land of The Last Frontier". It was a world apart, from southern California life! We felt that we belonged—we loved it!)

# We Chose Alaska

Now back to the property sale. The OTC price was seven thousand and seven hundred dollars! We paid them the five percent and were issued a ten-year contract. We were now property owners! Access is still by road—no bridge.

Later on, I found out that the DNR was only going to allow an individual to acquire up to six hundred acres—then he could no longer be eligible to participate in the land program!

Marcia and I had purchased this as a couple. This meant that as far as the DNR was concerned, we each had one hundred and sixty acres that counted in our totals. Not a very smart way to go.

We decided to change our style—from now on we would each buy separate parcels. We were on a limited budget for land purchases. I was still in school—income was limited. We would save enough for a down payment—then look into another purchase. We had faith that Alaska would be populated, in the future.

I only attended one auction. It was for property across Cook Inlet on Lost Lake. The lots had been surveyed, platted, and went all around the lake. A few pieces were already privately owned.

I invited a group of my fellow students, who were interested in what I had found, for a

# We Chose Alaska

breakfast at our home. Six of them showed—only one was interested enough to go to the auction with Marcia and me.

We bought two lots totaling about twenty-five acres. Our friend purchased the lot next to Marcia's. The price of our two lots was twelve thousand dollars.

My reason for investing in property—way across from Anchorage—was because I saw a Standard Oil Road map, of that time, that showed a proposed bridge across Cook Inlet. The distance to Anchorage over the bridge to Lost Lake would be about six miles. The distance by car, around the inlet, was about one hundred plus miles further!

That bridge has been the topic of concern, of many legislatures, all without success. The lake property is large enough for float planes, and just a hop from Anchorage. The area is Point Mackenzie—lately there's been a new port developed—with a rail head connecting to the main railroad system—just a few hundred feet from our hundred- and sixty-acre parcel!

# We Chose Alaska

19.

## Alaska Life (Part 4 - Waving of the Carrot)

My first year of teaching was drawing to a close. Both Marcia and I had our contracts renewed for the following year. Yipee! It was a very successful year. I really enjoyed my new teaching career and being at Dimond High School.

Things were very good. Summer vacation was approaching. The common joke is, "What's the best thing you like about teaching?" The cute response is, "June, July and August!" You don't get rich, but it's a wonderful job dealing with an equally precious raw material—our kids. Your kids really do become ours and they equally pull on our heart strings.

Another little cutie, about teaching kids is that teachers have a saying, "Don't believe everything your child says about me—I won't believe everything he or she says about you!"

# We Chose Alaska

One of the teachers in Marcia's school and his wife, also a teacher in another school, had gone to the State Operated Schools Office in Anchorage to look at the possibility of teaching in the 'Bush' schools (Alaskan native villages). He came back all excited and telling all about what happened during the interview with Merle Armstrong, the director of SOS (State Operated Schools). They had decided to become Bush teachers! They also piqued our curiosity!

Marcia and I decided to go to see Mr. Armstrong with the idea that we'd like to do something like that in the future. We made an appointment and met with him. He was a very warm and personable man. I can still remember his gray crew cut and gray suit as he stood in front of a large map of Alaska.

He explained SOS to us and when he saw that we were interested—he said, he'd send us to any available village of our choice—in whatever part of Alaska! He explained the pay scale, it was calculated by location.

The schools on the road system had the lowest salary and also the easiest life styles as a result. The ones in the Bush with more isolation brought in the highest. We chose the Bush schools. He pointed out that he needed

## We Chose Alaska

us for positions in Angoon, a Tlingit Indian village in Southeast Alaska.

On a map—it seemed a half a world away! The only access to it was by boat or float plane. He made his pitch and set the hook at the proper time—he sensed that we were vulnerable in our dreamy thoughts.

We told him we would love to accept. HOWEVER, we had already signed our contracts. He said, "You go back and ask your principals if it would be OK to back out and sign with SOS." We did and they were both in accord and very encouraging about our choosing such an adventure. The consensus was that they would do the same if they were younger.

We signed with SOS. I wonder if the director knew that he had us—before he even pulled out the carrot—when he said, "Hello, I'm Merle Armstrong!" The decision was made—the contracts signed and now— "WHAT?"

We first had to attend a compulsory six-week accredited indoctrination course at the University of Alaska, Fairbanks campus.

[One of the courses was to be of major importance many years later. I had allowed my certification to expire! It was a clumsy error

# We Chose Alaska

on my part. My superintendent approached me and asked if I was aware of this problem.

Without certification—he could not allow me to continue teaching. I blanched and got a clammy feeling! I hustled down to Anchorage to my old alma mater, Alaska Methodist University (AMU), and talked to the registrar. She told me that it just wasn't a matter of simply applying. My failure to recertify posed a huge problem.

I would now have to apply again and possibly must take college courses that were now needed for certification—that weren't available when I first became a teacher! I'm talking at least fifteen years ago! She asked for the transcripts of my post graduate courses.

I had been faithfully keeping my necessary course work up to date. I explained the situation to my superintendent and told him what was happening. He said, he'd wait for the registrar's decision before taking any further action. When she called the news was good—I met all the necessary course work!

The TESL course that had been taught that summer in Fairbanks would satisfy the only new requirement!] Phew! DI

The courses were to prepare newly hired teachers for teaching in the Bush. It consisted of all day sessions covering the aspects of

## We Chose Alaska

village life, as well as a course in TESL (Teaching English as a Second Language).

After the first four weeks—we were flown to our respective villages for a hands-on experience that would last a week.

On the home front, the next big item on our list was that we had to sell everything we owned in Anchorage—or put it in storage. We sold everything except a few personal items that we stored in a shed, at a teacher's home.

We timed it so that we'd be free to go when school started in August. There was no hurry—we still had to have some place to live in the meantime. The big items like the trailer, leanto, and VW van were the last to go. When you teach in the Bush—your housing and household goods are all furnished.

Our one-week visit allowed us to meet the school's custodian and arrange with him the receiving of our many boxes. We started to mail our personal items and all the food supplies we'd need for the school year, via the post office—a mind boggling job!

We shipped a whole case of eggs! They were tasting a little strange by the end of the year! We also shipped several cases of canned goods and dried foods. The items that stand out are a case of Chung King chop suey and one of chow mein. We liked them in California and would

# We Chose Alaska

frequently include that as a meal. Believe me—by the end of the year—before we left Angoon, we had a half case left of each that we gave away. We had developed a lifelong distaste for them! I still can't stand the thought of it—too much of a good thing!

We headed for Fairbanks in our old Volkswagen bus to attend our classes. Our dog, Nanook, came with us. We found a place near the university's power plant to chain him to a tree, near his small doghouse. He was used to being outside and settled right in—thankfully.

We registered and got our room assignment and class schedule. We met many of the teachers and became friends with a few of them. They were as excited, friendly and fun-loving as we were. (Or thought we were.) The classes were well structured and very interesting.

We decided to do some celebrating the weekend before heading to our villages. We (the guys and gals) wanted to go to a topless bar we'd heard about and have a few drinks. I loaded the van (thirteen of us) and headed for the club! We had a laughingly good time. It was the first time many of them (including Marcia) had ever been to a strip club. It was a revealing adventure!

# We Chose Alaska

On the way back to our dorms—we passed a lone hitchhiker who was thumbing a ride. We stopped to pick him up. As I asked someone to slide open the door, my passengers—in a jubilant disbelief—started to reorganize their positions.

When the side door was slid open—the hitchhiker stood there on the edge of the road with a very puzzled look on his face. All he could see were bodies. "Come on get in, there's plenty of room!" I said laughingly.

We were all in hysterics when the door opened. He also was heading for the university. It was one of those special moments where we pushed the envelope—rolled with the punch and adjusted. We made it work!

If you are going to teach in the Bush—you must be flexible. The Bush will either make or break a relationship. In a village, you find yourself alone—with each other—in a different culture and in a very isolated and rugged existence. Your mate is everything—or had better be! Sex does not always fill the bill! (However, don't give it up!) There has to be much more. You'll soon find out! Marcia and I have always looked at our village assignments with a certain awe and an appreciation of what a wonderful life we were living. How fortunate

## We Chose Alaska

we were. She was and always has been my all—I know she feels the same. Or so she tells me—quite often!

The time came to fly to Angoon. We flew from Fairbanks to Juneau and were picked up at the airport and taken to Channel Flying Service. We landed out of town a bit—in a small inlet and taxied to a dock where the local bus service would pick us up. That was someone who ran a VW bus and had a 'taxi' business.

He was called on his CB by the pilot and informed that we had arrived. The plane approached the dock to about fifty feet from it—slowly slid to a stop. The tide was low and the pilot helped us get off of one of the pontoons. We stepped into the mud and walked up to the dock. (It was strange for us. We'd never been on a float plane, much less, disembark in what I could call a bush version of a red carpet!)

We watched the plane taxi away—turn into the wind and start its takeoff. After a few minutes, all was very quiet as we waited for the bus to arrive.

Fact #1, we had arrived and the very first thing we were given was a full ration of the solitude and the majestic beauty of beach front living!

# We Chose Alaska

Rod, the bus driver, finally arrived! Later we learned that Rod had survived a very severe brown bear mauling while on a hunt. He was very lucky to be alive. He still had to periodically use a traction machine when the pain became too intense.

Fact #2, time in a village is highly relative, hence the term 'native time'. They don't view time the same as we do. When the spirit calls—it's the time! It took a long time to get a handle on that one—we did and planned accordingly. No big deal! No place to go!

RELAX. Don't worry about the fact that the area is known as the home of the big bear! It has a large brown bear population! The brown is the coastal version of the interior grizzly—much larger and darker brown.

The inlet that Angoon is located on is called Kootznahoo, which in Tlingit means home of the big bear (brown bears in that area)! They were formidable and nobody around to meet us! Gulp!

We were driven to the teacherage, after quite a while. There were six separate apartments, a large storage area and a laundry room with a wringer washer and a dryer. When we entered the building, we were met by Bill Somato, the custodian who was part Japanese and part Tlingit.

## We Chose Alaska

He had heard the plane arrive and knew we'd be on board. He showed us where we would be living. (A little aside here; he actually asked which apartment we'd prefer—remember this moment later on.) Bill explained the lay of the land to us. He was a warm and friendly person, who eventually became a good friend.

We spent the week exploring, eating and sleeping. Nobody came by to visit. Basically, there was nobody around! It was the fishing season, the village's main industry. Angoon had a population of about 425 people. Most of the men were out on the boats.

The remainder (women, children and old men) were out berry picking. The ladies and children would pick while the men stood guard with a rifle. Fact #3, this was going to be our new playground. A rifle would be our other best friend!

The usual berry picking ground was the area between the main (6th - 8th grades) school and the lower elementary (1st - 5th grades). The distance between the two schools was about a half mile right through the berry area along the fringe of forest. That was Marcia's and the other teachers' route to work!

All I had to do was cross the walkway (20') from the teacherage to my school. Which is

# We Chose Alaska

also where the principal's office was located. That is probably the main reason we were closer to the teacherage! (I jokes!)

Fact #4, the "I Jokes" remark is a standard native expression for, I'm only joking!

While there, we met our next-door neighbor, an elderly Tlingit lady. While on one of our walks, I saw that she was out in her front yard—fleshing a freshly skinned seal.

When a seal is killed, the skin is removed rapidly (skinned) with careless speed. Later the hide is fleshed to remove anything (fat or meat) prior to tanning. This process is much more meticulously done than just skinning.

I had said hello to her before as I had passed by. This gave me the occasion to approach her. I was sincerely interested in what she was doing. Evidently she sensed my sincerity and proceeded to explain the process to me. I was so lucky!

My neighbor was the one who did the fleshing when a seal was killed for food! She was a PRO—my NEIGHBOR—and she LIKED me! She took me under her wing and during the rest of the week taught me how to handle the hides.

This started me on a long journey into the curing and tanning of hides. I mainly did seal skins at first, later on, other animals that I shot

# We Chose Alaska

or trapped. I also put this information to good use—in another village. I used it to re-introduce the lost art of processing hides to both sexes of my students. (I'll cover that later in another story.) From then on—when I shot anything—I tanned it!

One day while I was working on one of the hides in her front yard—three little old ladies walked by, on the path. They looked at me—covertly pointed to one another—giggled and snickered at each other. I waved.

They ignored me, did an eyes front and continued down the path. I thought. "How cute." Their message was well understood by my neighbor friend. She explained to me that in the native culture the processing of hides was woman's work!

I chuckled. I was being made fun of. If only they had known that I, as an ex-hairstylist, could have done their hair—if I wanted! Then—we would see who would really be having the culture shock!

Fact #5, culture shock is just another person's values that are different from yours. That one-week visit was truly an excellent part of our indoctrination.

The time had come to reverse the arrival sequence. We had come, seen, met some people, made friends and were shown our

## We Chose Alaska

apartment. Our neighbor gave me a bunch of 'dry fish' that she had processed in her smoke house to take with us as a parting gift. That was as good as a diploma showing that we were somewhat ready for the new experience. We passed the course!

She handed me this large brown paper shopping bag that was half filled. It was a nice goodbye. She knew her seal skinner trainee and his wife would soon be back.

Saturday morning, we flew out on the same float plane in which we arrived. In Juneau, while waiting at the airport for our flight to Fairbanks, a group of us who were to teach in Southeast Alaska had a rendezvous and were discussing our village experiences.

I was standing next to the end of a long bench in the waiting room—chatting and listening. I noticed out of the corner of my eye—an elderly native lady was semi-leaning over the bench's armrest and was sniffing noticeably over my bag of dry fish. I nudged Marcia to draw her attention to what was happening! We smiled at each other—each of us getting the message—and continued our conversations.

We've had quite a chuckle about the aroma that we must have been carrying around. She probably couldn't imagine such a wonderful

# We Chose Alaska

aroma coming from that bag being held by one of those white men! (No insult meant. That's what we are and that's what we were called. They are 'natives' and we are 'white men'. (Pure and simple.)

I made sure the bag was well closed when we boarded the plane and put it in the overhead compartment.

Monday was the beginning of our final week at the university. We listened to all the other teachers' different experiences. Some of them would be teaching in very small villages without modern facilities. They would be living in small log cabins—rented from the villagers by the State Operated School.

Those accommodations were most times without running water, with a wood or oil stove for heat. Honey buckets were used for sanitation. They were picked up periodically by the village's disposal system—if they had one—and dumped!

The setup in Angoon was a primo accommodation in comparison to some of the bush schools. Beachfront property—great fishing and hunting. It was a real wilderness dream! Besides all these wonderful things, we had living quarters that were typical of a standard top rate apartment in any city.

## We Chose Alaska

The only thing missing was a boat! While there, I noticed a small skiff laying upside down, above the tide zone, in front of the school. Bill told me that one of the classes had built it as a project and never used it. The wheels in my head started to turn.

We couldn't wait to return!

20.

### Alaska Life (Part 5 - Liquidating)

Returning home to our little trailer—we set things in motion—selling our belongings. The Volkswagen van went fast with a delivery date to the buyer of just before leaving for Angoon. It was a nine passenger model with, as I previously mentioned, a capacity for more than that. It was in excellent condition with an almost new looking interior. I don't think I've ever had a vehicle with such a wide range of conveniences including camping room.

## We Chose Alaska

[On one of my archery deer hunts in northern California, I had seen another hunter who had driven to within a half mile of the prime hunting ground—he was camping in his VW van.

I had just finished a hike up to that spot and had been walking for over a half hour. Needless to say it made an impression on me, especially when it was time for me to head back down the hill.

Quite a way beyond where he was, I walked up to a small dirt road with a lot of water in the tire tracks. I noticed a bunch of deer tracks that were recent.

There was a small stand of alders that bordered the road. Since I was on my way back down to camp from where I had been hunting, I decided to wait for a while behind the alders. It was nearly dusk. No sooner had I settled—I saw movement across the field—I got very excited! Several deer coming my way made it to the tire ruts for a drink!

The alders were on a small rise along the road. That put me in a position directly above the drinking deer! Light conditions were getting poor.

They were so close, within eight feet, I feared if I drew my bow to take a shot—they'd

# We Chose Alaska

spook. I had a ring side seat, they hadn't a clue that I was there—a unique moment!

I was getting concerned about the light. I decided to take my shot. I was right! I no sooner started to slowly raise my bow and draw—the scene erupted into a disappearing act. I never got to shoot the arrow! I was disappointed but somewhat relieved. If I had been successful—I'd have been on that mountain for God knows how long!

I headed down and soon passed the VW van and said hello to that lucky son of a gun. He was settling down for the night and had started to cook his supper.

It didn't take long before the light was almost gone. It was getting difficult to see—every large tree on the trail was a concern! When you are caught in the dark and working your way down a mountain trail your mind, at least mine, goes into overdrive! It was slow going but I finally walked into camp with a wonderful story to tell.]

Now after that little rambling, it's time to focus on the main story!

It was time to sell the leanto. Someone in the park bought it. The trailer was next. It had been our home for four years—we had many good memories during that time. A person's

## We Chose Alaska

home is his castle—states it rather well. No matter how meager it may be—it is his castle.

We put that small space to many uses. I once overhauled the van's VW engine, using the kitchen table as a workbench. Another time—I put a quartered moose in our back bedroom. Then the pieces were put on the bunk bases, for several days while it cured. I then butchered it on the same table. Some of the memories were not as comical. Our stored meat suffered—the cold storage plant had a major fire.

One morning during the Christmas vacation, we were lying in bed, and of all things, we were discussing Einstein's Theory of Relativity. We noticed that the dark brown rivets that held the ceiling paneling in place had frosty white heads! The temperatures had dropped to around zero degrees.

All of a sudden—a loud hissing sound came from the bathroom area! What could that be? I sprang out of bed and rushed to the bathroom. Nothing was noticeable there. I got dressed and went outside to the area below it. I could hear a louder rushing sound!

I pulled back the trailer's insulated skirting panel in front of the noise. My copper water line was wrapped with a heat tape—evidently not well enough! It still managed to freeze

## We Chose Alaska

solid and pull itself apart at the brass shutoff fitting. Luckily, it did it on the trailer side of the line allowing me to shut off the valve and stop the flow.

Again during the winter—a problem had occurred in that same area—this time dealing with the sewer line. As I had said before, when we moved into the park, there was only one space available. It was on the road at the rear of the park, at the foot of a hill—adjacent to a boggy black spruce swamp.

We placed the trailer on six square concrete flat-topped pyramids for support to take the pressure off the tires during such a long duration. It was not uncommon for us to be subjected to all types of frost heaving. I think this probably played a role in creating a situation where the trailer's sewer line was pulled up out of the park's main sewer pipe.

I had noticed some water coming from that area and showing up in the bit of slushy snow that covered the ground at that spot. I pulled off the same panel and lo and behold—there was the end of the drain pipe sitting on top of a small brown glacier! It was a so-called crappy scene.

What to do? My analytical mind mulled the situation! Voila, I must return the trailer's dump line into the main sewer line! DUH! I

## We Chose Alaska

needed to get the proper tools for the job. An ice pick would have been handy, however refrigerators have just about killed that market. My next best tool was a large kitchen knife! Tool in hand, I crawled under the trailer (reluctantly) and started to chip away at the brownish icy mound!

Marcia was upstairs when our next-door neighbor Diane came to visit. "Tell her not to use the bathroom," I yelled to Marcia from down below. They were having a cup of tea and just gabbing about living in Alaska. All of a sudden, I heard Marcia say— "I just love living here."

I couldn't believe my ears! Evidently, she didn't have a clue as to the deliciously provocative scene below! There I was lying— on the brown icy frozen knoll! With every stab of the knife—the ice would splinter and fly everywhere. The chipping was taking place at the end of my bent arm only two feet from my face! You figure it out! I was definitely NOT a happy camper! Ah, memories! Some excellent—some not so! Nothing to do—deal with it.

We frequently had small earthquakes. Remember, this was shortly after the big '64 earthquake. The fact that the trailer was sitting on those concrete supports made the rides more exaggerated. If I wanted to tease Marcia, I'd grab the trailer's hitch and shake it vigorously—waiting to see her response! Sort of a small training session!

We were awakened during the early morning by some heavy shaking. The noise (like a freight train) is usually the first indication of an earthquake—immediately followed by shaking. These are usually very short in duration. The next wave is called the 'love' wave. This wave causes a rippling effect of the ground. The amount of damage caused by this wave is determined by its magnitude and duration. Watch out for that one—that's the killer/destroyer wave!

We sat up abruptly and realized that we were swaying from side to side rather aggressively. I thought, "The fridge!"—and headed to the kitchen. Marcia walked in—there I was in my birthday suit, spread eagle and pushing, with my arms forward, on the upper front of the fridge. My legs extended out behind me to increase my balance. She took one look at the scene and got a laughing spell! All ended well! We went back to bed.

When Marcia had flown in to be with me at Nunatak Cove, she told me that while I was gone, the ground thawed and shifted under the concrete supports! The back two had sunk so low that the whole trailer shifted its weight backward from the four front supports. This caused a movement of about six horizontal inches and less than two vertically downward, where the door was located.

Marcia had called Bob, our friend, seeking his help. He came over and crawled under the house. He had to jack up the trailer near the supports in order to reposition and level them.

When he told me what he had done and in what area—I knew the degree to which he had shown his friendship for us. At least he didn't have to deal with Marcia's, "I just love Alaska!" remark.

So much for the reminiscing. We bought the trailer for three thousand in California, lived in it for four years and sold it for twenty five hundred dollars—not too shabby. We had arrived here, basically ignorant of many of the skills necessary to survive. I had only a smattering of auto mechanics. I had acquired by trial and error—some electrical as well as plumbing knowledge. Both had dished up bad events for me—I was learning! I found out that when a disaster hits—don't hesitate—get a plan in place to remedy the situation! It takes away a lot of the stress. You need to override the anxiety. There will be anxiety— count on it!

# We Chose Alaska

The day before we were to fly to our villages, all the new Bush teachers checked into a hotel. We had an indoctrination session with a banquet scheduled for the next day. That's when we met a beautiful young lady—Jackie Gibson—new to teaching—she was also going to Angoon.

The next morning we were all bussed to the airport. The only possessions we had—were what we had in our suitcases. It was a whole new exciting adventure on which we were embarking. All the possessions that had been so vital to us—made us feel secure—were now put on hold or sold—I'd say it was liberating.

The only concerns that we had were our food and entertainment. The food was either from the trading post or from the post office! Not really a problem. We planned our food needs for the school year—quite a job. We took many boxes of various canned goods to the post office—we also sent a case of eggs. At least they didn't arrive scrambled!

The entertainment was a natural. The outdoors would provide an ample measure of it. It was much to our liking!

Goodbye, Anchorage. Hello, Angoon!

# We Chose Alaska

**21.**

## ALASKA LIFE (Part 6 - Angoon - Bush Teacher - part 1)

The title might give the impression that we were involved in some sort of plant life. The term 'Bush Teacher' is used for those who teach in remote regions of Alaska. It usually carries an aura of someone special in the field of education—said with great pride. Our status in a village is that of a very important

# We Chose Alaska

person. Our responsibility is also very special. We are there to teach their children. Of course while we're at it, there's nothing preventing us from experiencing the hunting and fishing that is so prevalent and abundant in village life.

We actually gained more of an understanding of bush life from them than any book or lecture could have given us. A good Bush teacher realizes that he is part of a puzzle and must become a good student of the people and their culture—in order to do a good job. Although this is only the first story dealing with our teaching in the bush—our focus and attitude never varied. We were there to teach the children, learn about the people, be happy, be friendly—and above all be respectful and noncritical.

From our Bush teaching days, we have some very dear friends who still hold a very special place in our hearts. We consider them part of our extended family, as do they. At the end of the story, I will have you read a Christmas letter that we sent to Marcia's mom. It will have a few details (population, etc.) that I won't mention here.

Flying into Angoon was a 'déjà vu' situation, except that this time, we had our dog Nanook with us. We landed in the same spot and had

## We Chose Alaska

to wait for the 'bus' to transport us to our teacherage.

First order of the day was to get Nanook settled in. I borrowed a small dog house for him to use at night. He settled right in and stayed close to home. We were lucky—he never had any problems.

The next project was to make some sense out of all the boxes that were stacked in our living room. We started in and when I found the box with our phonograph records, I started looking for the one that contained the player. It wasn't to be found. Evidently—it hadn't arrived yet.

I decided to go to the school and borrow the player from my classroom. I walked across to the school building and tried to open the door—it was locked! I knew the principal was there. I saw him through his office window just to the left of the entrance.

I knocked and waited. He came to the door, opened it about three inches, and said, "Yes?" I answered, "Hi, I'm Henry Milette. I just found out that my record player hadn't arrived with our stuff. I thought I could use the one from my classroom to have some music...." He stopped me short and said—"OH! You can't do that! That's state property!"—then shut the door!

## We Chose Alaska

What? Not even a hello nor a welcome? I thought, "What the hell just happened?" So be it. He's a little strange or maybe I just caught him at a bad time. I went back to our apartment and told Marcia about meeting our new principal. It was like some kind of joke. We chuckled. We pretty much had everything put away in a day. School was not due to start for a few more days.

When returning from a short walk through the village—I spotted the little dinghy that Bill had mentioned. I thought, "I think I'd like to get in a little fishing. I'll just check with the principal." BIG FREAKIN' MISTAKE!

I went across to the front door—same situation! "I'd like to do a little fishing and wonder if it would be OK to use the dinghy out front." "OH, NOooo, last year, the 8th grade students, made that as a class project and I don't have the authority to let you use it!"

I said to myself, "STUPID! STUPID! STUPID!" Not about him, but about me! Something told me that this would be a memorable year. I wish I could tell you that I was wrong. It WAS a very memorable year! I also had found out from the custodian, Bill, that the principal was quite miffed about the fact that we got our particular apartment. The

# We Chose Alaska

principal had wanted that one, because it was more secluded and looked out toward the side of a steep hill. However, Bill had already told us that it would be ours and he would leave it at that. Lucky us!

The day before the start of school, we had a faculty meeting. It was uneventful. He seemed very intelligent (and he was, according to a superintendent whom he'd worked for in the past). However, he was very uncomfortable on a personal level.

We found out that Marcia, Jackie and I, along with the principal, were the newbies on board. The other four teachers had been teaching there for several years and were well entrenched in village life.

It was during this time that Marcia became sick. We were warned that dinking the water in some villages might need some adjustment time and might cause intestinal problems. It was an easy step for me to diagnose it as 'The Angoon Crud!' No offense meant. Just a label. Case solved—tough it out and let it pass!

She did make it for the first day of school. The rest of the first week—she never seemed to improve and was too sick to teach. There was a substitute hired—to take her place. She had no formal training and a slight drinking

# We Chose Alaska

problem! It was not a very successful situation to say the least.

Marcia's situation deteriorated as the week wore on. She was only drinking hot tea with sugar and Tang. She just didn't feel like eating and the pain just kept getting worse. Finally, the weekend came, and I could be home with her during the day. Saturday night, Jackie came over for supper.

(Jackie's efficiency apartment was adjacent to ours and connected with a door between our bedroom and her main quarters for fire safety purposes). We became an extended family and gained a very wonderful lifelong friend. She spent most of her time with us rather than cooped up in her little apartment.)

We planned to fix whatever Marcia wanted for supper. Nothing sounded good. This time I insisted that she—at least—eat SOMETHING. She ate popcorn, ice cream and topped it all off with some beer! Later, during the night—I heard a cry coming from the bathroom—"Henry, PLEASE COME HERE." I could tell that it wasn't her usual tone—something was wrong! I rushed in and saw that the toilet bowl was all splattered with blood! WOW! All of a sudden this became a very critical situation. Here we are in a village on some remote island in southeast Alaska with the closest medical

## We Chose Alaska

help being a float plane ride away to Sitka, Alaska. I NEEDED to get help, NOW!

Early in the morning, I headed across the walkway to my school building. The only phone available in the whole compound was in the principal's office. As I approached the entrance, I could see him in his office.

The door was locked, same routine as usual with the reception. I told him that Marcia was very sick and passing blood and that I needed to call for a charter plane. I couldn't believe my ears! He said, "I can't let you use the phone for personal reasons!" INCREDIBLE!

I wish I could tell you what was exchanged between us—it's a blank! I honestly don't remember! I must have blocked it out, however, I didn't plead. I DID make my call.

The plane would be there—'as soon as possible'. Marcia packed some items for the trip in and we waited for a call notifying us of the pickup time at the usual landing spot.

Jackie, Tom Aubertine (teacher) and I were scheduled to go goose hunting by boat up to the flats at the head of Favorite Bay. The plane landed, we got Marcia off to the hospital in Sitka—to the west of Angoon. We headed up the bay, to hunt!

I can just hear some of you now! Of course, there was some discussion about it. Marcia

## We Chose Alaska

said there really wasn't any need to not go—once she was on the plane. Now with the passing of time and the telling of the story—her take on it is more like—"OH, I REMEMBER—you three could hardly wait for me to board that plane and fly away so that you could head up the bay!"—all with a chuckle, of course.

When she arrived at the hospital in Sitka, they discovered that her appendix had ruptured and had blown off its tip—not a good sign!

She was put on heavy antibiotics and remained in the hospital to stem the spread of any infection. They would operate to remove the debris only after the chances of getting an infection had subsided. While there she got a big CRUSH on her physician!

She was gone for ten days. Those were very long days for me. I didn't know how she was doing and had no way to communicate with her.

She came back home, many pounds lighter—very glad to be alive—and taught for the next two weeks. She had to return to the hospital and 'her doctor' to undergo the surgery. When she returned from Sitka, life slowly returned to normal—whatever that

## We Chose Alaska

was! We hadn't had a chance to find out what 'normal' really was—as yet!

When we shipped our belongings to Angoon, I had also shipped a 6hp Evinrude outboard motor. I was thinking about the skiff on the beach and thought an outboard would just fill the bill. Well, that was nipped in the butt! So there I was without a boat.

Tom Aubertine didn't live in the teacherage. He was married when he arrived in Angoon a few years earlier—but later divorced. Consequently, he had an apartment on the water's edge. He had upgraded from a twelve-foot aluminum boat to a twenty foot fiberglass skiff. He offered the use of his aluminum boat to me for our use. I gladly accepted!

This gave us the means to explore our marine environment. Angoon is situated on the west side of Admiralty Island between Juneau and Sitka. It is a marine paradise—it was OURS! If you want an understanding of what I'm talking about—Google Angoon, Alaska, to get a better feel of it.

Weekends were spent in one of the nearby bays, usually just exploring, camping, fishing and hunting. Most times Jackie would come along, however she did manage to fill some of her weekends by visiting friends in Juneau.

# We Chose Alaska

Things were going fine with the principal. He didn't interfere with our classroom performance. He mainly administrated—whatever that was.

I then found out that he had opened my mail which came from Alaska State Operated Schools! I was torqued and went into his office (where he spent all of his time) and confronted him. He basically told me, he felt—as the principal—that he had the right to open such mail! INCREDIBLE!

Bottom line—just as I was about to walk out the door—I informed him that he'd better not open any of my mail, unless he wanted to get sued! That was the end of that nonsense.

He went overboard the other way. He wouldn't even open the AV materials we had ordered—for the class—that he was to deliver to us when they arrived. No biggie. Life resumed as before—until the next traumatic event.

Teaching in Angoon was a great job even with the occasional outside of classroom confrontations—with you know whom. The kids were just wonderful and very well behaved. They were eager to learn and were at the door in the morning waiting for it to open. There were no discipline problems.

## We Chose Alaska

I wanted a special seal hunting rifle. I researched all the available catalogs and found one in the Herter's catalog—the very same one where I got my tanning supplies. I ordered a wooden stock of my choice—along with the complete barrel assembly for a 22-250 cartridge—a very fast and flat shooting bullet. You could custom build your rifle from all the available components.

I also started reloading my own cartridges. I bought several cans of powder and boxes of bullets. We had bought our third gun. I wanted to bring them up to the top of their accuracy.

I had entered a new area which I found challenging and very rewarding. There's a certain amount of euphoria when your shots are centered on a target—in a nickel-sized grouping! I spent a major amount of time increasing my accuracy. I don't want to wound my animal—a perfect kill shot is my goal. I hate sloppy work. I dedicated a lot of time—all enjoyable—improving my equipment.

One Saturday, I decided to go into Favorite Bay—seal hunting. I pulled the skiff ashore (see map 'Our Camp') and picked a spot to sit, watch and wait for a seal to come around. The spot was on the left side of the small inlet just

## We Chose Alaska

north of the name 'Favorite Bay' in the picture. That became our favorite cove.

I was very excited. This was going to be my first seal that would provide me with a hide to tan. Suddenly—I heard a 'fllrrrr' sound—like something surfacing and expelling an air and water mixture. There it was about thirty yards away! All that was showing above the surface was the top half of his head. It looked like a dome, the size of half of a large softball.

He spotted me and gently twirled away from where I was. I didn't know at the time—he was doing me a big favor. If you shoot a seal while he's facing you—the impact throws him backward and in so doing any air that he has in his lungs gets expelled—causing him to sink! I slowly took aim and squeezed the trigger. Time stood still as the sound of the muzzle and a (WHUMP!) were heard simultaneously—as the bullet's impact expended its energy. That same energy caused the seal to lurch forward, thereby capturing the air in his lungs.

I pushed the skiff from shore and went to the side of the floating seal. I put a loop from my anchor line around his tail and towed him back to the dock. When I got to the dock, I had one of the villagers help me lift him out of the water.

## We Chose Alaska

THEN, it dawned on me—now that I had the seal—I had NOTHING else with which to do my tanning. I didn't even have any fleshing and stretching equipment! I offered the seal to the person that had helped me. He was very surprised and pleased. He proceeded to quarter and butcher it without any concern for preserving the hide. This was strictly a food item. He never offered me a piece of the meat.

I found out later in another village, that native people do not offer seal meat to white people. The flavor is like nothing we've ever experienced—we do not like it! So they avoid rejection and simply don't offer.

I decided to focus on getting equipped to handle my next seal in advance of going seal hunting again.

I had done some stretching on my neighbor's fleshing rack. The fleshing rack is four poles fastened in a square to make a frame. Half inch slits are cut in the hide every several inches (depending on the size of the hide) all around its edge. Then a cord of some type is used to stretch the hide tightly. It has to be very taut to do a good fleshing job. I found that it was a very tedious process. I guess in the old days it was the only way to stretch the hides.

## We Chose Alaska

I decided to improvise and use a sheet of plywood and nails instead. Then I simply salted the hide down and let it dry until I was ready for the tanning process. I ordered tanning supplies from a Herter's catalog.

When the tanning supplies and a sewing awl arrived, I started tanning the dried hides. I found that the dried ones were more of a chore to soften than the fresh hides. They really needed professional equipment. I never did anymore dried ones.

I was tanning the hides immediately after the fleshing and making many items in the beginning such as small couch pillows. I graduated to making mittens, mukluks and vests, as I acquired my leather sewing skills. They were cherished Christmas gifts sent to our parents.

The next time I went hunting I headed back ready to be successful. I was slowly cruising along in the same bay just beyond where I had shot the seal and noticed a couple of sea lions feeding on what was possibly herring. That whole stretch of water goes from Favorite Bay out toward the village and then enters Chatham Straits.

There are usually large schools of herring that gather in those waters. It wasn't uncommon to see whales feeding on them—

## We Chose Alaska

just a few hundred yards from shore. I killed the engine and just watched the sea lions for a while. They appeared to have larger heads than the seals. They were fascinating to watch. I decided to take one back to the village and share it.

It took quite a while to get off a steady shot from the skiff. I was successful—it floated. I started the engine and moved up alongside the sea lion. OH, MY GOD! I was stunned at the size of it! It was almost as long as my skiff and nearly two thirds as broad! I slipped my line around its lower body. It was quite a chore to get it through the loop.

I towed it to shore and just before we got to it—I felt a sudden drag of the skiff. The skiff was afloat—however the sea lion had run aground! I slacked up on the line and got close enough to beach the skiff.

I got out and started tugging on the line, all to no avail. I couldn't budge the sea lion! I decided not to try pulling it back to the dock. If I had made an attempt to do so and if for some reason such as being beached—it would have lost its air, it would have sunk my skiff. It would have pulled the stern under from the sheer weight of its body!

I decided that I'd go back to the dock and get some help to process this submarine! At

## We Chose Alaska

the dock, there was nobody around—I waited what seemed an eternity and finally decided to return after lunch and try to butcher it into more manageable chunks.

I returned to where the sea lion had been beached. I hadn't given any thought to the tide—this was all new to me. I was surprised to see that the tide had risen enough to float the sea lion. It was nowhere to be found! Needless to say—I never shot another sea lion! What a waste of a beautiful mammal. He'd have fed several families.

Winter was setting in and the weather was getting rainier and colder. Our weekend seal hunting excursions became fewer. The entertainment turned to having dinner at Tom's apartment, or ours, and an occasional invitation to dine from the local trading post owner.

There seemed to be a division in the relationship between the native and non-native people. Nothing serious, probably just cultural differences. We weren't there long enough to get a genuine feel about that.

We did discover that the longer we stayed—the more open the natives seemed to be. The four of us were the main focus of our socializing. Christmas vacation was just

## We Chose Alaska

around the corner and we were looking forward to having a break.

We were getting better acquainted with one of our neighbors, Peter Jack. His son, Peter Jr., was one of my students. Peter asked us if we would like to go goat hunting during the Christmas vacation.

We gladly accepted. ☺

# We Chose Alaska

22.

## ALASKA LIFE (Part 6 - Angoon - Bush Teacher (part 2 - Jackie Gibson/Polasky))

I've recently received the pictures that Jackie had taken while we were teaching in Angoon. This is wonderful since ours burned in our house fire in 1999. I'm going to include some of her album's pages in this chapter. It's only fair that I very willingly pay her tribute by dedicating it to her, for being a very special person and friend; she was the major contributor of the very welcomed and necessary pictures that made it possible for me to put this chapter together.

This page is from her album with several aerial pictures of the village. Angoon is built on a small peninsula bordering Chatham Strait on one side and Kootznahoo Inlet on the other side.

# We Chose Alaska

This is a shot of one side of the village showing the weekly mail plane on the upper right. I thought it was wonderful; it looks more like a painting than a simple snapshot.

The water from Favorite Bay feeds into that inlet on its way to Chatham Strait, as seen in the next picture, the long straight line is the Angoon dock which is used for receiving supplies from a barge every two weeks, for the trading post and others who might have ordered things brought from Ketchikan.

# We Chose Alaska

For us it was a source of fresh fruits and veggies and ah yes, ice cream from the trading post. You had to get there to shop early otherwise the supplies that you were craving might be sold out! The picture is of Angoon Village. The lower elementary school is to the right, on a hill at three o'clock. The upper elementary school and the teacherage are not visible to the right of the picture.

There was a trail between the two schools that was called "The Ridge".

We had wonderful quarters. Jackie had her little efficiency apartment—ours was next door. We blended the two homes into one with an access door between them. The door was usually open or unlocked. We just enjoyed being able to make her a part of our life in Angoon.

## We Chose Alaska

Being a beautiful, single, young teacher proved to be the source of some very interesting conversations.

She's a very interesting—a very special person.

# We Chose Alaska

Marcia's class.

The two schools were a short walk from each other. My school—just across from the front door of the apartments—had grades five through eight. Marcia and Jackie taught over the ridge from the main campus. The class levels were grades one through four. Marcia taught second grade and Jackie had fourth grade. Their daily walk to school was along the ridge. During the berry picking season the ridge was a favorite picking spot because of the large expanse exposed to the sun. It was also a path through the outskirts on the edge of wilderness. Bear encounters? —a good chance! Gutsy for these two—you bet! Jackie's class is pictured below.

# We Chose Alaska

She also had pictures of two of our fellow teachers.
Tom Aubertine who was a close friend and made life in Angoon more pleasant for us.

Walt Demmert, a fellow teacher, on the right, a Tlingit who was a very friendly person, is shown here meeting with Bob Zuboff, a village elder. It must have been taken during

## We Chose Alaska

the holidays because Walt certainly does look very dapper!

Jackie, visiting Bob Zuboff at his home.

Jackie was very well received and accepted by the village elders. She loved visiting with them. A fine quality necessary for a good Bush teacher. This is one of her visits where she was allowed to wear one of their ceremonial costumes. She was a true ambassador. Kind of cute, which also helped! That's our Jackie.

When we transferred to Tatitlek—Jackie headed for Kodiak Island. There, she met her future husband, Tim Polasky, a Coast Guard officer. Their happy married life is still going on. They have raised and educated a very

# We Chose Alaska

beautiful family. She's always been a wonderful, gutsy person—hence an excellent: Friend, Bush Teacher, Wife, Mother—and Grandmother!

The Angoon School (upper grades) with a Totem pole at the entrance.

The pictures below are from a seal hunt that we, Jackie and Nanook our dog went on beyond the "Rapids", directly across from the village. We set up a blue nylon tarp as a cover in case of rain and made camp. We built a small fire pit at the edge of the tarp, far enough to get the heat but not the smoke. Then we fixed our supper.

## We Chose Alaska

I guess all the activity from setting up camp and the accompanying noise made the seals a little spooky about coming around. We got out our sleeping bags and foam pads for ground cover. This is rainy country so a ground pad that prevents the cold and moisture from penetrating up through the sleeping bag is a must for comfort.

We were fortunate; it was a nice weekend. I told Marcia if she got up before I did—to sneak up behind the rocks to the right and check to see if there were any seals.

Daybreak came and my honey was up at the crack of dawn as usual. She headed for the outcrop and suddenly! WHAM! A shot jolted us awake! As I was rushing over, I heard, "I got

# We Chose Alaska

it!" She hit it right between the eyes! As I approached: I saw it slowly sink from sight!

I took the skiff out to the spot where it had sunk—I found it—barely visible from the surface. The tide was up and we had to wait in camp for low tide to try and snag it.

We always had our fishing gear with us to provide us with some fresh meals. I rigged the pole with a triple hook and a sinker to make it heavy enough to maneuver across the bottom in order to snag the seal. It took several attempts before I managed to get the hook near a flipper.

Finally—I yanked, the hook held! I couldn't get too aggressive in pulling it to the surface—it might come off the hook. I VERY GENTLY—by hand, brought it in. This was quite a load—any hasty aggressive moves would have caused it to break the line. I managed to get it alongside and tied my anchor line around its tail. I headed for shore and pulled the seal up onto the rocks.

The 'Old Code of the West' rule, "You shoot it—you clean it." Marcia was up to the task—I walked her through it. She did rather well for her first time and really was eager to do it.

## We Chose Alaska

These are of Jackie target practicing, with Nanook, on the flats.

The dock is where the villagers kept their commercial seiners and smaller boats.

I truly appreciate Jackie for sharing her precious pictures for my story.
They brought back many beautiful and magnificent memories.

How fortunate we were to have found the courage that gave us such an adventure and opened such a beautiful chapter in our lives.

### 23.

## ALASKA LIFE (Part 6 - Angoon - (part 3 The Goat Hunt))

The days leading up to our Christmas break were just uneventful, I guess one could say we were experiencing normalcy at last. Our social calendar included dinners at each other's homes on weekends and if the weather was mild and sunny—day trips to Favorite Bay or an occasional two-day trip past 'The Falls'.

Living in Angoon felt good. The time for the goat hunting trip with Peter Jack Sr. finally arrived. We were scheduled to leave from the dock early, after breakfast. He came by to pick up us and our gear; we headed for the boat. We were very—very excited.

# We Chose Alaska

We boarded the boat. It was quite large for a seiner. The pilot house also included a large galley. The area forward and below was the crew bunking area where Marcia and I slept. The captain's quarters were just below the pilot house entrance. Peter evidently was a very successful fisherman. He was a very good man—well deserving of success.

He was a shy, ruddy complexioned, smiley man, who was extremely friendly.

His grins would show off his glistening gold capped teeth. His overture with this

## We Chose Alaska

hunting trip basically—started our acceptance phase by the village people. He was a leader—a family man—highly respected by his people. Divine intervention was in play and paving the way toward our fitting in.

We were on our way to Gustavus, a small fishing cannery town, about 85 miles north at the top of Chatham Strait from Angoon.
(The pin marker labeled 'Dock' at the upper left is Gustavus, as seen in this Google Earth photo. It was a full day of cruising.

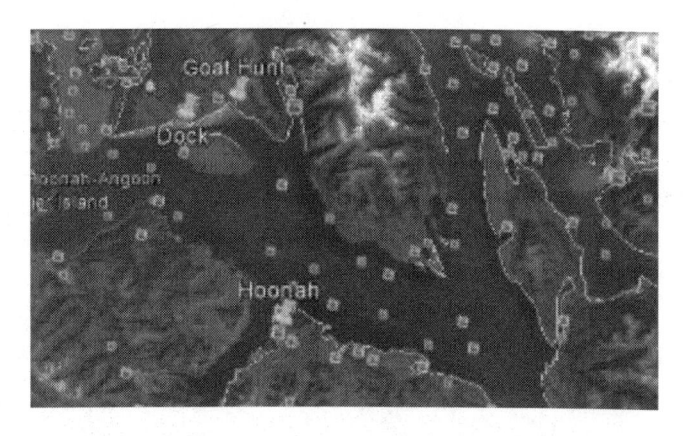

The weather was nice, the scenery was repetitiously enthralling. Snow-capped mountains skirted above the dark green spruce trees that descended to a thin brown shoreline resting on a blue carpet—unfolding all the way

# We Chose Alaska

around the boat and beyond. See the chart position of 'Goat Hunt' at the upper left of the above map.

Late that evening we arrived and tied up at the Gustavus dock. We all hit the sack after eating supper. We planned to rise early, eat breakfast and head east about six miles to a valley. The valley had a steady incline toward the upper part of the mountain.

During the night—sleep was interrupted by the sound of high winds—water splashing against the hull and the boat occasionally slamming against the dock—NOT good news! Morning came and we proceeded to do as planned. Peter Jack didn't seem concerned—why should we?

While Marcia and I cleaned up the breakfast dishes—Peter was out on deck lifting a twelve foot aluminum boat, and lowering it into the water using his boom with a block and tackle. We joined him—with our rifles and backpacks—when he was ready to cast off in the skiff.

Notice, I didn't say anything about the weather! It hadn't changed from the night conditions, except now we were experiencing a heavy drizzle along with the wind. Peter had a 6hp. outboard for power. It moved us along at a good pace. We couldn't travel at full throttle because the swells were large enough to warrant caution.

We were—heading out—with our backs to the rain—while Peter had to face forward—in order to navigate. He sat sideways most of the time, watching the shoreline and understandably not worried about other boats. (We were the only ones in town!)

After what seemed a very long time, we arrived at the valley. He reached the shore and held the skiff steady while Marcia and I hauled the gear up the beach. Then he took the engine off and we carried the skiff above the high-water line.

We geared up and headed up the valley. Peter went up its left flank and we did the right flank. He told us to find a good spot on the trail and wait and watch for game. The valley protected us from the wind. We reached a good spot—sat there and were graced by a light sprinkling of snow.

The forests of southeast Alaska are overly lush with a beautiful thick layer of green moss on both the trees and the ground. There isn't anything that doesn't succumb to it. It's brought about by excessive precipitation, moderately cool temperatures, and shade provided by the massive growth of the spruce trees—dominating the valley.

# We Chose Alaska

A trail is very easy to spot—you just look for a deep brown layer of trampled growth and topsoil. The constant tilling of the ground by the animals' hooves as they travel between the hill and the beach makes the trail.

We had been there several hours when Peter yelled from his side of the valley— "Let's go to the beach." Marcia and I started our downward trek to the rendezvous. When we reached the beach, Peter said, "If there had been some goats around, we would have seen some by now.

I guess we might as well head back to the boat and try again tomorrow." I know how a horse must feel when he heads back to the barn! Warmth, hot food and rest were all awaiting our arrival.

The trip back went faster and more comfortably since we were not bucking into the wind. We arrived soaking from the condensation. It was precipitated by regular rain gear and the cold air of the environment coming in contact with our hot humid bodies. It permeated our clothing. Hence the term—drenched to the bones!

There is only one material that can still provide some measure of warmth in those circumstances. Wool clothing is a must. You'll notice in some of the pictures that the old very

## We Chose Alaska

familiar red and black checkered wool shirts were part of our southeast gear. In the colder and drier parts of Alaska, wool gives way to down clothing. Moisture of any kind is a faux pas with down. Any moisture makes it lose its protection quality and places you in a bad situation. With down, you HAVE TO keep venting your vapors—stay cool and stay alive.

We returned to the dock, unloaded our gear and set out to tour Gustavus. It was a unique setup, more than likely typical of small island towns which have fish canneries as an industry. The population swells during the fishing season. When fishing is over it atrophies to just a few permanent residents. They weren't around when we were. It was nice to just be able to walk and stretch our legs. The sun even gave us a small break.

At the time, I wasn't aware of any involvement by the National Park Service. I do know that the park service did establish a base at some time. Our very good friends Will and Barb Tipton were stationed there for a few years.

The next morning, the weather was just as bad as day one. The wind had picked up and gave us the same problems that it had the day before.

# We Chose Alaska

After having spent our time in the same designated area and seeing no animals—we headed for the beach and the trip back to the dock. The weather was getting nastier and the winds were beginning to really gust! We decided that we would head for Angoon first thing in the morning. Believe me—I felt relieved to call it quits!

We were making that daily trek in that small skiff—it was a tense situation! We were new to being in a small skiff in times of bad weather. The only comfort is that we were always close to shore.

Now, I know that after being in many similar circumstances on some of our own trips by skiff in Alaska—I should have been petrified of the perils of the situation! We were six miles away from the dock—nobody knew that we were there—nor which way we went.

There was no one around to help. Capsizing would have dunked us into cold icy water, we would have had no way to survive once ashore! Hypothermia—here we come! Thank God for watching over us.

We left for Angoon with the winds howling at our heels and humongous swells pushing us along. That's called being in a 'following sea', rather than 'bucking into it'. A following sea is more dangerous than bucking the waves.

## We Chose Alaska

You have to be on constant alert to keep the boat from wanting to turn on its side as it enters the trench of the swell. This is done by correcting the rudder hard in the opposite direction of movement, just as you crest the wave. If you do it right and at the proper time—the boat enters the trench bow first and remains stable. If you don't do it right—then you have set into motion a very precarious situation—entering the trench with the boat heading sideways to it—possibly capsizing!

[I experienced that little scenario myself while teaching in Tatitlek, a small fishing village in Prince William Sound, a few years later. After being caught sideways in the trench—I learned very rapidly that it was frightening—I needed to correct the boat much sooner! Fastest lesson—I've ever learned!]

The weather seemed to have subsided a bit and appeared not to be as forbidding as the previous day's. The sun was shining and the wind was not gusting—but steady. Our southerly heading now took us on a course that cut across the swells that were still coming from the north.

We were bound for Hoonah—then eastward to Chatham Strait—then south to Angoon. The 'fetch' was so bad that Peter

# We Chose Alaska

decided to overnight in Hoonah and let the weather improve. The fetch is the distance over which the wind blows without interruption—or the time between two successive waves. I spent most of my time sitting on a stool next to Peter—at times, it felt as though I were riding a bronc!

The weather was bad for cruising—it put your reflexes in constant attention. I chose to stay where I had the best visibility possible. It lessens the chances of my getting seasick. Marcia, in the meantime—chose to remain below deck. She tells of looking out the porthole, over the kitchen sink. She was watching the panorama go from sky, to horizon, then to looking at nothing but solid water—then everything in reverse! She admitted that she was close to being sick—an extremely rare condition, for her.

I'd have been a basket case—had I been down there. Being seasick is a VERY unpleasant feeling. [On one of my first trips out from Norfolk VA—I almost lost my life when I was in the navy—due to being so seasick—in rough seas. I was laying across an ammo box—on the upper deck—dumping out what little I had left in my stomach, when the ship rolled heavily. I started to slide off of the box—headfirst—into the ocean! Luckily, one

# We Chose Alaska

of the guys from the radar shack came out to see how I was doing—he grabbed me by my belt—just above my butt and prevented me from going overboard!

He saved me—I was seventeen at the time! I would have been a goner in just a few seconds more! Now you know one of my big reasons for believing in Divine Intervention!]

Hoonah is a small fishing town. We docked and relaxed on the boat. We never did see a single person, all the time spent there! The village had a very long, high wooden dock. The tides in that area range from very high to very low; the dock has to accommodate accordingly.

There was a small boardwalk that fronted the town above water line that provided access to the few homes that we could see. The houses resembled grey wooden blocks—with weathered as well as withered sides with lush green roofs. It was a nice change from the view out of the boat's side ports while underway.

## We Chose Alaska

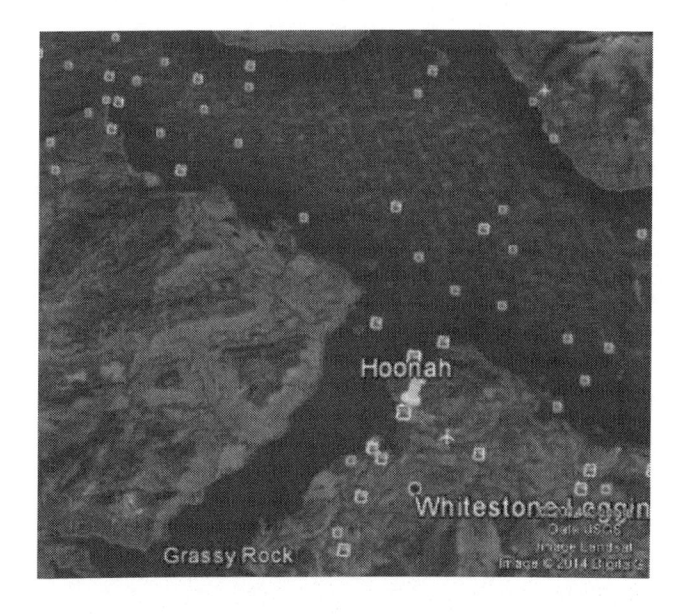

The repetitious oscillating—between water and sky—and the endlessly onward flowing waters—became very monotonous. During very rough sea times—while looking forward—the boat seemed as if it were up on a launch pad. The boat would start to shake nervously as it crested the swell, and then quickly and precipitously dove into the trench. Its forward motion was braked by the wall of water that it was trying to penetrate and sever.

It was nice being docked again! Overnight the winds subsided. When we were about mid-way to Angoon, we noticed a Coast Guard search plane that made several passes over us

# We Chose Alaska

and then flew off. We arrived at the dock in Angoon and unloaded our gear. We were very glad to be home safely. It was a wonderful adventure!

The next day, Peter came over and said that his wife had been worried sick about our having been overdue and the weather being so very bad. She had put in an emergency call to the Coast Guard in Juneau! Hindsight is always good. The several passes were probably flown while trying to get a look at the boat's name on the stern.

It was a trip that still evokes vivid memories and smiles. It was good to have had the opportunity to spend some quality time with a good friend and get to know one another better.

Both Marcia and I thank you very much, Peter, for the wonderful memories, and your gracious friendship. You provided our stay in Angoon with some very dear memories. That's a big plus.

# We Chose Alaska

24.

## ALASKA LIFE (Part 6 - Angoon - (part 4- Brown Bear Hunt))

Winter had come and gone and the time for hunting the spring bears had arrived. Around Angoon there is an ample supply of brown bears. Angoon is located on Kootznoohoo Inlet (home of the big bear in Tlingit). Peter Jack Sr. asked if we were interested in going on a hunt to Hood Bay, just a short distance south of the village. Map of Hood Bay, below.

## We Chose Alaska

The plan was to head out early after lunch. This time we were going in his fiberglass skiff, an eighteen-foot sport boat with a cuddy cabin. It was fast and comfortable.

We entered the bay and set up camp (Our Camp) in a small cove on the south shore of the bay. It was a gorgeous day, bright sunshine and virtually no wind.

Peter chose a spot to pull up and spend the night. We unloaded our camping gear and set up our two-man tent, just off the beach, in a small clearing at the edge of the woods. When you realize that you are possibly walking on a spot where no man has ever been—it makes you appreciate your experience more fully. I think the best word to describe the scenery is pristine.

Once that little chore was taken care of we headed to a small cove, (pin #1), where his skiff would be anchored while we headed up the beach. Peter had a good spot where we could hide and watch for bears. It was an old abandoned (Fish Trap) used in the early days before Alaska's statehood.

It was a humungous log structure, built at tidewater in order to trap the salmon that migrated up the bays to the spawning creeks. The fish—during high tide—entered the fish trap and were prevented from leaving by a

# We Chose Alaska

maze-like arrangement. Then the fish were scooped out with large nets and sent to processing ships anchored in the bays.

As we headed along the beach, we rounded a small bend that gave us a view of the next portion of the beach, (pin#2). Just ahead of us—about seventy five yards—was a huge Shira Brown Bear. The bear was feeding on some greens just at the edge of the woods. He was facing away from us—at a slight angle to the woods.

We immediately froze and crouched down. It worked! He didn't even know we were there!

We were in luck—the wind was in our favor—it kept our smell and our walking noises from him. It was a magnificent sight to behold. There he was with the sun shining off his amazingly jet black coat. You talk about awe—that's what that vision was.

The Shira brown bear is a unique creature. He is really a brown bear, yet his coat is jet black. His habitats are the glacier areas of southeastern Alaska. We had earlier decided that this hunt was to get a bear for Marcia. We were very excited—this was a very special bear to hunt!

We snuck up closer—the three of us abreast—Marcia in the middle—all was just perfect—just a little closer to ensure a good hit.

The tension and, I imagine, the adrenalin were in high gear. Suddenly and very slowly—the Shira moved his head—around the side of his body—to look behind himself. He must have felt our vibes—or something!

He looked directly at us and instantly—in a flash—bolted into the woods. His movement was so fast that it appeared as if he had snapped into the brush in just one lightning-like movement! It was all over—he was gone!

I still can see the piercing look that he had in his eyes when he turned his head. That's how close we got to him. We just pushed the envelope—and lost!

Disappointed but encouraged by such a quick result—we proceeded up the beach toward the fish trap which was just a short distance away. When we arrived at the fish trap the tide was going out—there was a lot of beach available to walk out to it.

We waited, hidden in one of the trap's compartments—waiting for a bear to come out of the woods. It was similar to being in a fort and being at the ready. The only difference was that we were the attackers lying in ambush.

## We Chose Alaska

The trap was a seaside musty and damp relic from the past—the upper portion was quite dry as it wasn't prone to being covered by incoming tides.

We waited and watched for what seemed an eternity for a bear to pop out of the woods. Finally—one showed up—Marcia got ready to take a shot.

This was not a Shira. It was another huge brown bear—lumbering out—from the bushes. Marcia had a 30-06 Winchester rifle and was shooting a 200gr bullet. That's a little bit of a heavy load for her. Most of her shooting was with smaller weight bullets, usually around 150gr. However, since we were after such a large animal, the 200gr was a prudent choice. What happens when you fire at an animal? The adrenalin flow renders the recoil blow almost unnoticeable—or so it seems!

She took careful aim and squeezed off a shot. We saw the bullet ricochet just before the bear! She's an excellent shot—the distance and the weight of the bullet probably played a role in her missing.

We returned to our waiting game until it was getting to be time to work our way back to the skiff. We headed back toward the spot

## We Chose Alaska

where we had seen the Shira and continued a fair distance past it.

We just glanced back there—in the hopes of seeing something—Bingo! There was another large brown meandering in the small creek—we had just passed!

We headed back to the creek with anticipation at the prospect of shooting a bear. We were still downwind and managed to crouch our way closer—we were setting Marcia up for another shot.

We had gotten rather close—closer than with the Shirah. The bear was meandering away from us—up the side of the creek. We must have passed right by where he was going to exit—onto the beach. We just missed bumping into him!

It was going to be a good shot as soon as he made a move to expose his side to us. The closer we got—the more we noticed that his pelt was not prime. He had evidently been out of hibernation for some time and had an awfully itchy shoulder! He must have scratched often and caused a few rub spots. You know how you have to scratch when you itch? Besides—he wasn't the Shira!

We were going to let him walk off—suddenly he stopped—turned around and slowly started toward us! He again crossed the

## We Chose Alaska

creek and was coming up our side—right for us!

He wasn't meandering anymore—he seemed cautious as he closed the distance. Thank God he didn't charge. We were still in control! It was getting too close for comfort (ours)! A choice had to be made.

Now, that I think about it there really was—NO choice! It was the bear's call. I waited until he had taken a forward step with his right front leg. This put his left leg toward the rear of his body and provided me with a good shot at his heart and his right shoulder behind it—I shot! The bear dropped to the ground as if a giant weight had smashed him down—he wasn't moving!

I stood up from my kneeling position and we all advanced toward the bear. I was told that when you shoot a bear and he falls with his claws curled under his paws that means that he's dead. As I approached—I could see that his claws were definitely not curled under.

I got ready to shoot again. Peter Jack told me— "WAIT!"

It seems that if you down a brown bear with just one shot—that's quite an accomplishment!

We very gingerly approached the bear—he surely was dead. The shot had gone through

## We Chose Alaska

his chest at a slight angle and must have hit his heart and possibly the spinal column—since he dropped so suddenly. I never felt the recoil—I was shooting a Winchester 338 magnum rifle and using a 300gr bullet. When target practicing, the recoil just about takes my shoulder off. ALL that disappeared in that moment!

We found ourselves running out of time. It would soon be dark and we had to plan accordingly. We decided to just roll the bear onto his back—spread his legs outward and leave him until morning.

That being done we headed for the skiff—never looking back. We got back to our camp—Peter pulled up to the beach as close as he could. Marcia and I jumped out with our rifles. We had boots on—the water under the bow was quite shallow.

I thought it was odd that Peter hadn't set up a tent. I got my answer as he wished us a goodnight and moved his skiff to deeper water and anchored for the night!

Marcia and I—with our usual sense of humor—quipped about the fact that he wasn't staying ashore. The bear population was very high! We slept very well, exhausted after such a memorable and nerve-wracking day.

# We Chose Alaska

Morning came and we headed back to skin our downed bear. We didn't bother to gut him because they are not considered good eating. Skinning didn't give any idea of the bullet's path after impact—gutting would have.

During this process—Marcia said that she was going to make a trip to the powder room. She headed down the beach for a short distance and then disappeared into the brush—very ladylike. When she came back out of the bushes and onto the beach—she headed our way.

At that very moment—a brown bear also came out of the bushes—about fifty yards beyond her!

It had no idea that she was there and just headed down the beach away from her! We didn't yell at her—we didn't want to alarm the bear and possibly change the scenario.

We were ready to shoot if need be—it was a somewhat surreal situation!

My darling didn't have a clue of what was going on behind her—that is the way we were going to keep it. She chuckled when we told her about our beachcomber friend—what a gal!

We finished our skinning job and cut a small piece of meat from the hind quarter. We thought we'd have some for lunch when we returned to camp.

Back in camp, we packed up everything except our cooking gear. We cooked the meat on a rack over the fire—it was HORRIBLE! It really didn't have the proper field dressing for meat quality.

It certainly hadn't been handled the way we would have if it were a food source. Spending over twelve hours on its back—everything intact—was not conducive to properly cooling down the meat. It's imperative that should be done. Our curiosity was satiated—our stomachs weren't! YUK!

We returned to Angoon, I prepared to tan the hide. I had saved the complete skull and was going to preserve it in case I wanted to use it in the finished product (rug).

I was told that if I put the skull into the salt water—off a dock—the sea lice would clean every bit of flesh off of it. I took it to Tom's dock and tied a rope around the skull and its jawbone.

After about a week, I went to retrieve my prize—I gingerly pulled up the skull and quickly found that I should have used some sort of basket to hold it. Not only had the lice devoured everything but bone—they had also eaten the very ligaments that hold the bones together—also the gum material that holds the teeth in place! I pulled up the upper portion of the skull with several teeth missing—it was a complete fiasco! I threw it back in and chalked it up to experience. I really didn't need it to recall our trip.

## 25.

### ALASKA LIFE Angoon - (part- 5 - Time to Move On)

Spring in the S.E. Alaska wilderness is as close to nature as you can get. Winter is behind you and the weather is becoming nicer by the day. We started making some weekend trips to an even more secluded area.

That's the area above the falls that dump from the upper bay out of Kootznahoo Inlet, right across from Angoon.

# We Chose Alaska

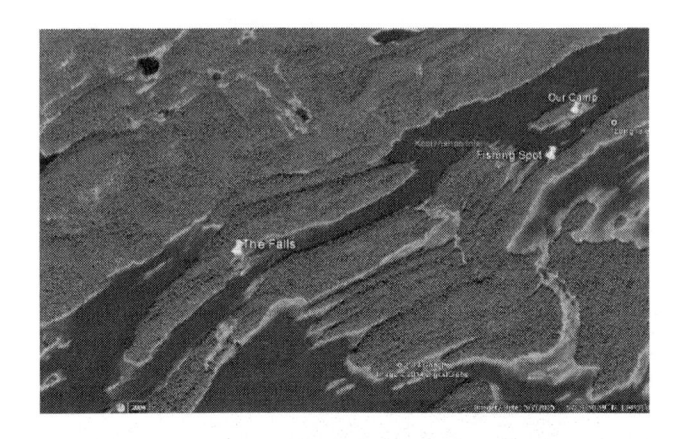

Travel into that area was a little tricky. When the tide—a large one—came in to fill the bays it turned the rocky gut into a roaring fall—facing up the bay. And when the tide was going out— the falls faced toward the inlet—with the same ferocity.

This meant that with our little 6hp. outboard—if we planned on going into the bay—we had better pick our time for doing it safely, whether close to high tide or low tide. That way we didn't have to buck the current nor duck the rocks of the falls. When we decided to leave, we just did the reverse.

I did find myself on a trip—with our dog Nanook, heading up to the bay as the tide was halfway out. I could not make any headway—the engine was not strong enough to counter the speed of the outgoing tide! It was a virtual

# We Chose Alaska

stalemate! I had to pull ashore and wait for slack water before proceeding further.

On a later trip, Marcia and I were going to camp for the weekend and do some fishing. Basically—just getting away. (Now isn't that a funny remark?)

By this time we were quite experienced, with the 'when'—to manage the falls. We set up (our camp) on a stretch of beach. The weather was very pleasant. The location oozed of—this is all yours—ALONE. It was an awesome feeling. It was—as they say—priceless!

The next morning we took the skiff across to the other side to our (fishing spot) and commenced to enjoy ourselves. The rainbow trout fishing was good and more than ample.

I'm funny about my fishing. If I spend too much time and don't get any bites—I quit because there aren't any fish to be had. However, if as soon as I drop the hook—I catch a fish—and that is the pattern, I get bored and quit. See how fickle I am!

You can only catch so many fish for lunch. I guess that means that I'm more of a subsistence fisherman than a sports fisherman. That works for me. The same goes for the hunting.

# We Chose Alaska

We were sunbathing and enjoying the ambience—when we heard the sound of an outboard engine coming from the area of the falls. What the heck! Way out here?

The sound kept getting louder and louder. We watched to see what was going to appear.

From around the point to our left—came a very large skiff (maybe about plus 20' long). At the bow was a very large (fat) man leaning forward with his left foot perched up on the bow—he looked like an early automobile hood ornament.

He was dressed in his hunting regalia and wore hip boots that were rolled down below the knees. He was wearing a sort of safari type felt hat and was hunched over in a cocker spaniel spotting position. He didn't have a tail; however, he had a very impressive rifle slung over his right shoulder. Behind him were two elderly men—wearing the same kind of gear. However, their hats did not shout, "Here we are!" They had their rifles snuggled between their legs with the barrels sticking up—they were ready!

Marcia and I remarked about the fact that we were seeing this semi-comical scenario on this one excursion—it was very entertaining. It drove home the fact that—after all—we were in prime bear country. That had never entered

# We Chose Alaska

our minds. By then we were so used to just going out and enjoying ourselves that bears were no longer a threat. We were, however—well prepared for that possibility. It's a bit like worrying about getting killed in a car accident or in a plane crash. Chances are slim and—you can't let it bother you— "Live life!"

As they approached our spot and pulled up to the beach, the guide asked, "Seen any bears?" I answered, "Nope."

He looked around as though he were searching for something. He asked, "Where are you camped?" We pointed across from where we were and said, "Over there, down on the other side." I could sense his bewilderment.

Here we were—two people in the midst of his prime hunting ground! What the hell were we doing there? AND—I imagine that he also thought of how all this would play out with his two clients. After all you don't hire a guide to take you on a big game bear hunt just to wind up chatting with a couple of schoolteachers in your killing field!

They left, after a while we could hear the sound of the motor trail off below the falls. The next day, we broke camp and headed for home—clearing the falls with ease—and armed with a new memory.

# We Chose Alaska

As Bush teachers, you could put in for a new assignment around the first part of March. The SOS (State Operated Schools) policy urged you to keep moving from one village to another—at least every three years. It prevented you from becoming involved politically in the village. Everyone who wanted to be reassigned had to submit a request. You could also list any preference you might have.

Earlier, we had an administrator visit the school. She mentioned that Tatitlek, a smaller village in Prince William Sound, was going to be open for selection. When we put in our transfers, we requested it. Tatitlek had about eighty (+ or -) people and it was a two-teacher school. Perfect!

One reason we wanted to leave was to have a closer working situation with the village people. Peter Jack and his family were wonderful. The others were more stand-offish. However, the ice was breaking. More and more people extended their friendship toward us, primarily because as spring arrived, the village had more and more functions for getting people together.

One day, we heard a knock on the door and when we answered—there stood four of the men we had gotten to know—leaders in the village. We invited them in and offered coffee.

# We Chose Alaska

They had heard about our transfer request. They came to ask if there would be any chance of changing our minds! We were touched. However, the idea of having our own school in a small village was now a very exciting reality. We warmly thanked them for their very nice and well appreciated gesture. We had been successful here and this was a sign—their seal of approval.

The end of the school year (graduation) was a big deal. The village had, I guess you'd call it—a very nice cultural evening, followed the next day—by the 8th grade graduation.

The village shaman and elder wanted a brown bear hide for the evening presentation. One of my students knew about mine from the hunt with Peter Jack. He asked me if I would let them use it—I agreed.

While things were being set up for the evening festivities—the shaman asked—"Who bring this?" He was standing in front of my bear hide—pointing at it. My student pointed at me and said—"That white man there!" I chuckled!

Here I'd been that boy's teacher for about eight months—he couldn't have said— "It's Mr. Milette's". There was a slight element of prejudice that existed in the village—which

# We Chose Alaska

may have contributed to the slow pace of our acceptance.

I have to touch on the prejudice part of my last paragraph. Several students were not full-blooded Tlingit. One of them was in Marcia's class. She was the principal's daughter. She was a cute, very intelligent student. The other students didn't address her by name—they called her "white girl". In order to try and fit in she would dumb down and not be as responsive as she was capable of being.

The other student was in my class. He was a jovial, energetic and also an intelligent student. His name was Vernon and he was the child of a Tlingit mother and an Eskimo father. He was living with his grandfather—he appeared to be in need of some TLC. He also was being discriminated against—because of being part Eskimo.

In the villages, it is common practice for the teachers to have visitors during the evening or weekends, from the students or the village adults. We'd hear a knock at our door. When we would open the door, the usual greeting was, "Come to visit."

On one such visit, by the adults, a couple came in, sat down on the couch and for about fifteen awkward minutes. No conversation was

# We Chose Alaska

exchanged—they just watched! When they left, they got up and just walked out the door!

Vernon appeared. He was—our one and only student visitor—in that village who came for a social visit in the evenings. He came often and we enjoyed having him around. It probably filled some void in both of our lives. We developed a friendship.

Over the Christmas holiday he and I went looking for a tree to cut and haul back to our apartment. He was there Christmas morning and we gave him a gift—much needed socks and a wool cap.

He later came back and presented us with two small round red colored match containers the shape of a miniature nutcracker. Marcia attached red yarn at the top to hang them on the tree. We still—every Christmas—are reminded of him when we decorate our tree.

All was going very well until one day in the spring. In class, I scolded him for misbehaving. I didn't think anything about it except that he had to be disciplined.

At first I didn't sense that anything was wrong—I had only scolded Vernon. He must have thought it was more severe than it was. It must have appeared so—to him!

As time went on, he wasn't coming around anymore and his behavior in class was nothing

# We Chose Alaska

out of the ordinary. Our friendship just passed into oblivion. I've always wondered if there could have been some other catalyst that caused the rift—perhaps parental pressure—or our leaving. He had a strong sense of survival and probably acted accordingly. He loved us—we were leaving!

You ask, "Why didn't you approach him and talk to him?" As I mentioned, it never occurred to me that there was a problem. I had some twenty students that shared my attention. I can't say anything in my defense—except that I should have and would have—if given more time. I thought he'd get over the class incident in due time. I was wrong! It was too close to the end of the school year.

That experience with Vernon reinforced my philosophy about what being a teacher is all about. Teacher first—friend second—both with respect and heart.

Many years later, when a new crop of teachers was joining our ranks, things got looser between student and teacher. The first time one of my students referred to me as Henry—I recoiled with—"My name is Mister Milette, I am not your buddy. I am your teacher!" That didn't mean that I didn't love the little turkey! The relationship between teacher and student is VERY SPECIAL.

# We Chose Alaska

There was a special meeting held in the principal's apartment across the hall from ours. It was during an administrator's visit.

Jackie had a concern about the prejudice in her class and how to handle it. After she had made her statement, the administrator said that she hadn't seen any prejudice during her classroom visitations. The principal chimed in—"There is no prejudice in our school!"

Marcia was so stunned at this revelation, she stood up in angry defense of Jackie and informed them that—"INDEED there IS!"

Frustrated, she said, "In fact your own daughter is a target of it, in my class!" She sat back down, in tears, after having given her opinion. That wasn't the end of it.

To make matters worse the administrator retorted—"Evidently, you are too emotionally unstable to teach in the Bush!" That pulled a pin in my Marcia's grenade—she had heard enough—she 'blew up'!

"How could he have known? He never observed my class while, in session!" She was so furious that she stomped out of his apartment! When my darling gets very angry, she cries! I know from experience!

The meeting concluded very shortly thereafter. As for the stability, Marcia lasted another twenty very successful years before

## We Chose Alaska

retiring. We are still living in the Bush—thirty years later! Unstable—Not. Crazy—Possibly!

[One warm spring Saturday night there was a party going on at one of the houses in the village. It was the first time we'd ever become aware of one.

Evidently, a couple from the party, had decided to take a walk along the boardwalk that went from the main part of the village, past the front of the school and the teachers' quarters, and on to a couple of houses beyond.

We had been in bed for a while—when outside our window we heard a commotion. It was a couple who had stepped behind the teachers' housing—probably to find some seclusion.

The rear of the housing was carved into the side of a hill and had about a twelve + foot clearing along its side. They must have found it to be a perfect spot—for whatever reason. At first there was a lot of anger going on with loud harsh words and accusations of misconduct at the party—along with some struggling sounds. Then—there was silence! We thought they had moved on.

Then, we heard the sounds of moaning and groaning accompanied by some heavy breathing—sort of like a crescendo leading to—for lack of a better word—a climax! As

## We Chose Alaska

married couples—we didn't need to ask ourselves what was happening! I've heard the old saying that the line between hate and love is a very fine one. You might say that theirs had snapped! The whole scene was really comical to us. Isn't it funny, one man's love making, is another's situational comedy! Sad to say it wasn't at all erotic, for us—just comical!]

The next morning, Jackie crossed over into our apartment after breakfast and asked, "Did you guys hear that noise outside our windows last night?" We said that we had and had quite a chuckle from it.

She continued, "What did you think they were doing?" I said that they had argued and then had sex! She said with concern, "Really! I didn't know what to do.

Since it was dark out, I lit a candle and put it on the windowsill for them!" That's OUR Jackie! We had another great moment to log into our memory bank! Our dear sweet Jackie got to hear unfamiliar sounds easily recognizable by married couples.

In preparation for the graduation—I was to give a speech since it was to be my 8th grade class that was graduating. In those days when the students graduated from school, they left home for the rest of their education.

## We Chose Alaska

There were two places where they were sent. One was the Chemawa Indian School in Oregon and the other was Mt. Edgecumbe Indian School in Sitka on Chichagof Island in S.E. Alaska. You can see that this was a very traumatic and important event.

Dr. Walter Sobolef PhD, was to be the special guest speaker. He was a fantastic leader in the Tlingit community, as well as the state. He was a pastor and a very charismatic spiritual leader.

I wanted to do something special for the occasion. Since I love languages, I decided to ask Peter Jack if he would coach and help me translate my speech into Tlingit! As far as I knew that had never been done by a white man!

He agreed and we set off to do the task. The moment came—I walked to the podium and began to give my speech in my best Tlingit! When I had finished—I proudly returned to my seat, accompanied by warm applause.

Dr. Soboleff came to the podium and said, "That's the first time I've ever heard a speech given in Tlingit—with a French accent!" The roar of laughter was as stimulating as was the applause! It was very nice!

# We Chose Alaska

Take a deep breath—grab your mate's hand—put a smile on your face—keep joy in your heart.
"GO FOR IT!"

Look out Tatitlek—here we come!

26.

## Tatitlek – The Transition

When we returned to Anchorage—after our school year in Angoon—it was time to plan for our new assignment in a small village in Prince William Sound. We were contacted by State Operated Schools and offered a one week—all expenses paid trip—to be 'Bush Teacher Consultants' in the Rural School Project (where we attended last summer). It was great fun sharing our experiences and answering their questions.

We were glad to have had the privilege of being asked—as unstable as we must have been—according to Marie, our 'wonder'-ful visiting administrator! Our principal was sent

## We Chose Alaska

to a one teacher school in a Southeastern logging camp—perfect!

Our new station in Tatitlek would differ greatly. We didn't have to order and ship a full school year worth of basic food supplies. We would have access to the grocery store in Valdez about 27 miles away.

The only way in or out of Tatitlek was by boat or float plane. Another benefit was that we would have road access once in Valdez to the mainland of Alaska—principally Anchorage.

Prince William Sound is a relatively young geologic formation. Not too long ago, in geologic time, the Sound was subjected to the erosive pressures from the many huge ice fields and glaciers that covered it.

It is in a major rain and snow accumulation area due to the flow of the warm, moist Japanese current. The moisture laden current pushes up against the cold air of the Chugach Range. That causes precipitation.

The picture below still has remnants of the glacier covered range. Many glacial striations are visible on the many rock outcrops around the shore of the Sound.

Prince William Sound was originally Chugach Eskimo territory. This link is very informative in explaining the chronological

# We Chose Alaska

prehistoric phases of the Peoples of Alaska (South Central).
(http://www.alaskool.org/resources/regional/sc_reg_pro/population.html)

The first explorer to visit the Sound was Capt. Cook in 1778. Five years later, 1783, the Russians entered the Sound in search of furs, namely fur seals which have amazingly luxurious pelts.

Since the Russians came from the west, they would have stopped in Aleut villages along the way up the Aleutian Chain and practiced some sort of conscription—to get the men needed for their fur seal hunting expeditions.

I imagine the request probably went something like this, "Come with us, leave your families, or we shall kill you and them!"

Who can refuse an offer like that—especially with those magnificent health benefits?

They were put to work in badarkas (Russian for small boat), a kayak style sealskin boat used in harvesting fur seals.

These same men were most likely quartered in the villages of the Sound while the Russians returned home with their pelts. It was the common practice. Otherwise, the people of Tatitlek and Chenega would not be saying that

# We Chose Alaska

they are Aleuts—but rather that they are Chugachimiut Eskimos.

The people of the Sound do consider themselves to be Aleuts. We know how the Aleuts got there. The mystery is what happened to bring this about? I believe it was a peaceful assimilation of the two cultures caused by an overwhelming number of Aleut men becoming integrated with the Chugach people. Or maybe it wasn't so loving and peaceful! We'll never know.

When the present people of the Sound say that they are Aleuts, I fully believe them. They bear Russian family names and speak Aleut from the contact with the Russians fur traders and the Aleut people.

There are a few with English names who would have come in contact with U.S. Army. Lieutenant Henry Allen's expedition in 1885. His mission was to explore the Copper River area via Prince William Sound.

No matter what they are—they are some of the nicest people that Marcia and I have had the pleasure of knowing. We've made some life-long friendships. I hope that will be apparent in my future chapters on Tatitlek, and the people of Chenega.

When we arrived in Tatitlek, we found out that the March 1964 Earthquake had caused

# We Chose Alaska

serious devastation in some areas of the Sound. The village of Chenega had been completely destroyed by a tidal wave. A third of their population was lost in an instant. The remaining people were transferred to Tatitlek until they were able to return to their own newly established village in 1984.

We had the honor of getting to know some of these wonderful and brave people as they co-existed with the people of Tatitlek. To us they were one and the same. Prejudice was not a factor. I've included a site for the history of the Chenega people. (Chenega.com/history)

I've marked these places with yellow pins (no colors in photos) in order to familiarize you with our new environment. As you can see it brings to mind the comment, "We've died and gone to heaven!" We were so blessed to have been given this assignment.

Here is a closer look at the Valdez & Tatitlek area and the surrounding glaciers, in the picture below. The word PARADISE is quite fitting to describe our new playground.

## We Chose Alaska

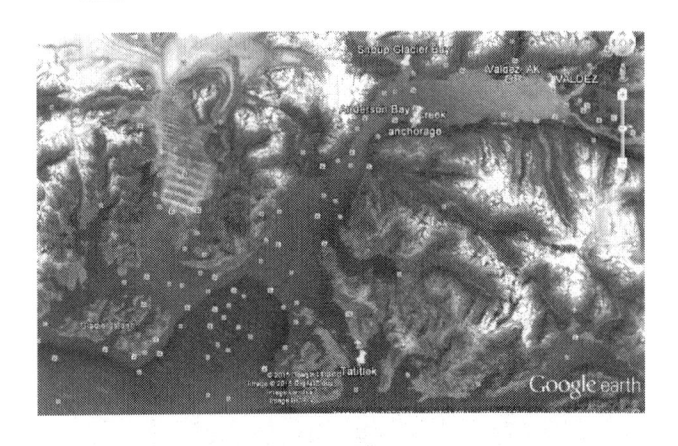

We took a trip south to California and back East to visit family and friends for a couple of months.

When we returned to Anchorage, it was time to start acquiring things that we would need for life in our new environment. It's quite obvious that a boat was in this case a utility—a need instead of the usual toy—and a want!

In those days the Seattle Sunday newspaper was accessible. Boats, cars or whatever were very expensive in Alaska. A case in point was the new Chevy pickup that we originally drove to Alaska, I sold it after having driven it for two years for a thousand more than my purchase price.

I learned that lesson early on. I happened to see an ad from a Seattle boat dealer who had a boat that would fit my needs. It said that there was minor damage to it. I called and was told that the damage consisted of a light circular scratch pattern that was done by someone's shoe on the top of the cuddy cabin. I was assured that it was a brand new twenty-one-foot Bayliner with a four cylinder Mercury inboard-outboard engine. I did what comes naturally for me. I took a chance and made the purchase. They shipped it to Anchorage on a freighter. The cost was not exorbitant.

The day it arrived, I went to the docks and there it was sitting on a cradle, already unloaded and ready—for transport to Valdez. Here's where my memory is a little foggy. Although I can vividly see the first look at our boat, in my mind, I can't remember how it got to Valdez. I asked my friend Bob Rood if he was instrumental in the move.

He and his wife Ruthanne were our best friends at the time. I just talked to him yesterday to help me fill in the blanks. I asked, "Is your memory still good, or are you now an old senile bastard—who doesn't remember anything?" He assured me in a very verbose manner that he was as sharp as a tack! He didn't remember anything about it—therefore it probably was not he.

We are in the same boat! No pun intended. That part of my story shall remain a mystery. [I

# We Chose Alaska

would like to note here that in Marcia's Christmas letter—you will read the rest of the story that will solve the mystery!]

While we were at the small boat harbor in Valdez, we met the Londagins, Herman and Maxine. They had a (plus) thirty foot, live-aboard-if-you-want boat. We became very good friends. Occasionally on weekend trips, we would go to Valdez on our boat to shop and spend the nights with them at their home. We felt like family. They were very warm people.

Their story is very fascinating. He worked for the Dept. of Transportation (highways) and Maxine was a school secretary. The house they lived in was originally located in 'Old Valdez', the town that was obliterated during the 1964 Alaskan earthquake. It was one, of a few houses, that was relocated.

Their home had the atmosphere of a loving and friendly haven. After they retired, Herman and Maxine moved to Hawaii. We still look back very fondly on those days spent with them.

Herman offered to take us and our supplies, on his boat to Tatitlek! "What's not to like about these wonderful people?" Once there, we headed for the school, hauling our stuff to our apartment. We went through all the rooms

# We Chose Alaska

and buildings, checking on what we had inherited. The school had four areas—two large classrooms on one side and on the other—a large kitchen with a serving counter for preparing and serving snack lunches. There was an adjoining guest room, with its own entrance, for state visitors on business, such as school nurses, visiting dentist, carpenters, mechanics or whomever. Our two-bedroom apartment encompassed the remainder of that side.

Everything seemed in order until we hit a light switch—nothing happened! Of course not! We had to 'turn on' the generator! There's always a catch!

The generator house was a large outbuilding that had two exhaust mufflers sticking out of its side. The building contained two rooms. The larger one had two diesel generators and occupied about 80% of the building. The other was a 'water room' that contained two large square steel water storage tanks 8' x 8' x 7' high and a chlorination system on the house feed line.

Tatitlek is in an area of massive precipitation. It rains and snows a lot! Needless to say, water was not a problem! "Yeah right!" Just in case of a dry spell, (hindsight: We had a problem with water in

# We Chose Alaska

December!) there was a feed line to the tanks from a small lake up above the village. We never used that one.

Just in case you didn't perceive the problem while reading about the generators, I'll tell you what it was. I knew what diesel generators were and that they made electricity for us to have lights. However, I didn't have a clue on how to operate them! Herman came to the forefront as if he had a new toy and said—"Let's get it going!" I asked, "You know how to operate these?" "Sure—it's easy."

I suddenly realized why they hired me for the job. Not only was I going to teach, I was also going to run the place! Didn't these people know that I used to be—a hairstylist?

Herman did save the day and showed me what needed to be done. Luckily, any servicing was done by state maintenance employees on a scheduled basis—during the summer. I only had to check the oil and coolant levels.

We proceeded to bring our new home to life and move in. In those days, as I mentioned for Angoon, when you taught in the bush, all your household goods except sheets and blankets were furnished—a turn-key operation. The kitchen and living room were quite large, as were the two bedrooms. A

## We Chose Alaska

very large kitchen area had a wringer-type washing machine and an electric dryer for doing our laundry.

I asked where I could moor the boat, when it arrived from Anchorage. I was shown a floating buoy that was about a hundred or so yards from the beach. It had a line that went down to a heavy chain that was wrapped through a caterpillar track gear—that's a lot of weight. I couldn't wait to see our boat riding—tied to its mooring!

In those days anything that you did in Alaska always took time. I hadn't given that any thought when I started looking for a boat. You had to develop patience—tolerance—and acceptance of the situations. I didn't have a boat in time to make my journey to the village. It was due to arrive in a few days. Here comes 'Divine Intervention—again—Herman to the rescue!

We spent a couple of days in the village, setting up housekeeping, before going in to pick up our boat. We needed to get back to Valdez and on to Anchorage. John Borodkin, the village council president, took us in his skiff to the "Bartlett" an Alaskan ferry that serves the waterways of the state. The Bartlett stopped a few miles offshore, for customer pickups.

## We Chose Alaska

When fully stopped, from its bow, the ramp was lowered and John pulled up alongside. We could hear the captain, over the loudspeaker, informing the passengers (tourists) all about who we were and what we did. He mentioned that the marine system was one of the very few ways for us to reach civilization.

Well, I'll tell you—heads were popping up all over the rails above—with cameras in hand, no less! Ever feel like a curiosity? We still don't know what they expected to see—Tarzan and Jane, maybe?

Back in Tatitlek, with our boat, we were settling in and would soon be open for business. We were greeted VERY warmly. The people couldn't do enough to help us whenever or wherever they could. Their friendliness and acceptance of us was captivating. Little did we know at the time that we would forge some very strong friendship bonds—along with memories that would linger in our hearts and minds way into old age?

We spent three wonderful years at Tatitlek. This chapter in our lives will comprise stories that are not necessarily chronological—except in the fact that they fall between the years 1970 to 1973. As you know all our pictures and notes were lost in our house fire in 1999—so we are

# We Chose Alaska

relying strictly on our memories and the letters that Marcia wrote to her mom. They were saved and passed on to us, after her mother's death.

Thank God! He hasn't deprived me of my memories. As for the rest of the body—He probably took a well-deserved break!

Because of Tatitlek's isolation, there was no administrative entity that I responded to except the Head of State Operated Schools—the very same person who hired us for Angoon. It was a very unique situation.

The following year, the problem was solved by tucking us under the wing of the Glennallen superintendent who was about a hundred and fifty miles away. That was twenty-seven miles by water and about a hundred and twenty-five over land.

That move made it possible for me to implement a few programs that I wanted to do while there. I finally had someone I could talk to, for equipment to improve my teaching goals.

Communications in the village were limited. There was one short wave radio located in John and Chis Borodkin's home. John was the village council president, a very influential man in Tatitlek who took his responsibility very seriously. He was very

# We Chose Alaska

involved in what was happening to the village and his people. He was a good role model. That is the sign of true leadership.

Mail came every other week by float plane in the summer and by boat in the winter. There were no local radio nor TV stations. The newspapers mailed from Anchorage, arrived fourteen or more issues at a time, weather depending! I hardly read any of them—it was overkill—who cares about old news, anyway? We were wholly involved with village life and the people—our sole focus. We were in another world and loving every moment and aspect of it.

The fuel for the generators and the school furnaces was brought in the spring. A large fuel barge from a larger tanker would pull up close to the beach. A fuel line was brought up to the tall round fuel tank in front of the generator building. The tank must have been at least ten feet in diameter and twelve or so feet in height. The fuel was pumped to the feed line valve for the tank.

It was my job, in order to keep fuel contamination down, to bleed the tank's bottom valve of all the water. The water came in from the leaky tank tops or the fuel line as it was dragged through the water before the fuel transfer was started. That meant that I had to

# We Chose Alaska

open the main drain valve and let the water gush out until I noticed a slight sheen on it. I then closed the valve until the next fuel time. It was amazing how long and how hard that water flowed—before the contaminated water showed up!

Not knowing what to expect, I felt a little apprehensive the first time I did it. Ignorance is a heavy burden! A huge responsibility doesn't help the situation, either!

The village people would go to Valdez or Cordova with their boats and fill fifty-five-gallon drums with fuel oil or gasoline. Once back at Tatitlek, they'd hoist them up onto the main dock and roll them to their homes—a very costly and labor-intensive project.

The source of food was either a trip to town to stock up on supplies—or subsistence gathering from the many plentiful food sources of the Sound, such as fish, kelp, herring roe on kelp, clams, king crab, berries, all types of waterfowl, seals, bears, deer, and mountain goats. I'm sure I've left some out. We also participated in the subsistence lifestyle alongside our friends.

When a family came in with their load of supplies, it was a community effort to haul it from the dock to the proper home. These runs were usually done for the most part after the close of the fishing season and some, to a lesser degree, just before the Christmas season.

We were introduced to steam baths (saunas) by our friend George Allen. Dispersed throughout the village were several steam bath houses. Each provided a place for the many family groups and friends to bathe.

Usually, the structure was located a safe fire distance from the house. They were made of plank and plywood construction with the main chamber containing benches, clothes hooks, and five-gallon fuel cans with tops removed, which were filled with water. There was a healthy supply of cord wood for the stove. The stove was constructed from a 55-gallon fuel drum. It stood on end in a 2x6 framed box filled with small rocks and sand to insulate the floor against the hot barrel bottom. It had a door cut into its side for placing alternating levels of firewood and igneous rocks. The fire was lit at least three hours prior to taking a bath.

George's steam bath was on the left side of the shed about five feet from the entrance. It was constructed using five sheets of plywood. A rectangular container was made with four of the sheets and the fifth one was cut in half and nailed to the container on each end.

# We Chose Alaska

The right side of the front sheet had a piece cut out of it to make a door. The cut piece then got hinged back on to the long side. Voila! A steam bath!

While the fire roared and the barrel stove glowed a dull red—the large water cans placed around and on top of it when the fire was lit—provided us with hot water for bathing.

I remember my first view of the fire chamber as George opened the door to extract the crimson rocks. They were glowing a deep fiery red and seemed to sparkle as the draft of cool air entered the chamber. I had never seen rocks that glowed red before. I had seen many pictures and videos of lava in my geology classes. This was totally different. I could feel the heat. They almost said, "Go ahead, touch me, I just dare you!" No way, Jose!

The hot rocks were scooped out, one by one, and placed inside the sauna with a shovel. They were put in a large, galvanized tub that was snuggled directly into the back right corner, just in from the makeshift door. To the left of the door was a low narrow bench that extended to the side wall, where it met up with a shorter one. It was a flipped 'L' shape. We sat on these while bathing.

The schedule was that the men go first. The women and children bathe next. Each group took about an hour and a half to complete its turn. We went into the steam bath for about 15-20 minutes, to just open our pores and release the body's toxins. We came out and sat and socialized for a while; then we returned for a final washing and rinsing. The women followed the same ritual—which took longer!

When there was need of more heat (steam), someone would say—"Spill-em!" Then one of the small tin cans, used as a ladle, was picked up, dipped into a water bucket and the water was splashed on to the rocks. They used to love to do this to newcomers. They didn't spare me the pleasure of this treatment.

They spilled them so much—I had to drop to the floor to get cooler air—to breathe. It made them happy! The resulting dropping curtain of hot steam would drive anyone not used to this bathing style—to head for the floor. It didn't matter much because the steam always managed to follow you down. You'd just have to get used to it! They relished those moments. It was entertainment! We would do two rounds in the steam bath, divided by a cooldown period.

If there were more people than the steam bath could accommodate, the others would go into the sauna for their first time, after the first group. The second round was to wash yourself

# We Chose Alaska

before heading back out to the bench. This was a great time for socializing. The bench time was used for talking about whatever was pertinent, while you cooled down enough to get dressed.

I could see the smoke from the steam bath house from my classroom window. "Ah great—steam bath time!"—I would think to myself. It was usually just before four o'clock that the men and the boys would go to the bath, as part of the first shift. Then, when they were finished, the women and the very young children would congregate for their turn.

Marcia, at first, was reluctant to take a steam bath. She felt too intimidated and refused to go. I think she finally got tired of seeing me come home—glowingly flushed and raving about how great it was. It took a very long time for her to decide to join the women. It wasn't until the middle of December when she took the plunge! (You'll get to read her story when you read one of her letters.)

Most times (we) would be fixing supper around six o'clock. This meant I would finish the supper preparation on steam bath days. Even to this day, our principal bathing method is a sauna. We bathe every other day, or as needed, and have ever since that first time in

# We Chose Alaska

George's steam bath. Steam bath time is family time and community time. There were several steam baths going on in the village at varied times. Each handled a family unit and friends that were close.

Marcia's main apprehension was shyness—I never raised any objection about the fact that she didn't participate. I knew that she was in turmoil about it. When you live in a village situation, the one thing you don't want is conflict. I knew that by keeping my mouth shut—to understand her predicament—she would, at her own pace, join in. It's such a wonderful way to bathe. Your pores open, under that steam, and your body gets a chance to purge some of the toxins from your system.

One of the things that is touted as wonderful during the steaming when your body is extremely hot from the steam bath, is to go outside and roll in the snow!

I tried it once and it wasn't a problem. Your body is so hot that it counters the cold feeling! Been there done that—once—that sufficed! Steam baths are a definite part of our lives. We both became hooked! It was also a MUST for the first house that WE built a few years later. I was able to use the technology that I had learned—however it (steam bath) was a fiasco!

## We Chose Alaska

1. Temp. 31°

Wed. A.M.

Dear Mother & Earl -

The mail boat came in yesterday - and with it came the Christmas box from you. Also the red material. Thank you ever so much. The material is beautiful! The card for the National Geographic came too. Thank you again.

We got a few cards - yours included. Imagine the next mail boat - on the 29th - will have a lot more.

Hope your things get there on time. We just sent our Christmas letters out yesterday. Sorry I didn't get cards made this year. Don't know where the time goes. We made the letter extra long, as you will see, to help make up for the lack of a

# We Chose Alaska

2.

card. I did make cards for many of the people here in Alaska – mainly other bush teachers and the people at Angoon. The stuff in our letter would be kind of "old hat" to them.

Didn't get the dolls for Lori and Lisa made either. Had quite a time trying to get the material from Sears. Will still try to do them though.

We haven't heard a word from Bob and Ruthanne since they left here. They had planned to come back the weekend after Thanksgiving – but the weekend was pretty bad. We thought we'd get a letter yesterday – or a message on KYAK – but neither came. They're probably real busy too. They plan to go to Hawaii and San Diego for vacation. It's almost impossible

# We Chose Alaska

3.

to get in and out of Tatitlek now —
unless you have a big boat —
(bigger than ours). No planes come
in, in the winter and the ferry
was supposed to stop running
yesterday for about a month
for repairs. The weather changes
so quickly, that you're really
taking a chance with our boat —
that is, you can get to Valdez,
but could be weathered in for
days before you could come back.
Guess that's one of the exciting
things about living here!

 Henry mentioned the steam
bath in the Christmas letter. Well,
I took my first one last Saturday night. It's wonderful! — And
seems to be great for dry skin.
I took it alone — but of course
the custom is to take one with
the other ladies. Sylvia Allen said

# We Chose Alaska

4.

that they had talked about asking me - but were afraid to. Can't imagine why, but as much as I wanted to take one, I was scared to death they'd ask me - and you know how inhibited I am! Have decided that it's so great though, that I'll forget my inhibitions!

I enjoyed it so much, that I got partically dressed once - then undressed and went back in. Henry was in George and Sylvia's house. I was there so long, that they began to wonder if I was all right.

Got another letter from Judy De Vito yesterday. They're probably back in Phelps by now. Spence's dad has a brain tumor, so he had to go back and take over the business. They had only been here

## We Chose Alaska

5.

four months. They hope to come back eventually. Judy said it doesn't take long to learn to love this place (Alaska).

Your stove and refrigerator sound nice — especially the self cleaning oven — and self-defrosting refrigerator. They are not my favorite jobs either. I've found (from one of the native gals) that spray oven cleaner works very well on the top of this stove — so it's not really too bad a job.

Our snow has really melted down — and we had some rain again. I hated to see the snow go, but we really needed the water. It was very low — and for so early in the winter — that was bad!

Have to go get some breakfast ready for Henry — big deal — toast,

6.

peanut butter, and jam! Speaking of toast — Do you like rye bread? I have a no-knead recipe for it that is delicious (if you like rye bread!) I like caraway seeds so much now. — but isn't that what Grandma Barnum used to use — and I always turned my nose up?

Got to run!

Love —

Henry & Marcia

P.S. Hope you have a wonderful Christmas!

P.S.S. Am enclosing one of the card I did make. I made 10 different pictures this year — then repeated them several times. Nice!

27.

## Tatitlek – First Year

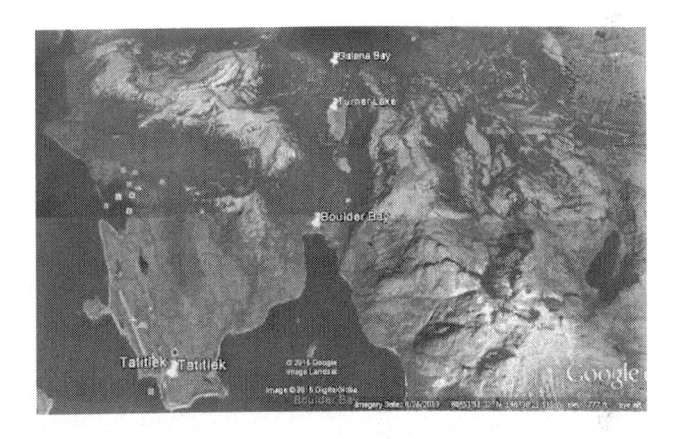

We settled in and started to enjoy our new life in Tatitlek. We explored, camped and fished. The magnitude and the beauty of the wilderness surpassed our last assignment. There were many snow covered mountains and beautiful nearby bays to explore. I wrote to Bob and told him that they needed to come for a visit. It was agreed that they would come for Thanksgiving. "Great!" We had a wonderful time with them. The story will be mentioned

## We Chose Alaska

in the attached letters. I don't want too much redundancy in my stories!

The one exciting highlight,—other than seeing them—was when we were returning from a hunting trip to Fidalgo Bay. All of a sudden, as we neared the point to the bay—we hit some large swells. I couldn't gauge their magnitude—I didn't throttle down soon enough. We weren't slowly introduced to them. It was a, "Hey! Where did these come from?" moment.

The next thing I knew the boat was flying off the top ridge of this enormous swell! Staring at us, just ahead, was a wall of water! I immediately throttled back to stop my forward speed! We were in the air! I doubt if that had any effect until we hit the oncoming swell.

Does "SWOOSH" mean anything to you? Then I stepped up the speed enough to maneuver the boat, up and down the oncoming swells, until we got back into calmer waters. We had a great time and plans were made for them to return in a couple of weeks. Bob is an avid outdoorsman and had just had a taste of paradise—he WAS coming back!

One night when the wind was howling—the worst I had ever experienced—I looked out the window and barely saw that something was going on with our boat. I was having a

# We Chose Alaska

rough time making anything out due to the darkness. I was hoping that I could see something because of the light coming from the corner of the school building.

As I was looking, I noticed Illene Totemoff, our neighbor, bent forward, holding a Coleman lantern—pushing against the wind—while working her way up the path toward the school. I still see that vision as if it were yesterday—it was eerie!

I quickly headed for the door to let her in. I opened it and saw that she was frantic. "Henry, your boat is drifting and the men are on the dock! They want you to come." I was stunned!

I got my gear on and headed for the dock. As I went down the path, some of the men were shining their spotlights at our boat. I could see it clearly. It was even eerier!

There is a mostly submerged reef, carved by glaciers that eroded the beach area, way earlier when Prince William Sound was mostly ice covered. The reefs still showed wear striations on their surfaces. The boat was dragging its mooring!

The wind was trying to push it towards the outer reef! Luckily, the waves coming from the open waters and crashing over that reef caused a pushing wave action—countering the wind! It was actually saving the boat from destruction! There it rode— stuck between hell and high water!

I got to the dock and George Allen said that he would take me and David Totemoff, the school's custodian, to our boat. I knew David. He was a young, robust, pleasant young man and a good choice for the task. We took along a long rope which was tied to the dock. David tied the other end to the bow of our boat.

I started the motor and when all was running well, I said, "OK". He released the line that was tied to the mooring—away we went! We headed for the leeward side of the dock. George adjusted the distance on the rope that he had previously given us. The boat needed it to ride safely, until the storm subsided.

The next day I took my SportYak dingy and paddled to the boat. On the boat, I had a battery-operated pump which took care of the excess water from the rain. That was a plus.

The brand-new white nylon canopy—had been ripped from the aluminum framework! All that was salvageable was the small intact canopy piece which covered the front part over the cuddy cabin! At least the two chairs and the pilot station were still kept covered.

It turned out that as time went on, I probably would have removed the part that

# We Chose Alaska

the storm tore up. It would have been a major pain in the butt! It looked nice; however, it was a nuisance. Its intent was for cruising comfort in a more placid and less critical environment. This was to be a 'work' boat—in Alaska.

The mooring was returned to its original spot and our boat followed suit. Can you imagine the strain on the boat's cleat and line! That caterpillar gear was being dragged, along with our boat—halfway towards the dock!

In a storm you must take what gets dished out—make the best of it. Finally, all was well again. It didn't look as majestic as it once did. That full canopy made a gorgeous picture sitting on top of that turquoise hull. C'est la vie!

It's time to mention the boat's name. By this time, we had become good friends with George and Sylvia. I loved teasing Sylvia. She would often counter with, "Ayah, Henry!" So, when it came time to name the boat—up popped the word—"Ayah".

I was told of the many times the village people would get a giggling charge, when I'd get on my marine radio and say, "This is the Ayah!" The word was a very common expression among the people—something like 'golly'.

## We Chose Alaska

Due to the high winds and the cold temperatures of winter, our exploring adventures came to a halt. We could only go by boat to a couple of the closer bays. However, at that time of the year there's no place like home.

Life became routine. The men would go toward Seward—goat hunting on their large seiners. George came back from such a trip and had had success. He brought home a beautiful huge goat. I immediately jumped into my tanning mode and asked if I could have the hide. I broke out my Herter's Catalog and ordered my supplies. It became something that I could share with my students.

This is a great cross country skiing area. The snow was moisture-filled and made an excellent base for trails. Marcia and I had put our skis away when we moved to Angoon. We were used to doing a lot of it while in Anchorage—which also has good snow, for cross country skiing. In Tatitlek we made a ski trail up and over the hills behind the village.

The schools at the time had special access to military surplus equipment sales from the bases near Anchorage. We ordered some military skis for the students. It became very popular. Even the younger men would test their skills on the slope directly behind and

# We Chose Alaska

above the village. They had a ball! The hills were suddenly alive with energy. We had to restrict their use of the skis. The skis were for the students, so the young men could only use them during the time school was in session. There was no problem with after school hours because it got dark just when school let out. In winter, the sun comes up around 9:15 am, and sets around 3:30 pm.

Sylvia bought regular skis for herself and their two older boys, Russell and Gordon. We planned a cross country ski trip for the five of us, from Boulder Bay, across land, to a forest service cabin on the shore of Galena Bay. It was to be about a two-hour ski trip from bay to bay. George took us in his boat to Boulder Bay and dropped us off. (See p. 287)

The plan was to ski over to the Forest Service cabin and wait for George's arrival—and then return to the village. We skied through a sort of saddle formation between two hills. There was a small lake in the middle—the best part of our trip. A lot of the terrain was a challenge with shrubs and small trees and boulders obstructing the way. The lake was a very welcomed flat unobstructed plateau. The boys did very well. They were real troopers.

## We Chose Alaska

We arrived at the cabin and had a short wait till George arrived. It was a very nice and memorable trip! The weather was fantastically clear and sunny. The air was crisp, but it soon didn't matter. We were feeling our bodies' heat up because of the skiing. It was a working exercise. It was really the ultimate in a cross-country ski experience—for all. We were very proud of our accomplishment

Weekends were ski days. Marcia and I had made plans to meet three of our students, Wayne Totemoff, George Selanoff and Kevin Gregorief, up on the hill to ski the trail into the back country behind the village.

We had skied our way around the back side of the hill and were looking down the trail which led to the bay. The trail passed through a very narrow stretch of brush about half the way down the hill. I went first to break trail for Marcia and the boys. I started to head down and as I approached the brush patch, I saw that I had too much speed to pick a clear path.

As I neared the patch—I started to use a slowing down maneuver—"The Snowplow".

## We Chose Alaska

It's basically a move where you crouch and bend your knees, spread your legs, and at the same time your feet should point toward each other. The maneuver makes you do a plowing action which in turn slows you or stops you, depending on the angle of your skis and the amount of force you use.

I wanted to slow down and pass through a narrow-cleared area ahead. I didn't notice the one little stubby branch, sticking up out from the snow, uphill from a row of brush. The row looked like a short, thick wall, drawing my attention away from the little branch.

All of a sudden, the middle of my left ski near the binding—found that little sucker dead on! It stopped my forward motion—on a dime! My left ankle took the brunt of the impact—I felt a sharp snap! My momentum flipped me forward and sideways! I made a spinning nose-dive, as my body was jerked out of balance! Frustrated, embarrassed, covered in snow and in pain—I couldn't get up!

Marcia and the three boys rushed down to where I was lying. What to do? Whatever it

# We Chose Alaska

was—I couldn't stay there. George, one of my eighth graders, said that he knew where there was an ahkio, (pictured) a military snow sled for dragging supplies. It is shaped like a large banana peel half, made of fiberglass and extremely rugged.

He soon returned and I was loaded onto the sled. The three boys took me on a wild trip down the hill! Believe me that was not an easy feat. They were highly capable of taking care of me. There is a strong work ethic in the village. These boys were used to doing tough jobs.

The downhill portion back to the village was a challenge. They had to keep ahead of the slippery ahkio and its load. It wanted to go faster than they could. None of us was wanting such a speed! All in all—it was a very bouncy ride—but they did it—got me home in one piece. They were wonderful young men!

News has a tendency to spread fast in a village. John Borodkin heard about my accident and came to see how I was doing. We looked at the leg and couldn't tell whether it was a very bad sprain or a fracture. Illene had a pair of crutches and an elastic bandage that she loaned to me. I wasn't of much use around the house! I imagine that

# We Chose Alaska

accordingly, romance would have been a big No, No! Sort of, "the mind is willing and the flesh is weak!"

I went back to work on Monday morning. I sat at my desk with my foot resting on an open drawer. By then the ankle had become very swollen. I heard that Illene and Steve, her husband, were heading into Valdez for groceries on Tuesday. I asked if they could take me in to see Valdez's only doctor, Dr. Schunk, at the hospital.

Winter is a heck of a lousy time to get a broken leg. Walking on ice is enough of a challenge, never mind—on crutches as I was soon to find out! It's more of an inconvenience rather than a pain.

This is Marcia's letter to her mother, written on Nov. 30, 1970

## We Chose Alaska

1.
Temp. 17°

Nov 30

Dear Mother & Earl —
   Mail tomorrow — hopefully!
   Thank you for the Thanksgiving card!
   Just finished my laundry a few minutes ago (It's 7:50 P.M. now) still have stuff drying. Since the colder weather set in, I can't run the dryer while school is in session. It's too much for the generator with two furnaces and the lights on. Even if I have to be doing it at midnight though, it's much, much better than going to a laundromat!
   Well, we had a few Thanksgivings! We let school out at 12:15 on Wednesday and headed for Valdez by 1 P.M. in our boat. The weather was fine going in. We ran into a little wind — but

# We Chose Alaska

nothing bad. We stayed with the Londagins, of course. They're such marvelous people!

Bob, Ruthenne, Robert Clarke and Pierre got there around 10:30 a.m. Thursday morning. The trip back out here was pretty rough! The wind was blowing pretty hard — consequently we ran into some very choppy water.

On Friday, Robert Clarke stayed here with Carol and Norman Vlasoff and the Roods and we went to Landlocked Bay to look for the goats and seals. We've seen the goats every time we've been there, but couldn't find them then. (Bob really wants a goat.) Henry shot one seal. Bob shot a couple of times, but missed. We also went to Fish Bay. It was a

3.

beautiful, calm day.
  We had our Thanksgiving dinner, Friday night, after the movie - around 10 P.M. in fact.
  Saturday, we set out fairly early to seal hunt at Gull Island - across Vidalgo Bay. When we were about half way across, the swells started rolling in and the wind started to pick up. By the time we got across, they were huge - and there was no getting anywhere near the island. So we beat it to Snug Cove Bay - then finally back across Vidalgo and into Nah Bay. It stayed windy - but you're somewhat protected in the bays. No luck with the seals - so we headed back out. The swells were huge there by that time too. Henry was going pretty fast - and

# We Chose Alaska

4.

we literally flew over one of the breakers. Scary — & but funny too. After that we

slowed down considerably. The swells were at least as high as our ceiling Henry says — and that is 9 feet high! How would you like a ride like that, Mother? Earl, you'd probably love it!
　　We came back on past Tatitlek and went to rummage around Ellamar — the old deserted cannery. Quite an interesting spot. We needed spent lots more time to see everything — but it starts to get dark by 3:30 — so we came home.
　　The wind kept picking up — so we couldn't go anywhere in the boat yesterday — and Bob and

5

Ruthanne couldn't get out of here. We went for a long walk — really chilly with the wind — very invigorating!

Back to school again today! The Roods left on the ferry around 12:30 P.M. — so did the high school kids who had been home for the vacation. The "Little Dan", one of the big fishing boats, took them all to the ferry. The Roods were kind of moaning about losing a day's pay, but knew they were taking that chance when they came.

As far as we know now, they're coming back next weekend. They'd use their 2 personal leave days — one on Friday and one on Monday — so they can take the ferry here and back. They're pretty impressed with Tatitlek. Bob said that when

## We Chose Alaska

6

he sees all we're doing, he feels as though they don't do anything.

Am enclosing a picture of our boat — and Judy's letter. (Don't need either back.) Our boat has an aqua interior.

How much do we owe you for the stereo? Henry said it was sent to you C.O.D. Sure is nice to have it! If I've forgotten something in what we owe you — let us know!

Got to run! Take care.
Love —
Henry & Marcia

Oh — by the way — Hey, Lafayette sent us a whole new stereo — so now we have two turntables, four speakers, two covers!

How was your Thanksgiving?

## 28.

## Tatitlek – The Holidays

Christmas vacation was fast approaching and it wasn't going to be joyful for me—rather a big pain. I had hoped that there would have been signs of healing as the days passed. No such luck!

When I heard about Steve Totemoff's trip to Valdez, I thought maybe I should go and get the leg looked at—it might be a long time before I got another chance.

Dr. Schunk had an enormous responsibility! He was a kindly elderly person with a good sense of humor. He had a calming sense about him. He liked to joke. He was personable. We headed in and I was taken to the hospital while the Totemoffs shopped.

Dr. Schunk x-rayed my ankle area where all the swelling was concentrated. He had a nurse to assist him to put my leg in a cast; however, he did all of the work except gathering the equipment for the job. I felt as though I was in good hands—I was the only

## We Chose Alaska

patient. I was swiftly taken care of—by late afternoon. When I walked out the door, on crutches, I was really on my own! We didn't have medical facilities in Tatitlek!

I began my wait to be picked up for the trip back to Steve's boat. The specific memories of that day in Valdez pale in comparison to the trip back home. I look back on that last sentence and the word 'home' is exactly how Marcia and I felt about our three years of teaching there. We lived there and—it was our home.

[Valdez is one of the most impressive 'Winter Wonderland' scenarios that I've ever seen—on a sunny day—that is. You've got the blue of the bay butting up against shoreline. The heavily snow-covered mountains basically start somewhere above the beach, all the way to the peaks. Top this off with a clear blue sky or a partly cloudy sky and you have an almost perfect alpine picture.

Valdez is known for its heavy precipitation—all year round. In the warm months, you'd better have your rain gear nearby. In the cold months, snow accumulation can reach up to thirty-six feet!

People have to put up sheets of plywood to cover and protect the first story windows! You can virtually walk up from the berm along the

# We Chose Alaska

road to the roof top of a single-story house! You're talking serious winter 'snow'.]

Sometime, early in the day before we headed back—the weather had already turned—it was snowing heavily.

By the time we crossed Jack's Bay it was dark and the water had gotten rough. Wayne, another of my students, went up on the bridge to be with his dad. His dad was in a jovial mood! He'd had several drinks, while waiting for the shopping to get done.

The visibility was better on the bridge than in the pilot house. The mood was very tense. Illene's body language expressed the concern about our safety. She was nervously sitting—then suddenly jumping up—trying to see out the cabin window, and then immediately sitting back down again.

There wasn't much to see—it was pitch black out there! In one of her maneuvers, she had forgotten that I was sitting with my outstretched legs on the bench to her right.

She plopped right down on my legs! She didn't need to be more upset—but she was! It didn't help the situation. She apologized and I told her that I hadn't felt a thing. The cast did its job! All was well. There was some chuckling about it. The whole scene had a sense of

# We Chose Alaska

slapstick humor. Humor always has a tendency to calm!

Things on the bridge weren't going very well. There was a definite lack of humor up there. Wayne and his dad could not see where to turn—into the Tatitlek Narrows at Rocky Point! It was the entry point that led to the village. The only navigation aid, they came upon was the buoy at Bligh Reef—past the narrows!

I figured that Illene had done that trip so many times in her life—she had a gut feeling. Too much time had elapsed before taking the usual left turn after Rocky Point. They had overshot their course and were heading into the Sound!

Knowing where you are is good. Getting back to the turning point into the Narrows was still a challenge. If you missed it once—couldn't you do so again? Wayne and Steve successfully found their way back. As we turned right into the Narrrows—the mood lifted. We had safely passed by Bligh Reef!

[Years later, Bligh Reef is where the Exxon Valdez ran aground March 24, 1989.]

The trip was much longer than usual. I don't remember what time we left Valdez, but it was dark. That really doesn't tell very much—at that time of year it gets dark at

# We Chose Alaska

about 3:15 in the afternoon! I know, according to Marcia's letter, that we got back home at one thirty in the morning. Valdez is about twenty-eighth nautical miles from Tatitlek—a normal two hours and a half trip—which took about six hours!

When we arrived, Wayne tied the boat to the mooring and got the skiff ready for a run to shore. Their first concern was to get me onto the beach. Then they could unload the groceries, the other passengers and their dad in the area in front of their house.

Wayne helped me get into the skiff. When I got out of the skiff, he made sure that I didn't get wet. I headed up the beach and noticed that because of the snow level, I couldn't go left nor right to get to the walkway, about twenty feet above.

There was only one way—it was straight up—through about two feet of freshly fallen snow! I had to lie down and use my crutches to clear and pack down the snow out of my way!

I had to keep my cast from getting wet while crawling up—not an easy thing! I traveled short distances, about half my body length, until I reached the top. I picked myself up with great difficulty and used my crutches—as they were meant to be. I walked

## We Chose Alaska

on the walkway to the school door. My darling was VERY glad to see me! I was a sweaty, wet and a VERY happy person to be back home!

Life continued, hampered by my new handicap. It was a low key time of year. The big excitement on the horizon? The two Christmases that we were enthusiastically awaiting. The first was our traditional Christmas on the 25th of December. The second was the village's Russian Orthodox Christmas, celebrated from the 7th through the 9th of January.

We thought it was to be the only excitement! Yeah right!

As my friend George and his son Russell (Rusty) pulled away from the dock, on a lazy afternoon—he had apparently forgotten that I had my boat moored in his path! His skiff struck my boat about four feet back from the bow, just in the front of the cuddy cabin and along the starboard outside edge, where the deck and the hull are joined!

The calm was once again broken! George was distraught. He apologized and was very embarrassed by the episode. I told him that it was OK and I was glad that he wasn't badly hurt in the crash. Rusty was fine, but George was standing at the outboard motor control and was flung forward by the

# We Chose Alaska

sudden impact—thereby injuring his leg. He made arrangements to take our boat to Cordova for repairs.

His timing was impeccable! It took two months until the repairs were completed and the boat returned to its usual mooring. It was just the length of time needed for my fracture to heal! Even had I wanted to—I couldn't have used our boat. It was up on cribbing in a shipyard, high and dry—quite safe!

Another case of Divine Intervention! Now, both the boat and I would have to wait while our injuries slowly mended!

# We Chose Alaska

"16° - temp

Dec. 28, 1970
Monday P.M. (late)

Dear Mother & Earl -

Boy - this sleeping late is great! Have decided that teaching four primary grades is really tiring - at least for me.

Lots of news. First, thank you so much for all the Christmas gifts! Henry is really pleased with his compass. The gloves and slip are so pretty - and the fruit cake - delicious - we had some for dessert last night - right after some home made clam chowder - which was yummy too. I made it with creamed corn, onions, celery flakes, canned potatoes, and a few potato flakes for thickening, clams (which Henry dug quite a while ago and we had frozen) and garlic salt, pepper and butter. So easy - and so good! The

2

box with the dish cloths, pickles, etc., etc., etc. (!!!) got here before Christmas too. George Allen went into Cordova for groceries and brought back a bunch of it (mine) I haven't opened any of the jars yet — know they won't last long once I do.

Henry's tea pot is perfect. Remember. I bought two cans of tea at that little shop at the Mall — plus I had saved the tea strainer you gave me. Those three things were to Henry - from Santa — also some of the nuts you sent. I hid the rest till after Christmas day.

Sylvia and George Allen gave us a box filled with tangerines, oranges, pears, apples, bananas and pecans. Also Sylvia gave me a cute blue hat — she crocheted

5.

it. I think she called it a popcorn stitch.

John and Chris Borodkin gave us four coffee mugs on a rack – and a long knitted scarf (beige) to me from Glenn – their youngest boy who is in my 4th grade.

I'm going to save the plum pudding and have the Borodkins and Allens over some night to have some with us. Sylvia said she had never had any – but she'd always heard about it at Christmastime – and it sounded so good.

Henry broke his leg – near the ankle a week ago last Saturday. We were out skiing way out back of the school. Luckily we met 3 of the kids out there and they started off with us. We were all at the top

4.

of a pretty good hill and Henry was the first to start down. He didn't go far — I was right behind him. He thought it was sprained. One of the kids came back here to the school and got the toboggan — and really gave him a ride back. ~~Elene~~ Totemoff had an elastic bandage — and crutches, so we wrapped it up. He went to class Monday — but came in and laid down during recess times. We were through with school Tuesday at 12:15 P.M. The Totemoffs were going in to Valdez in their big boat to pick up their oldest daughter and do some shopping. They were ~~able~~ already on the boat ~~went when~~ Henry decided that maybe he should go in and have it x-rayed. They planned to come back that

6.

same night, as I puttered around here till 12:30 A.M. making some big Christmas decorations for the Allens and Bowdkins – and trying not to be worried. It had been snowing for several hours – and I finally decided that they were going to wait in Valdez for better weather – and I went to bed. They arrived at 1:30 A.M. Because of the snow, they had been lost – and the trip took six hours.
 Consequently, we're having a pretty quiet vacation. He has to go back in to Valdez in about four weeks to have the cast taken off. Normally the doctor would x-ray it every week – but under the circumstances – that's next to impossible.
 Sylvia and I went snow-shoeing.

6.

along with a following of kids on skis, to get Christmas trees on the 23rd. More fun. I've had never been on snow shoes before. We had had a real heavy snow fall - in fact it was snowing then. The trees all looked gorgeous covered with snow - but not so pretty when the snow was shaken off. The one we kept, looked pretty spindly - but the two Olsen kids and I fixed it up with cotton (for snow) and it looks quite nice.

The day before Christmas, I mixed up a double batch of sugar cookies - and a big batch of ginger cookies. I cut (mostly Christmas trees) and baked the sugar cookies and whatever kids happened to be in here at the time - decorated them. You know how I love to.

7.

do that. Just wish I'd get an earlier start one of these years. Guess the hustle and bustle adds to the fun though. The kids of course thought they were wonderful. They ate cookies here and then we sent plates full to several families.

Christmas night, being Friday, of course, meant movie night. There was a big crowd (many high school kids are home for the holidays) and the movie was very good - a real tear-jerker called "Bridge to the Sun". Everyone was trying frantically to wipe his eyes before the lights came on after the last reel.

We invited all of the Borodkins (six of them) and the Allens (five of them) to come in for ice cream, Christmas cookies, ~~nut~~ apple sauce-nut-cherry

8.

bread and tea or coffee after the movie. Fun!
Don't know if I told you that we bought an electric ice cream freezer. While I was up to my neck in cookie making, and telling the little kids how to make frosting on my left — older kids (boys) were on my right mixing the ingredients for ice cream — and needing just as much help with the recipe. Henry was here sitting at the table - with the freezer — but really couldn't be of much help since he couldn't walk around. We made two batches - but that meant four different sessions with the freezer since one batch was too much at a time. Anyway - it was all well worth it. Delicious! We made vanilla when we first got the freezer — and maple (with

# We Chose Alaska

9.

maple syrup) a couple of times. But this time we made ~~mool~~ mint - with chocolate chips in it - and made it green with food coloring. That was our favorite kind when we could buy it in Anchorage - and it was by far the best we've made yet.

3:40 P.M.

Am back again after some skiing and a little lunch - and towel folding. (am doing washing)

Mentioned a while back that I had mixed up a batch of ginger cookies too. Finally got around to bake those Saturday. There were 50 cookies. I cut gingerbread boys and girls mostly - plus a few bells, trees, a star, a big Santa and angels. I don't have cookie cutters here with me - so just use a knife - and really think they

10.

come out just as well - or better. I used that egg-yolk "paint" from the December Good Housekeeping and their other decorative icing. They're the best I've found yet. I worked on decorating till 11:30 PM - and of course loved every minute of it. Really made them fancy. I have frozen them - to give out for Russian Christmas - which is celebrated for three days - January 7th, 8th and 9th. I just hope that freezing doesn't spoil the frosting.

Dorothy finally wrote. She sounds happy! Also, she sent pictures of the kids.

The day before Christmas, we were over at George and Sylvia Gillin's (Henry had walked with the crutches - while I had nervous prostration.) We did good to deliver

11.

the Christmas decoration. It was real windy and George's float had been dragging, as he was not taking care of it. He come in saying that he had some bad news for us. He had an unsold Christmas tree and some other trash which he was heading out with and he ran into the side of our skiff. He must have really rammed it because he hurt his leg when it hit. We've looked at it with the binoculars, but haven't seen it up close yet. Guess it's pretty bad. He's going to take it into Cordova to be fixed. Poor guy was just sick (George, I mean).

Rusty just came to invite us to dinner (Sylvia & George's oldest boy) so had better get ready.

Think I told you that the National Geographic card came. Chuck

12.

you again for everything. Hope your Christmas was as merry as ours was. (And it was! — even with poor Henry's leg.)
    Happy Birthday, Earl!
        Love,
            Marcia & Henry

P.S. I still haven't heard a word from the Roods since they left her — thanks giving. Assume that no news is good news.
    Maybe on tomorrow's mail boat.

## 29.

## Tatitlek – The Christmas Letter

*Season's Greetings*

*from the Malottes*

THIS YEAR STARTED RATHER QUIETLY EXCEPT FOR THE SHOTS THAT BAGGED A SEAL AND TERMINATED AN 8 DAY GOAT HUNT IN THE EXCURSION INLET AREA IN SOUTHEAST ALASKA, WITH PETER JACK, OUR

WE WERE HAVING SUCH A GOOD TIME THAT WE DECIDED TO STAY THE MAXIMUM AMOUNT OF TIME THAT WE HAD PLANNED. PETE'S WIFE, HOWEVER, GOT WORRIED AND PUT A CALL IN TO THE COAST GUARD AND INITIATED A SEARCH.

WE WERE CROSSING CHATHAM STRAITS, UNDER CONDITIONS OTHER THAN CALM. MARCIA AND

## We Chose Alaska

the kitchen under control. She was stretched out on a bench amidst a conglomeration of coffee grounds, mustard, salt, pepper, and all the accessories necessary for a choice smörgåsbord. Pete and I were in the pilot house, wondering if the Coast Guard plane overhead was out looking for someone. It circled the boat several times and then headed toward Juneau. We later learned that they were indeed looking for someone — us.

Spring came, and the brown bears started coming out. We went hunting, one weekend, with Pete, just seven miles south of Angoon. That was a fantastic weekend. We spotted many brownies and even sneaked up to several. We got as close as 50' to an enormous bear that was grazing. I was quite proud of Marcia. She was right alongside all the way.

The next evening, I had to take one that turned and came toward us. I didn't want to shoot because the light was too poor to have a good look at his coat. He took the decision out of my hands though. One shot forward of the right shoulder toward the left center rib cage brought him down for good.

Pete had mentioned that a way to tell whether a bear is dead or not, is to notice his paws. If they are palms up, then the bear is dead. You

2.

# We Chose Alaska

Guessed it! Mine had palms down and I had to check to be certain it was dead. What a hairy deal.

While in Angoon, I started tanning seal skins and making mocassins. I even tanned my brown bear hide - which was a considerable savings.

We put in transfers for a two-teacher school. Our luck held out and we were assigned to our present village.

This past summer, we took a short vacation - to California and New York. We also spent one week at the University of Alaska in Fairbanks, as consultants in the training of "bush teachers".

Finally the time came to head for the bushes. I made arrangements in Valdez with a stranger (now a good friend) to take us and our supplies into the village by boat.

Once our supplies were stored for the winter, we made plans for getting back to Valdez. We were taken to the ferry, "Bartlett", by John Borodkin, the village council president, in his skiff. The Bartlett stopped a few miles offshore, lowered the ramp, and we pulled up alongside. On the loud speaker, the captain started telling the passengers (tourists) all about who we were and what we did and that the marine system is one of the very few ways for us to reach civili-

# We Chose Alaska

ZATION. WELL, I'LL TELL YOU, HEADS WERE POPPING UP ALL OVER THE RAILS ABOVE — WITH CAMERAS IN HAND, NO LESS. EVER FEEL LIKE A CURIOSITY? I STILL DON'T KNOW WHAT THEY EXPECTED TO SEE. TARZAN AND JANE, MAYBE?

THE BOAT WE HAD ORDERED, ARRIVED IN ANCHORAGE BY BARGE. WE TOOK DELIVERY OF IT, RENTED A TRAILER, AND BOB ROOD HAULED IT TO VALDEZ FOR US. WE SET OUT FOR TATITLEK A DAY LATER. OUR TRIP TO THE VILLAGE WAS PLEASANT AND THE SOUND WAS CALM. OUR BOAT IS A 20' CRUISER WITH A 120 HORSE MERCRUISER INBOARD-OUTBOARD. IT IS PROVING TO BE COMFORTABLE, ECONOMICAL AND PRACTICAL FOR THE WATERS OF PRINCE WILLIAM SOUND.

TATITLEK IS A SMALL VILLAGE ON THE EAST SIDE OF PRINCE WM. SOUND. THERE ARE ABOUT 60 PEOPLE HERE, INCLUDING OUR 23 STUDENTS. WE ARE LOCATED IN THE CHUGACH ESKIMO TERRITORY. THE PEOPLE CLAIM TO BE ALEUTS. HOWEVER, THIS IS ENTIRELY POSSIBLE DUE TO THE SHIFTING OF MANY OF THE ALEUT PEOPLE DURING THE RUSSIAN FUR TRADE DAYS.

THE PEOPLE ARE VERY FRIENDLY AND MARCIA AND I ARE ENJOYING OURSELVES IMMENSELY. WE TAKE PART IN THE "VISITING" THAT EVERYONE DOES. I HAVE BEEN GIVEN AN OPEN INVITATION TO TAKE STEAM BATHS WITH THE MEN. THE STEAM BATH IS A 4'x8'

4.

# We Chose Alaska

BOX WHERE HOT ROCKS ARE PLACED IN A TUB IN ONE CORNER - AND NEXT TO IT, A TUB OF HOT WATER. YOU THROW WATER ON THE ROCKS TO INCREASE THE STEAM AND HEAT IN THE BATH. YOU SCOOP WATER FROM THE HUGE TUB WITH A CAN AND POUR THIS ON YOURSELF TO EITHER COOL OFF, OR TO RINSE OFF THE SOAP AFTER WASHING. THE BATH ACCOMODATES 4 PEOPLE COMFORTABLY. WHILE WAITING TO GO INTO THE STEAM BATH SECTION, YOU SIT AROUND A STOVE MADE FROM AN OIL DRUM, WHERE THE ROCKS ARE HEATED, AND JUST CHAT. IT'S A NATIVE VERSION OF THE SAUNA BATH.

WINTER IS HERE AND ITS ARRIVAL DREW THE ATTENTION OF THE ENTIRE VILLAGE. WE HAD WINDS UP TO 150 MPH. AND OUR BOAT STARTED TO DRAG ITS MOORING — A 350-400# STEEL GEAR FROM A CAT GRADER. IT SKIRTED A REEF BUT LUCKILY WAS NOT SMASHED AGAINST IT. WHEN A LULL IN THE WIND GAVE US A CHANCE, WE TOOK A SKIFF ALONGSIDE AND DAVE (A VILLAGER) AND I JUMPED ABOARD OUR BOAT. WE HOOKED A LINE TO THE BOW AND THE OTHER END TO THE PIER 150' BEHIND US. LETTING GO OF THE MOORING LINE, WE DRIFTED PAST THE PIER, STRAIGHTENED OUT, AND RODE OUT THE REST OF THE STORM IN SAFETY.

WE NOW HAVE A CROSS-COUNTRY SKI TRAIL BEHIND THE SCHOOL. A ONE WAY CIRCULAR RUN TAKES A

5.

# We Chose Alaska

little over an hour. It's splendid — peaceful. The feeling is beyond words. We are fortunate to be allowed such a close communion with nature.

We wish all of you a Merry Christmas and a Happy New Year!

Sincerely,

Henry and Marcia

The following are "space-filler-uppers" and perhaps items of interest too!

1. We have mail delivery once every 2 weeks — if lucky — by boat.
2. Our living quarters are actually a part of the school building itself. We just have to walk across the hall to our classrooms.
3. Our water supply — rain.
4. Power — our own generators.
5. One of the sources of village entertainment — the Friday night movie which is shown here at the school. Films are ordered from Anchorage.
6. We would be most happy to have you come and spend some time with us. The welcome mat is always out!

6.

# We Chose Alaska

30.

## Tatitlek - Russian Orthodox Christmas

Greetings! It is forty-five years after the writing of the enclosed letter! I now know what 'ZIPPED ON BY' really means! When the enclosed letter was mailed, I had a full head of dark hair and a broken leg! Now I sit here and I still have a full head of hair. However, for some odd-ball reason, it's pure silver! It has nothing to do with my getting old—merely a passing of time!

I would like to mention a very unique moment that happened during Russian Christmas. At the end of the Star celebration— we wound up at home for the evening. There was a knock at the door, it was George and Sylvia who had come to invite us to his uncle's house for a party. We gladly went.

It seemed that the entire village was crammed into a very small house. It was! Music was going on and lots of conversations were scattered among the rooms. Drinks were being handed out from the

## We Chose Alaska

kitchen area. David Totemoff was the one who approached me and asked, "Would you like a glass of hot wine?" I said, "No, thanks." His expression immediately went from jovial to almost apologetic for having asked such a question.

There was a definite change. I realized that he probably thought I was a non-drinker and he had offended me! I read the body language and quickly added. "Do you have any cold wine?" "Yes—wait right here."—he said, with a miraculous recovery to his old self! He was a happy camper again! The wine was delicious. It was a very happy occasion.

There are those that are called to serve their fellow man, by what they consider a higher power by being teachers in the villages.

Not the exact reason for Marcia and me. We loved teaching. Teaching in the 'Bush' gave us a golden opportunity to see Alaska and meet its people.

We've been blessed—however we do drink wine! We can party with the best of them. We just don't party with the worst of them.

The house was rather cute and basic in its own way. His uncle was quite elderly and pleasant—he lived by himself. The light was subdued and came from Coleman lanterns. He

# We Chose Alaska

didn't have electricity due to the high cost and the burden of obtaining it.

All of the activity was in the living room and the kitchen. The music was a bit loud. One very nice thing, to non-smokers, such as we—there were few, if any smokers in the village. I don't recall any circumstance where I was bothered.

It was very nice being invited to a Christmas party. What was particularly nice was the fact that they cared enough to include us in their village life. It was our first—full village gathering. It was very festive and simple. There was a good feeling that emerged from all that were present.

This was a very special gathering and filled with the holiday spirit toward everyone. Smiles were the norm. For us, it was a feeling of acceptance and fraternal love that permeated the atmosphere. What a wonderful way to finish the special day. We headed home shortly before one in the morning—exhausted and happy. We take our relationship with the village people very seriously.

This is a star from Tatitlek. The Star is a celebration of the spirit of Christmas. It was brought to Alaska by the Russian traders, in the 1700's. It represents the Christ child and is spread to each of the homes. Originally it

## We Chose Alaska

spread to the local people of the villages, primarily villages that had a water route access to them.

The people visit each home—by going house to house with the Star. It is called 'starring'. The Star had a large pin-wheel shape that spins on a shaft and is kept in constant motion. This Star is held by Maxine Totemoff's grandson.

It is elaborately decorated with varying bright colors, mostly foils of silver and gold.

## We Chose Alaska

There is a religious picture icon on the front of the shaft. The stars are very festive and ornate—as they should be—for such a joyous occasion.

As the Star spins, the people sing songs, about the nativity. At the proper time somebody yells, (something that sounds like, "sprazdnecum"—in Russian). Then things come flying out of wherever the family members are—into the crowd! Everyone is diving to where the goodies are landing. It's a friendly 'free for all'! It's like a distribution of good cheer.

We put $5.00 bills in balloons and inflated them and stuck them to the ceiling. It's a very happy "ruckus", with everyone vying for the goodies. Most of the homes threw out food items and candy. Marcia managed to collect two full grocery-sized paper sacks, before it was all over.

The next day, I started to go through all our goodies, Marcia had gathered. At the party, I heard about Willie Totemoff, a village man, who was housebound, in a wheelchair. We felt sad that he couldn't participate along with everybody else in the celebration.

I made a mental note of it. The next morning, we took the items that we (It was really Marcia, I had my broken leg to protect!) had gathered (feverishly grabbed), from the homes visited on the rounds with the Star. I managed to amble along as we delivered the goodies that we had gotten for him. He was very grateful.

# We Chose Alaska

*1*

Sun eve.
Jan 10, 1971

Dear Mother & Earl,

Whee-e-e-e! What a hectic four days we've had! But great fun! Thursday, Friday and Saturday were the Russian Christmas holidays. Each night "the star" is followed by all of the villagers from house to house. At each house there is a religious center with a candle burning. The center is usually one, or several, religious pictures (Nativity scene, last supper, etc.) It is also decorated with Christmas lights, balls, tinsel, etc. As the star (made from wood ~~and~~ covered with paper) is twirled, everyone sings in Russian or Aleut — for about 15 minutes. At the end of the singing the leader says "Prauz-nee-kume" ← phonetic spelling which means Merry Christmas. Then things really pop. Gifts are given out.

*very pretty →*

2. Everything imaginable -> much fresh fruit, candy, pop, canned goods, whole pies, frozen meats, detergent, money, tissue, fresh cooked crab and more, more, more! If there is something that is fragile, they pass it out individually during the singing. Otherwise, everyone dives for the stuff as soon as they hear "Prauws-nee-kume"! They have goodies on the floor & on the ceiling (taped). While everyone's scrambling for that, they start throwing other things from various hiding places — sometimes at you, to you, or out the windows. There are also often special gifts for certain people. Every house is a mess when it's left.

There are two stars — a little one for the kids and the larger one for the adults. The kids go around first. As soon as they finish, the adults start.

The first night, Henry and I didn't go. We went to George and Sylvia Allen's

3 and just watched to see what it was all about. Then Friday and Saturday, we made the complete round. Henry had to sit it out, of course. He'd head for the kitchen each time - even then it (the action) would get a little close sometimes. Many times he'd be sitting holding his leg (in the cast) up in the air. At first, I was a little hesitant about entering in - but it wasn't long before I was right in there fighting too. My left hand is one huge black and blue spot - as are both my knees and a place on my right hip. It sounds terrible, I'm sure - but if you could be here and know these people - it wouldn't seem bad. And if you could hear them singing - everyone - old and young - male and female - it's beautiful! They really sing from the heart, too.

Friday night was the longest - from around 5 P.M. till 1:10 A.M. We were both ready to drop. Last night, I took my back-pack to carry the loot in - sort of as a joke. I filled it twice!! Had to come home and empty it after the fourth house! The amount of stuff they give away is unbelievable. But in reality, they're just trading since everyone goes to everyone else's house. Each family goes ahead when its house is next in line.

We filled a big box up this morning and took it down to Willie Totemoff. He's an old man, crippled, who lives by himself.

Friday, we had a Russian Christmas dinner, here at the school, which was a smashing success. I sent a sign-up sheet around to all the ladies asking them to donate food. Their response was overwhelming! Henry was in charge of the meat. He had his boys build a huge barbeque place out in front of the school and they cooked a whole deer, plus two legs (deer). We had hoped to have seal meat too, but nobody

# We Chose Alaska

5 got one. We also had salads (tossed, macaroni, and potato), corn and creamed corn, pickles, rolls (I made them) and butter, cakes, pies; jello. Also coffee, tea, Tang and grape drinks and Kool-aid. What fun – and every one was starving, so things tasted all the better. Almost everyone in the entire village came – plus several people who were here visiting for the holidays.

Very little mail came in on the last mail boat. The weather had been so bad that planes hadn't been able to land at Cordova – and the mail for Tatitlek has to go there first. The boat should be here again Tuesday, so we expect to have lots of letters – and Christmas cards (we hope).

We still haven't heard from the Roodes. Of course – no mail has been in. Sure hope everything's okay with them.

Henry frosted my hair again the day before New Year's. It really came

# We Chose Alaska

6. out nice. He also gave me a fancy hair-do. Haven't had it fixed in such a long time - really feel spiffy!

We had the Allens and their three kids over for dinner tonight. It's the first time I have" entertained here - other than serving coffee, tea, ice cream, etc. I was a little nervous, I guess. But everything was fine. We had roast pork, potatoes, onions & carrots cooked with it, peas, apple sauce, gelatin salad with cabbage in it that I'd saved for ages for such an occasion (the cabbage is what I saved for so long - not the whole salad!), fresh rolls - right out of the oven, home made pickles (yummy!!), Tang and coffee. There was pie, too - given to us. But everyone has seen so many pies the last few days that none of us wanted any!

School tomorrow, so I'd better hit the sack. Henry's already there. Think he's getting a cold from all the running in and out - following the star.

# We Chose Alaska

Mon. a.m.

7. Hope you'll forgive the "copying" - but wanted both you and Henry's mother to know all about the holidays.

I thought for sure I'd have Lori's and Lisa's dolls ready for this mail boat. I didn't realize we'd be so involved in the activities. Have made quite a few doll clothes for each of them - but haven't finished the dolls. Oh well - no rush, I guess.

Am sending that lovely slip back - hope you can exchange it for a 32. Don't know what possessed me to tell you 34 (and that is what I said - it wasn't your mistake). Hate to send it back - it's so pretty - but I just don't fill it up!

Have to tend to my washing.

Take care - write.

Love -

Marcia & Henry

Sept. 20

Sorry the copier didn't work very well. Hope you can read it.

31.

## Tatitlek - Life Goes On

Now that the celebration of Russian Christmas was behind us, what next? Winter! For Tatitlek that meant cold and snow. Prince William Sound is located at the convergence of two very distinct air masses, the warm moist Japanese current from the south, and the cold dry air from the northern interior of Alaska. A perfect storm zone in between!

The only things that went on were the occasional hunting trips for food. The two main sources were deer, which were plentiful on the many islands that are in the Sound, and mountain goat who dwell on the mountains toward Seward on the Kenai Peninsula. Locally, clams were plentiful.

On the map, the area surrounding the cities of Valdez, Cordova and Seward and the outer islands that form its southern border, is basically Prince William Sound.

# We Chose Alaska

This episode will deal mainly with activities that are generic to life in the village during the winter months. Our concerns are the basic necessities in life—no matter where you live.

In Alaska, especially in a village situation, you only have yourself and your neighbors (friends) to call on for help. This whole 'Bush situation' was completely new to us. In Angoon, we had all that taken care of—just call the maintenance man and—end of worries! In Tatitlek, I had to learn quickly and thanks to friends—I had help. As you'll read about in many of Marcia's letters.

# We Chose Alaska

John Borodkin, and Joe Kompkoff, who replaced David as custodian, were both very influential in helping to restore water to the school building.

This particular winter had turned brutal and I hadn't ever used, nor had the knowledge (more importantly), of the existence of the heat tape under the school building. When the temperatures called for such measures—it was to be plugged in! Remember, there was no manual that went along with my new job!

You would think that some sort of information book would have been available. As I recall, three years later—I didn't leave a manual either! John and Joe were certainly my guardian angels on that one. It was, in retrospect—to be the last time that such a chilling experience would occur! I was learning.

Earlier in the fall when the fuel (for heating the school and powering the generators) was delivered—my new role was loud and clear—I'm the maintenance man.

In reality, this was a teaching position for two teachers who were certified for grades one through eight. My certification was for secondary education. I suspect that they jumped at the chance to hire Marcia and that I was accepted! I would be able to handle the

## We Chose Alaska

everyday functioning of the physical plant—or at least—they probably hoped so!

The most important position is the teaching of the beginning grades—Marcia's grades. That's where the real expertise was needed. Teaching the upper grades is somewhat easier. If you are an excellent teacher and you like people, then you should be able to handle any grade you're given—in your area of expertise. I learned more about basic facts that I was going to teach in elementary grades—than I could have ever imagined.

Being bilingual put me at a disadvantage. I was fluent in both French and English—but early on—I lacked the nuts and bolts of the languages. I went to a bilingual school and the early grammar years were basically all in French. Having taught in the elementary grades allowed me, even to this day, much to Marcia's dismay, to spew out the rules for proper English—when it's being misused. It's a game with us. However, for me to try and teach the little ones in the beginning grades is downright petrifying!

Joe was a single parent who was raising two of his boys. He was a jovial happy-go-lucky sort of guy. He always sported a huge smile and robust laugh. He also became a good

## We Chose Alaska

friend of ours. George extended his family umbrella to include Joe who was basically his sidekick. I had the pleasure of going on a deer hunt with the two of them. It was a lot of fun. Lots of laughing and joking. The times spent together were always that way. George was just a happy person. He had a wonderful wife, great kids and many friends. What's not to be happy about? He was my best friend.

One day at lunchtime, I dropped by George and Sylvia's house. I know some of you are thinking, "I'll bet he had that planned!" Well in my defense, it was midday and I imagine that I needed to talk to them about something very important—or at least that's my story and I'm sticking to it! Besides, Sylvia is a fantastic cook and that makes any motive justified.

Sylvia was serving a salmon head casserole. [During the fishing season, the salmon heads are not wasted; they are loaded with very important nutritious vitamins and minerals. The heads were cut off from the bodies just behind the gills, split into halves, from the nose on back. The gills were removed before storing. They were put in a five-gallon bucket, alternating between a layer of salt and a layer of split fish heads, until the bucket was full. They were stored in a cool place. When ready to use the heads are sweetened (soaked in

## We Chose Alaska

water and refreshed several times to remove the salt). Once sweetened, they could be used in various dishes.]

I was sitting to the right of Sea Lion Murphy (Joe's nickname). We were well into the meal and I noticed that Joe had laid part of the fish head (the part containing the eye) to the right of his plate—thinking it would be safe. It's not something that a white man would eat! Sylvia had the same concern the first time she served Marcia and me a seal meat dish. It's just not a taste that exists in our culture.

We ate heartily. It was totally different, however very good! My favorite seal meat became the liver! I always hated regular beef liver cooked by my mother. It was always overcooked and very chalky tasting! I found that seal liver, cooked medium rare, eaten with a nice raw onion, was the best gourmet experience—I ever had eating liver—I was hooked!.....Now, back to Joe.

I could see that eyeball looking up at me! Not Joe's, but the fish's! Close to the end of the meal, that eyeball was still staring me down! I thought myself, "If he isn't going to eat that darn thing, I will!" SOooo, I reached over—swept up the half head—eyeball looking straight at me and with a (sscchhhuukk!)

## We Chose Alaska

sucking sound, I swiftly removed it from its socket and swallowed!

"HEY!" Joe shouted with a sideward unbelieving glance! "I was saving that until later!" Needless to say, laughter erupted all around the table. I understood fully what I had just done.

However, the eyeballs are such a fantastic delicacy—I wasn't going to just sit there and watch it get thrown out! There was absolutely nothing to be done. No sooner had he heard the sucking sound—the eyeball was already on its way to my stomach, the point of no return! I apologized.

There's another cute story about Joe's youngest, William. He was visiting us—as was the custom with many of the children—on weekends. Marcia had just pulled a couple of pies out of the oven and put them on the table to cool. Lil' William bellied up to the table—for William that was eye level. He could almost rest his nose on the table's edge. He was so darn cute. You could almost read his mind. He was completely enthralled about the whole scene. His focus was on the pies; ours was on him and the whole lovely scene.

Marcia informed him that he was definitely going to get a piece of pie. He provided us with such a warm memory—he

# We Chose Alaska

certainly deserved one. There are many such memories of visits by the kids. They were all very much a highlight in our lives. Isn't that right, Thelma and Gus?

I had to go back into Valdez for the cast removal on my leg. The news was not good. The leg wasn't healing as it should! That kept me from doing any trapping for the rest of the season—one of my main forms of physical exercise and enjoyment.

The exhilaration that I felt out in the wilderness, all by myself, was superhuman. The sounds and the scenes that unfolded were way better than any 3D movie! In simple terms, it was an equation of two parts: me + nature = JOY. You look, you listen and you keep your mouth shut! The sounds are deafeningly impressive!

George and some of the men went on a goat hunt and returned with some wonderful fresh meat. They were gone several days aboard his seiner. I imagine I'd have been with them if I not had to teach school—also one little minor detail—a broken leg in a cast! What a wonderful adventure to have missed out on! I still drool about the golden opportunity to gather goat hides for tanning!

George, Joe and I went on a deer hunt to Hichinbrook Island, southwest of Cordova.

## We Chose Alaska

We went on George's seiner and spent a few days.

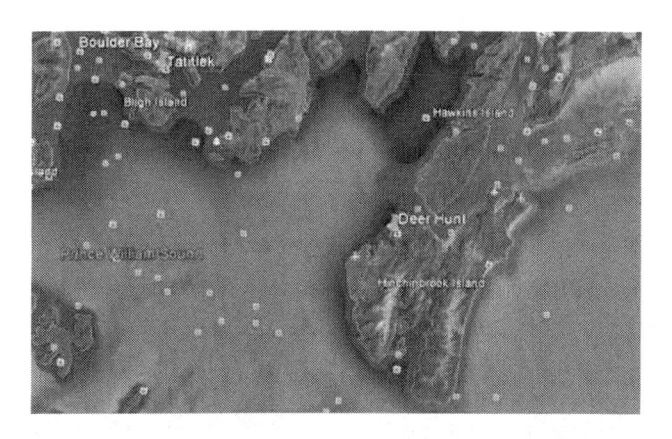

We pulled into a bay and saw three grizzly bears rummaging around in a creek leading into the woods. Only George and I were looking at the beach—Joe had gone below.

BANG, bang, and bang—three shots went off—in rapid succession! Joe had his rifle! He scared the heck out of us! He really had a huge fear of grizzlies—they were where he wanted to hunt! Luckily, he didn't hit any—before they hastily bolted to safety.

We headed for another bay—anchored and got ready to go ashore. George had towed his small gillnetter skiff, behind the seiner, for going ashore. When we got ashore—George and Joe went to the left of the valley—I went

## We Chose Alaska

to the right. It was a spectacularly nice day, plenty of sunshine and just a slight breeze.

I worked my way up the valley, near the edge of the woods, looking for deer. Hopefully, NOT for bears. It really wasn't a major concern. However, the events of the last bay were still very fresh in my mind. There was no need to wonder if there were any bears on the island? After some time, we all returned. George and Joe had been successful—I hadn't been!

We went back to the seiner and fixed supper. Later, we saw several deer emerge from the woods onto the beach. The sun had just set, so the light was diminishing. We very quietly got into the skiff and paddled quietly to shore—down-wind from the deer. They didn't know we were there! The slight wave action muffled any sounds we might have made. We each got to shoot a deer! I was finally successful! If I can see them, I can hit them.

Another of my invitations to hunt was from Steve Totemoff, our next-door neighbor. He was planning to go duck hunting, in front of the village, in Tatitlek Narrows. This was a major food source for his family. Steve was a very quiet man, except when he had a few

# We Chose Alaska

drinks. At those times, he was quite vocal and lively!

This was quite an invitation. He must have put his shyness aside in order to ask me. He came to the beach with his skiff to pick me up. I got on board and sat down in one of the seats slightly forward, to balance the skiff. We headed out for the narrows to spot ducks.

A short distance out, he saw a group of about a dozen ducks! He stopped the skiff and asked me to take control! I didn't understand why. He told me to go toward the ducks while he went to the bow. The idea was to flush them into the air—in order to shoot a few—while they were taking off.

I was pleased not to have to shoot at them. One big reason, I'm a super shot with a rifle. When it comes to a shot gun, I've never gotten the hang of properly leading the waterfowl. In other words—I am a lousy shot!

I have another duck hunting story. George had dropped me off, with my shotgun, on a slight peninsula projection into Fish Bay, to the east of Tatitlek. The idea was that he would go to the head of the bay and flush out the geese that were resting on the flat. My job was to wait, listen and when the geese were flying over the peninsula—shoot! Sounded like

# We Chose Alaska

a plan. I had no idea at that time, how bad I really was with a shotgun!

When he arrived near the flats, George fired a shot—the geese headed for open water. He must have had an inkling due to past hunts, that the geese would take the flight path over the peninsula. I could hear the geese honking, louder and louder, as they approached.

I couldn't see them coming because of a stand of large spruce trees that ringed the peninsula. The honking got louder—not too far away! The moment arrived—I saw them coming low over the trees! There were many! I started shooting—all my five shots—not a hit! It was a magnificent sight—the geese—NOT my shooting!

This goose hunting trip deals with my method of hunting. I had been shooting rifles for many years, with good success. Being in the villages gave me the perfect venue. I got into doing my own reloading and increasing my accuracy. My rifles all had very precise ammunition. I've always considered that I'd be a good sniper—I was! That's the philosophy behind this one story. I used my 22-250 rifle for waterfowl.

One evening, my brother Norman, Marcia and I went to Fish Bay in our skiff. When we got as close to the flats as we could, Normand

# We Chose Alaska

and I took the dingy to the head of the bay. We stayed near the shore until it was too shallow for the dingy. I got out with my hip boots on and followed the beach to the flats.

When I got there, I found a perfect spot to conceal myself. The geese had not yet started to make their way to the head of the bay. My perfect spot was a nice sized spruce tree right on the edge of the beach. It had plenty of low hanging branches that provided a fantastic cover. Normand headed back to Marcia and the skiff.

I settled in under the branches which were spread out enough to give me good cover and a great shot.

I heard the faint honking of geese in the distance, approaching into the flats. It got louder and louder, until the geese started swooping down onto the beach for a landing! I waited quietly—made no movement at all. They looked as if they all had special resting spots. They coasted directly to them, hovered slightly and landed.

I picked out a nice sized goose, nearest to me, with a sideways profile. I aimed right behind the left eye. I shot—the goose slumped forward—dead. The beach exploded with the flurry of many wings! The geese headed back out to sea.

# We Chose Alaska

The only problem with using a rifle, you get only one shot—no more! One goose at a time is really enough. I picked up my goose and noticed a log on the beach to my right, in the direction of the boat.

The boat looked further than it was when I left it. I sat by the log and rested my rifle beside me. Nothing to do now, but rest and wait. I thought I'd take a little snooze until Normand showed up.

All was calm and quiet. I became aware of some muddy, clop, clop sounds nearby on my right. I slowly turned my head in that direction and saw a black bear entering the mud—another coming out of the trees! I grabbed my gun and slowly stood up. The first bear noticed me and started to run across the flats—heading for the other side.

I started to chase him. I wasn't gaining—nor could I get a good steady running shot at him. I said to myself, "Why are you running after him? You can't catch him—just stop and aim." I hit him right behind the left shoulder. A perfect shot. I gutted and dragged him to the log.

We both waited for Normand. When Normand showed up, he helped me carry the bear to the SportYak for the trip to the skiff. Marcia was surprised when she saw our extra

# We Chose Alaska

passenger. Life is full of unexpected events—it's amazing. We went out for a goose and returned with a bounty of organic meat. It was part of our life style—a real treasure. It was late enough in the season so that they were no longer eating fish. There is nothing tasty about the bear meat when they're on a fish diet.

We brought the bear into the water storage room in the power plant building. Hung him from two by fours between one of the tanks and the wall. After about five days we brought it into the school's kitchen for butchering. There was a little bit of meat loss due to the bullet's impact behind the left front leg.

The kitchen was an excellent place to do the job. It had large counters with a large table in the center of the room.

Cutting the meaty sections went very well. When it came to cutting the T-bone steaks, I ran into a small problem. I didn't have a meat cutting saw! I thought about it and came up with—I could use my skill saw!

Bone shouldn't be much of a problem—my blade was very sharp. I started cutting across the rib cage to limit the length of the steaks. My next cuts were to the top of the backbone, spacing my cuts to make good sized steaks. I was then going to cut the individual steaks in

## We Chose Alaska

half by cutting the back-bone again—that should give me two good steaks.

When I had done a few of the initial cuts across the back-bone—everything seemed to be going well. I glanced up from my work for a second—I had a problem!

As the blade did its cut—it also sent a halo of red meat into the hall and upward across the ceiling overhead—Whoa! Needless to say my steaks didn't include any bones—just plain cuts of meat.

Cleanup was not an easy chore—lesson well learned!

# We Chose Alaska

14°

Jan. 25 - A.M.

Dear Mother & Earl -

Hope I can get this finished so that it gets in the mail on the & Valdez run.

I finally finished Lori's and Lisa's dolls and they will go out in this mail. I'm sending them to you - so you can have a look at them. What a ball I've had making them - as you'll be able to tell when you see them. You might tell them that they shouldn't try to comb the hair - or take out the hair bows. I forgot to mention it in their notes. It doesn't really matter - but they'd have trouble fixing it again, probably.

Boy, we've really been having some cold weather. Yesterday, we got up and Henry came out to make coffee - no water. - frozen line somewhere. He, John Bowdken

# We Chose Alaska

and Joe Kompkoff spent hours mending heat tape, soldering, crawling under the building, etc. They finally got it thawed — late yesterday. It was frozen again this morning (although it has really warmed up and is snowing a little bit), but Henry went out & plugged the tape back in and it thawed in a very short time. (Then he went back to bed!) Guess it's kind of touchy and he didn't want to take the chance of a fire.

George Allen returned from a hunting trip yesterday — he left last Wednesday with 3 other guys. They got 9 goats! So it was quite a successful trip. Boy, his boat was really iced up by the time he got here. Guess they had a rough trip back.

## We Chose Alaska

3.

So glad you liked your Christmas gifts. I made an apron and pot holder like yours for Henry's mother too - only hers was ~~gold~~ with a pineapple pocket.

Henry's back at his stitchery. He made both of us a long pair of seal skin mittens - really neat. We should be getting some nylon material on the mail boat tomorrow. Then he's going to line them with down.

Lunch time:

Henry is due to have his cast taken off and had planned to go in to Valdez with the mail boat - but with this weather, he has decided to wait. I'm really glad that he's not going. When we first came here, I remember the people saying that travel in the winter is terrible - if not impossible. They

# We Chose Alaska

4.

sure know what they're talking about.

I made some pickled herring Friday. Had had it soaking in salt brine for around three weeks. Mother, you probably wouldn't appreciate it, but how about you, Earl — do you like it? Man, it's really delicious!

We still didn't hear anything from the Roods on the last mail boat — that was since Thanksgiving weekend! Henry was worried and I was fit to be tied! So John B. called someone in Cordova on his radio and they, in turn, made a collect phone call to the Roods or the Camerons - we still don't know who they talked to. Anyway, the message back to us said that they were fine.

8.

Something must have happened in San Diego - for them not to write at all. At any rate — I'm sure we'll have a letter tomorrow.

Henry went with John B., last Sunday - a week ago yesterday and checked Steve Cotenoff's crab pot. So - we have quite a few crab dinners in our freezer now. Really yummy!

We're down to one generator now. This morning, right after school started, one of them began to act up - the lights were blinking, etc. Henry went out and said that it was really knocking so he shut it off and started the other one. Joe checked it this afternoon and they think it's the rings (most likely) or pistons or valves. Of course, we have the

# We Chose Alaska

6.

two new ones setting out in front of the school. Guess this may encourage them to send someone out to get them installed.

You know that napkin ring (I guess that's what it is) that I took from Daddy's duffle bag. I always thought that it was supposed to be black with the silver design — but for some reason, last night, decided to try silver polish on it. It's really pretty! I've also cleaned two sets of the little salt and pepper containers. What a job that is! Don't know when I'll get at the other two sets.

Please save the fancy plates and fruit server set for me. Am really attached to all those little doodads — and I use them occasionally too!

Can't think of any other news. Have to get some clothes out of the dryer. Take care, love —
Marcia & Henry

# We Chose Alaska

Feb. 8, 1971

                      Mon. A.M.
                        Feb. 8

Dear Mother & Earl- Just a quickie to go out in tomorrow's mail. Will try to write more for the boat when it comes back through on Thursday.

    Henry went in to Valdez a week ago last Wednesday afternoon to have his leg checked. It has not healed as fast as it should have. The doctor said that he was not getting enough vitamin C— so he gave him some pills to take twice a day— and told him to drink milk. He had already taken the cast off before he ought to or it. would probably still

## 32.

## Tatitlek - The Allusion

The divorce and the aftermath were very amicable. Charlotte, my ex-wife, and Marcia, my present wife, were and are still very special persons. They, from the first meeting—became friends and still are. I guess that's not common—however not impossible.

On a warm and sunny Saturday in April, I was looking out our living room window toward the Narrows. I noticed a small skiff, coming from Valdez rounding the marker buoy and heading for the dock. As the skiff was tied up and the lines secured—out emerged a very impressive figure—an Alaska State Trooper.

You'd think that living in Alaska would make this a common sight. While living in Anchorage, then in Angoon on Admiralty Island, we didn't see any troopers. Anchorage had its own police force. If you

## We Chose Alaska

traveled out of the city you could occasionally see a state trooper in his cruiser.

As he walked up the dock toward the footpath that fronted the village, I lost sight of him. I remember thinking, "I wonder who's in trouble?" Moments later—he was knocking at our door! I imagine the village was all abuzz—wondering what I had done!

I opened the door and said hello to him. "Are you Henry Milette?" Perplexed—I answered, "Yes." "I'm here to serve you with these court papers!" He handed them to me—turned and walked away!

There was a rift between the two parts of our family that came to a head that spring. We had to contact an attorney in Cordova, Alaska. The rest is personal history that had a very rocky road. Not uncommon in most divorces. However, time is a great healer!

Speaking of time, (March 1971) we got a letter from Vernon. He was my "teacher's pet" while in Angoon. He needed us and I guess we needed him at that time. He was like a son to us. He had a rough existence as a half-breed—part Eskimo and part Tlingit Indian. We took him under our wing, in our home life. We hadn't heard from him since leaving Angoon.

# We Chose Alaska

It was just wonderful to hear that his life had changed for the better. He was now living with his mother. This was such good news.

Evidently, he had come to terms with understanding why I had to discipline him in the classroom—shortly before our departure to Tatitlek. That had always bothered me—leaving there with things as they were. He had closed us out.

We loved that unkempt and neglected little guy. I can still vividly, in my mind, picture exactly what he looked like. He always sported that humongous smile that pushed up his chubby little red cheeks—supporting his expressive big dark-brown eyes.

He could have been a poster child for an Eskimo. We bought him winter clothing for Christmas. He gave us two little nutcracker, matchbox tree ornaments. We still hang them on our tree. Every year—he is fondly remembered by both of us.

Another exciting thing happened that spring. It was a welcomed one. Yeah! The Roods wrote and said that they were planning to come to visit us! They now had three children. San Diego must have been really great! I gather they didn't spend too much time watching TV for entertainment! We had missed them.

# We Chose Alaska

Sunday eve.
March 7, 1971

Dear Mother & Earl –

Where does the time go? Less than three months and school will be out for another year.

Sorry that I never did get another letter written for the last mail boat, just not much news.

Thanks for the calendar. Hope business is still good!

Have finished two of my dresses now. Thinks I'll save the blue plaid material and get a different pattern. Still have the pink and the red to do.

We really had a couple days and nights of snow – and now for the past week or so, it's been pretty cold. According to the reports we've heard on the radio, you've had your share of snow again too.

Seems like there's constantly something happening with the Diemer situation (Lorene & Henry & so). We haven't heard one word from the kids since we saw them last summer – and I told you those circumstances – but we've heard plenty from Charlotte, her attorney, etc. Finally, I got a letter in the last mail from attorneys in Anchorage whom they had been saying we owed several thousands of dollars plus interest, etc., etc. etc., a week ago last Wednesday, Henry went into Cordova to see our attorney –

368

# We Chose Alaska

2.

We haven't heard anything from Thor as yet. He said he'd contact us by "Bush Pipe-line" - the radio program - if he needs information in a hurry. He (the lawyer) has offices in Cordova & Anchorage both. We don't know exactly what they're after - but if it's the adoption business Henry has decided to let them go ahead, I guess. He really spent some sleepless nights - but it seems the only way. Of course we still don't know for sure, but that it can be settled pretty soon.

While Henry was away (two days) I had all of the boys in my room. I was a little nervous about it at first - but can see now it would work out pretty well. It was even kind of fun. Since then, Henry's class has been coming in nearly every morning to sing with us. I was afraid the 7th and 8th graders (all boys) might not appreciate our 1st & 2nd grade songs - but they don't even seem to notice.

Am going to have my class make waffles one of these days. We were talking about them one day (they were mentioned in a story we were reading) and most of them didn't know what they were. I brought them into the apartment and showed them the waffle iron. Have been asked several times when we're going to make "them things." It's really good for them. And they love all parts of it - measuring, mixing, and dish washing and wiping bring just as much pleasure as the actual cooking. And of

course eating the finished product is
out of this world — even more so if
it is shared with the big kids (Henry's
class).

Will send you one of the "books" about
teeth that my class made. Will have
to explain a little bit though. Had planned
that it would tell more about proper
brushing, visiting the dentist, good foods,
etc.— but as you can see the red tablets
were the leading title. After we [chewed?]
the kids each [chewed?] one of the tablets,
red stains remain on any place that
they did not brush properly. The
beauty on the middle left hand side of
the cover is none other than your
daughter, drawn by Phyllis Cotemap.
Did you ever notice that I have such
prominent ears?

Am reading Wuthering Heights again —
and really enjoying it. How the English
language has changed since the 1800s!

Henry's working on a pair of mukluks,
a new design. I made a seal skin
decorator pillow this past week. It's the
first that I had used the sewing awl —
kind of fun, but hard on the hands.
You asking about a price for the slippers —
figure about $20.00 a pair. Henry also
made a pair of 9 mittens for Nadine
and slippers for Homer, (the Londagins in
Willy) last week. Guess I won't lose
them though.

> 4.
>
> We finally got a letter from Vernon Mendelook the boy from Angoon (part Aleyot - part Eskimo). He's in Washington living with his mother now and sounds quite happy. We were really thrilled to get the letter!
>
> Have to get a book order ready to go, so will close for now.
>
> Lots of love —
> Marcia & Henry

## Tatitlek - Spring is a Coming!

Spring is a tug of war between warmer days and colder days. You get to treat that time of year as if you were on the exit end of a tunnel. Every day—no matter what—you know that the season is changing for the better. Your spirit is being lifted in tandem with the longer

## We Chose Alaska

days. No complaints as everything comes back to life. Funny thing about 'life', the actual daily living of it—isn't determined by the weather—but by events.

Illene came to see me about a situation that had come about. Our dog Nanook had broken into their rabbit cage and killed a rabbit! She also informed me that it wasn't the first time. Evidently, he had done it sometime in early winter. Wow!—that was not acceptable behavior. We had a problem. What to do about it? This was a very good and gentle dog. All owners believe that about their own. We were no exception. I agonized about what to do.

Where the heck had this come from? Nanook's roots were simple. He was the product of a female husky and what we thought might have been a German shepherd. His mother had been chained to a doghouse in the swamp across from our street—one hundred yards to the right.

In those days, where we lived was quite a distance from the edge of town. He might have had some wolf in him. Who knows?

# We Chose Alaska

Then I remembered an episode that had happened when Bob and I had gone on a goat hunting trip to the Kenai Peninsula.

[I had taken Nanook along with us. We headed south on a Saturday for a day hunt. On the way to Resurrection Pass area, we came upon a large semi-truck hauling a load of domestic sheep. It had gone off of the steep shouldered road and was laying on its side!

We stopped and investigated—nobody was around. It was a very peaceful scene. There didn't seem to be any blood involved in the cab area. The truck was hauling sheep south from Anchorage. The trailer's cargo door had been sprung open, most likely by the torquing motion of the impact—or maybe the driver to save the sheep.

The hills were alive with the sight of grazing sheep. Bob and I decided to investigate further. We headed up the hill toward the sheep with Nanook alongside. Bob and I spotted a big sheep and decided to tie it up. We thought that if the recovery efforts didn't work out—as far as the sheep were concerned—we would come back and see if 'our sheep' was still there.

First we had to go back to the car and get a piece of rope. I completely forgot about Nanook. When Bob and I returned to where

## We Chose Alaska

'our sheep' was last seen, we heard the sound of a sheep in agony—further away! We rushed toward the sound. About fifty yards later—there was Nanook! His jaw had a good bloody grasp around the sheep's throat! I called him off—not soon enough the sheep was in a bad condition. It had been bleeding badly.

Bob and I talked about dispatching it. One very foolish thing was that neither of us had bothered to pick up a gun for protection. This was wild country and it was just a matter of time before the bears would have a field day. They probably wouldn't have recognized the smell of domestic sheep; however, blood is blood.

Now we had a different problem. How to put that sheep out of its misery? No problem for Bob. It wasn't his dog that did it! I hate to see any animal suffer. Even to this day, I never take long shots at game. If I'm going to shoot, it's going to be a kill shot.

I used the only thing at my disposal—my hunting knife. The sheep's condition made the situation urgent! I severed its carotid artery—much to Bob's dismay. "Gee whiz, Henry!"—he spoke out. The sheep was gone in seconds—as I held him steady. I didn't enjoy the task—however I was up to it—the responsibility was mine.

# We Chose Alaska

We hid the dead sheep since we didn't have any room to haul it to town. We only had Bob's VW bug. We planned on going back the next day with a pickup truck. When we did, everything had been cleaned up! The truck and the sheep were all gone—no sign of anything—including our hidden bloody sheep!]

Now with this in my memory—I couldn't overlook the rabbit incidents—I had a responsibility to act properly. In the next few days, a couple of the boys (no need to mention names) were heading for Valdez in a skiff. I approached them and asked if they would take Nanook to town with them. I told them—"Don't bring him back!" They agreed. I watched as they rode out of sight around the bend of the Narrows leading to the Sound.

That was a very rough time for Marcia and me. That night we held each other and cried. He had been an excellent dog. He was our first and only dog. We still think fondly of him.

March was the time in the State Operated School System to put in for transfers if you desired a new school for the coming year. Mr. Greene, our superintendent, informed us that we were able to stay on in Tatitlek. He was

# We Chose Alaska

sending new contracts for us to sign. Great news for us!

We got word that the Roods were coming to visit. Yeah! That was welcomed news for us. Bob wanted to do some seal hunting. We made a trip to Valdez to pick them up.

I mentioned earlier that we had two new Cummins diesel generators, sitting outside of the power plant building, waiting to be installed. In late March, they sent someone to do the job. It was a circus! These guys must have been a special breed. One wondered, when you saw them, how they ever got anything done. Nevertheless, we were getting two new generators and that meant an end to our poor power source. These were magnificent plants—we were very thankful.

The herring started showing up in the bay in huge numbers, accompanied by the usual entourage of sea birds who feed on them. In the Alaska interior, we have snow buntings, small whitish and brown birds, whose flocks swoop and dive in aerial maneuvers as they head north. In the Sound, the herring introduce the coming of spring. Everything comes alive.

> The Roods' visit and Vernon's letter were frosting on the cake—for March.

# We Chose Alaska

Wed. A.M.
March 24

Dear Mother & Earl —

Happy Birthday, Mother. I hope you have a happy day — and am sure you will!

Well, yesterday was mail day — and we got lots of good stuff. 2 letters from you, another one from Lori, one from Marian Strickland, 1 from Kenny's mom, 1 from Vern Menadelook and one from David & Joan Gideon — in California. They were at our wedding reception. You might remember him by his flashy sport shirt with the Trojan horses on it! They wrote at Christmas time and then again to let us know that they were all right after the quake. They're really good people, but we haven't gotten to see them except our first trip down to Calif. from here.

We let school out at noon on last Wednesday and took the skiff into Valdez. Had a good trip - smooth all the way - which I'm always thankful for. The bay right outside Valdez was filled with slush. Henry stayed at the dock while a guy came and worked on our radio (we have a Pearce-Simpson) and I went on to the grocery store to shop for us and for three other families here in the village.

We spent the evening and night with the Londagins. Bob and Ruthanne and the 3 kids and Pierre arrived Thursday morning. We were really loaded down for our trip back - but again, it was

# We Chose Alaska

quite smooth. While they were here, we spent a good part of the time out in the skiff — hunting for seals. We tried to go to Columbia Glacier, but by then Valdez Arm was really rough again. We probably could have gotten there all right — but didn't know whether or not we'd be able to get back. People here in Tatitlek baby-sat the little ones and Robert Clarke just stayed here and played with the kids.

We planned to take them back to Valdez Sunday, but when we got out in the Arm it was wild and wooly again, so we turned around and came back. They stayed then till Monday noon and went back on the ferry. We had Monday off too, so just kind of lounged around. We're wondering if we're becoming hermits. It was wonderful to see the Roods - but just as good to wave goodby. Isn't that awful? Oh well, we'll be thrilled to see them come again, too!

Three guys arrived Thursday to begin work on ~~the~~ putting the new generators in. They've moved them into the rooms now and are doing whatever work has to be done there. Many of the native guys are working too. They're also painting the school (inside) and the apartment. They're going to start the apt. today - so have been bustling around trying to put things away, etc. It's really bedlam, but will be nice to have freshly

## We Chose Alaska

painted rooms!

Am really rushed, so won't get your check in with this letter. The goat skin did arrive yesterday — so think you have sent everything we've asked for. Can't thank you enough. I know how I am about getting things ready to mail, so am particularly thankful!

Want to get this to the P.O. so had better cut it short.

Take care. Write.

Love —

Henry & Marcia

P.S. Got one new student yesterday. Now if we can get one more, we'll have our quota. We also got our contract yesterday. Mr. Greene, our superintendent, says he wants us

~ To stay another year! ☺ ~

# We Chose Alaska

April 4, 1971
P.M.

Dear Mother & Earl—

Another new month. Wow! The last couple of days haven't been very springy though—cloudy, blowy and snowy. The temperature, however, is slowly but surely rising.

Two of my African violets have tiny buds on them. Guess they've been resting up all winter.

Before I forget. When I wrote to Lori, I went into detail about the mail boat, etc. and the fact that the letter to her wouldn't go out until April 9th (she should have the letter already.) You could tell her that one of the men from the village went into Valdez and took the letter with him.

# We Chose Alaska

"Have started on my pink dress. Think this pattern is even easier than the first one I used. Of course working with plain material, rather than plaid, makes quite a difference too.

Have also done a little drawing in the last couple of weeks. Was going to order some frames from Sears, but have decided to wait till we make a trip into Anchorage. (When we were in Valdez last, we couldn't even see our car. It was buried under the snow.)

Can't remember if I told you that the guys came March 18 to begin work – putting in the new generators, painting etc. One of them, apparently the head man was so drunk that he literally couldn't stand up. I will

# We Chose Alaska

he had been heading for here for six days - but had spent those six days in Cordova just boozing it up. Man, he was a mess! One of the others was nearly as bad. He wasn't even supposed to be working out here (they're supposed to use native help from the village only), but must have been drinking with Al (the head guy) and been hired over a bottle of something or other. The third guy, who was out here earlier this year, was okay.

They really got a lot accomplished while they were here though. - they left on the 29th. Six of the native guys worked too. Boy, the new generators have a lot of power. No more worry about overloading them - now

## We Chose Alaska

it's the opposite — Making sure we have enough things on.

The entire inside of the building has been painted. I take that back — all except the closets — most of which are like Fibber McGee's I'm sure. Must say my housekeeping leaves much to be desired! I always like to think that if I weren't working things would be different — but honestly doubt it! Oh well, what's a messy closet, or two, or three?

Have to get to bed. Will write more in the A.M. Good night!

Hi again — but it's P.M. again, rather than A.M. The evenings are starting to come in now, as I spent some time this morning watching all the seagulls,

# We Chose Alaska

5.

cormorants, grebes, etc. while they were "fishing". There was also a crane over on the point that really fascinates me. Today is the second time I've seen it. When it walks, it's almost as though it's in slow motion. All that was about 6 o'clock - by 7 A.M. they had all cleared out. Guess by then there were too many people out and about to suit the birds.

Today Sylvia sent a vest over to me with Rusty (her oldest boy). She knitted it. It's so pretty - red. She's been making them like crazy and I've really admired them. Gee - I was so surprised. What a gal she is!

It really snowed again today. Real wet though - so we're getting some water in our tanks.

# We Chose Alaska

Have my class making paper mache Easter eggs - big ones over balloons. We did them last year too - but don't remember that they were so messy. It sure is fun though (that is, in the eyes of a nut who likes to puddle around with that kind of stuff).

Can't remember now what I owe you money for. If this check isn't enough please!! let me know. Probably one you for some huge item that I've forgotten.

Henry's leg is still swollen after all this time. He has been wearing the Ace bandage again the past week or so, and that seems to help quite a bit.

Not very newsy again this time, I guess. Take care - write.
    Love - Henry & Marcia

## 34.

### Tatitlek - Summer is a Coming!

Spring was always a welcomed season. The temperatures started to warm. You could actually feel the heat of the sun when it shone. It was still too rough to go on outings in our skiff. Easter is a time of celebration. The people are Russian Orthodox and quite religious. The women have a custom of making what is called "Easter bread".

These are elaborately decorated loaves with all sorts of brilliant frostings that are consumed by the family and shared with

# We Chose Alaska

others. Sylvia made a beautiful bread for us loaded with raisins, pineapple, and almonds. There is a virtual baking frenzy—in all the homes in the village. It's not exactly a time to be on a NO SUGAR diet. It is a time of family and church celebration. The breads and colorful eggs are brought to the church—to be blessed. We willingly participated—since we were treated as family.

The celebration started on Saturday, April 18th, with a midnight church service—another one on Sunday morning at ten—we attended both.

The same day, after the church service we went on a day trip to the Columbia Glacier with George and the family. The ride over had large swells—not too rough for his seiner. On the way, before making a right to the entrance of the glacier, we made a left. George wanted to show us a sea lion rookery.

It was quite a large rocky outcrop, covered with many sea lions. Some were swimming apprehensively in the water. Many seemed not to give a darn! It was the largest concentration of sea lions I'd ever seen! We didn't stay too long.

## We Chose Alaska

We headed to the glacier, a short distance away, and anchored. The long swells had caused some nausea due to the constantly slow side to side, rolling motion of the boat. The boys were getting a little queasy.

On the way from the village, Sylvia cooked a delicious chicken dish for our supper. Marcia had brought canned ham, pumpernickel bread, a blueberry and a cherry pie! We weren't going to go hungry! It was a calmer trip back home in the evening—a fun day.

The next day, the herring spawn on kelp beds agenda was in full swing. The whole bay in front of the village, and the dock, were areas of frenzy. It so happened that the right time happened to fall when we had a school day—also a good low tide!

The money is extremely lucrative in harvesting herring roe on kelp. The kelp is sent directly to the Japanese corporation's distribution center. All the necessary work in processing the roe is done in the large temporary building on the village's dock!

Entire families were gathering the kelp in the quickest time possible. There were planes flying overhead that looked for large areas of herring spawning in the kelp beds and relaying

## We Chose Alaska

that information to its supporting boat captain. The individual boats hire their own pilots. There were a lot of boats competing for this lucrative prize.

I saw the writing on the wall—attendance would be minimal—my available students would be collecting herring spawn! "When in Rome, do as the Romans do."

I canceled the morning session for my grade levels! Henry Jr. and I joined in! I took my skiff and borrowed a kelp rake from George and earned over $150 in about 2 1/2 hours. That was a good infusion of cash for us.

The rake was made of rebar. It was shaped like a traditional rake, except the head of it was more massive. A rope was tied to a short piece of rebar rounded into a small circle on the end.

You find a shallow spot where the kelp is covered with herring roe. You can spot it because the whole area is covered with the whitish green roe—you can't miss it. The rake was thrown out over that area and dragged, snagging the kelp. We had a large wooden box in which to put the raked kelp.

When the kelp is harvested, it usually is fastened to a rock on the bottom. When you

# We Chose Alaska

pull it up, it either breaks away or pulls the smaller rocks up along with the kelp. Then you have to cut the kelp away from the rock and return the rock to the bottom where it came from. This allows the kelp to rejuvenate.

The first day of the harvest is the best—it slowly gets harvested out—then it's on to a better spot. You have to harvest the roe before it 'eyes out'. That's when the roe is starting to develop a fetus— it looks like a tiny eyeball! The eyeball look is the first indication—it's time to quit—it's unsaleable.

Besides selling the roe on kelp which we harvested—we also put some up for our own use. It is salted in layers in a five-gallon bucket and stored in a cool place until ready to use. It is an 'excellent' addition to any fish chowder— or a tasty snack heated in butter. The next day we had a full attendance when the school doors opened.

George picked a time of very good weather, when he towed our boat into Cordova for repairs to the damaged hull. It took several months before I went in to get it. Happy days again!

Spring slid into summer vacation. Usually, we'd make plans to travel south during the

## We Chose Alaska

summer months, but due to the strained family relations, we decided to stay in the village. It was nice not to have to deal with changing school locations. We were home.

During the spring I decided that I'd like to build a kayak. It would be easier and far more fuel efficient than our skiff for exploring the nearby bays. In those days there were two types of collapsible kayaks on the market. One day, as I was looking at a magazine, I noticed a small ad showing a picture of a family who had a kayak perched on the luggage rack of their station wagon, (SUV for you youngsters)!

I knew the size of the station wagon, so I just made the transition to figure out the size of the kayak. This gave me close approximate dimensions needed to build my plans.

When I was young, I did some model airplane kits and the technology was the same for a boat. I drew the ribs to support the longitudinal stringers and then covered the whole thing with crepe paper—voila, a plane or a boat!

We had to make a few trips to Anchorage to buy the materials for the kayak's construction. We needed: plywood for the ribs, twelve-foot planks for the stringers (which I'd later saw into one and a half inch strips), aluminum

# We Chose Alaska

window screening to cover the framework and fiberglass cloth and resin to saturate the screen skin.

I had no idea if the screen would be a good base. In fact, I had never done fiber glassing before! I studied how to do it. It was all I could think of that might work. I lucked out—it was perfect. It didn't allow the semi thick resin to saturate through and drip. The visible inside layer of screen stayed neatly shiny—as it should have.

I had a perfect location for the project. Since school was out for the summer, I used the main hallway between the classrooms and the rest of the school building. The hallway was about twelve feet wide and went from the front door all the way to the rear door of the school building, a distance of more than sixty feet.

I improvised from my original drawing because I wanted a double keel at the rear half of the kayak for stability and a transom for mounting a motor. The keel was the trickiest. Doing one keel is basically simple—two is another matter. When all was done the kayak was sturdy and functional.

The fiber glassing shouted inexperience! The finish could have had more work—with the proper tools—which I didn't have. It was

# We Chose Alaska

sufficient. Performance wise—it was a pain to row. However, my 6hp Evinrude motor handled it very well.

My brother Normand, who was retired from the Air Force, came to live with us during the summer. He made it an annual event—winter in California—summer in Tatitlek. It was nice to have him around. The kayak and he became good friends. Normand was in his element. He loved to fish—fish he did!

We heard from the attorney that the case had been dropped—good news! A few weeks later, a request came that we take Henry Jr.—to live with us. Evidently, he became too much to handle. We sent for him.

The news just kept getting better. We got a letter from Marcia's mother that she and Earl (Marcia's stepfather) were flying up for a visit! When they arrived, we were at the Anchorage airport to greet them. We headed directly back to the village. They were impressed by the beauty of the majestic mountains all along the way between Anchorage and Valdez (our home port to Tatitlek).

Henry Jr. had arrived from California by then. We decided to take a day trip in our boat to the Columbia Glacier—just across the Tatitlek Narrows and northward about a half hour from home. The right-side picture below

## We Chose Alaska

is entering toward the glacier from the Sound. Since 1971 the glacier has ablated and regressed greatly to a much further distance than seen in this picture. You were confronted by the glacier as soon as you rounded the point. Hence, the left side picture. All the pictures of this trip were taken by Earl Dunham, Marcia's stepdad.

Entering the Columbia Glacier inlet.

I decided to combine the sight-seeing trip into a real adventure for them. I was going to have them experience a seal hunt! As I said before, seals are plentiful in the waters, in front of the glacier. It wasn't long before we got close enough for a good shot. We then proceeded to a small cove near the glacier to field dress the seal.

I showed Henry Jr. how to dress the seal. I salvaged the organs, pulled the small intestine from the body and made small slits in it about

# We Chose Alaska

every foot. I merely pulled the intestine between my thumb and folded fingers.

The water helped to flush and clean out the intestine. "WHY?" you ask. It is made into a large, braided sausage, boiled in seasoned water and cooled when ready. It makes great lunchmeat. The other delicacy was seal liver. I never liked liver until I ate my first piece of seal liver. Medium rare along with a raw onion is a gourmet item—in my opinion.

In the picture Henry Jr. was doing his job of

# We Chose Alaska

holding the line to the boat. He had improvised. He was cold and instead stood on the line. The bay was very calm—a gorgeous day. I had just pulled out the seal's intestines and was doing the necessary slits for the final cleansing to make sure it was completely void of any matter.

I brought the seal aboard and transported it back to the village where I showed him how to butcher it. Nothing was wasted. We shared the meat with others and I did my usual tanning to make seal skin items.

Next, we took a land camping trip up to the Denali Hwy. with Marcia's parents. It was a total disaster! The road, I mean! After only about sixty miles we decided to stop and fix supper and set up the tents for the night. We had had enough of the rough road treatment in that old rattly van. We called it a day. This is a picture of her mother peering out of the tent in the evening.

## We Chose Alaska

Chuckle, chuckle. What's with the rain bonnet? It must be a girlie thing! The next morning, we ate breakfast and decided to head back to Tatitlek and comfort. Enough of the wilderness—besides the weather changed drastically. A large front would be coming in with heavy rains. We got back to the village—everyone was very happy to have that rustic experience over and finished!

A few days later, we planned their return trip to Anchorage. NOT that easy—it turned out that the heavy rains had caused serious flooding damage and the closure of the road to Anchorage. Earl became very anxious about the whole situation. We thought about our alternatives and Marcia decided to accompany them to Anchorage—by water! If that hadn't

## We Chose Alaska

been an option, there were always flights from Valdez to Anchorage—very costly. The only way there was the ferry between Valdez and Whittier—then the railroad to Anchorage.

This would be the most economical way and they would get to see a lot more of Alaska—very picturesque. It was a win-win situation. Earl was not one bit happy about the situation. You talk about adding anxiety on top of anxiety. He was a nervous wreck on the trip to Valdez from the village and the resulting change in plans. They had a good time; however, they never came to visit again! C'est la vie!

Marcia's & Henry Jr.'s mukluks—I made for Christmas presents. They were very much appreciated during the heavy part of winter. We really had to watch the temperature to make certain that it wouldn't be detrimental to the seal skin leather. Most of the time in Tatitlek was not cold enough for mukluks (Eskimo boots).

# We Chose Alaska

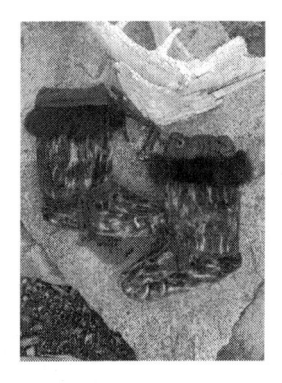

## 35.

### Tatitlek - 2<sup>nd</sup> Year Ahead

Before I write about the second year of teaching in Tatitlek, I need to mention an event that mentally slipped by me before I finished my story. It was early May and the bears hadn't made an appearance from their winter dens.

Marcia and I went on a weekend trip to Fidalgo Bay just southeast of Tatitlek. It was a camping trip and, just in case we'd see a

## We Chose Alaska

bear, we brought our rifles. Port Fidalgo somewhat resembles an upside-down boot. We found a nice, flattened area for our camp site just about where the ankle meets the top of the foot. It was a small rocky outcropping jutting slightly into the bay.

As we looked around the area, we found a nest with five or so goose eggs—more than likely Canada geese. (Never did see the parents, hopefully they returned after we had gone.) While there, we respected the area and stayed well away from the nest.

There isn't much to do when you plant yourself on a rock and just observe the scenery—a very wonderful thing. We could ponder and appreciate the very wonder of being the only two people in that area east of Tatitlek. The main events were meals, sunbathing and looking at the opposite side of the not-so-distant shore for any bears that—hopefully—might show themselves.

Several of our meals were from a seal that had come near us. We were in tune with eating seal liver by then. The hide and the rest of the meat could wait until our return to the village.

Sunday morning, we woke up and started to fix breakfast before heading back later that afternoon. While lazily enjoying the warmth of the morning sun, we spotted a nice sized black bear browsing by a small creek across the bay.

The mode went from enjoying the magnificent peace and solitude, to ecstasy! We changed focus and made our move to approach the bear.

We made our way over in our boat at a very slow speed. We didn't want to spook the bear. We figured that we would land 'downwind' from it with the dingy.

We dropped anchor just a short distance from shore. The closer we got to shore—we saw that we were in luck. A large tree had fallen from the bank toward the shoreline. It had been there for quite some time—the limbs were missing and no bark remained. We didn't realize how much protection it afforded us.

# We Chose Alaska

We started creeping towards the bear. (He couldn't see us nor smell us! = We couldn't see him nor smell him!) The equation was very fluid. He beat us with a better nose and ears!

We crawled toward the creek—very thankful for the downed tree. When we arrived at the tree, we glanced over it to see the bear. It was just about a hundred feet from us and had no clue that we were there! There was a good breeze coming toward us and he was feeding on greens and facing away from us—a great shot angle!

Marcia looked over the tree—slid her rifle into position, took aim—and fired! This was the moment; we were calm and in control. The bear sprung forward for the bushes and trees as if he'd been struck by lightning.

We now had a situation. The wounded bear ran into the woods! The problematic area had to be entered! We listened intently for a while for any sounds that would give his position away.

He was hit. That was certain—we heard nothing! I decided to walk into the brush and follow his tracks into the woods. About twenty-five feet from the edge of the woods—I found him! We dragged him back onto the beach and gutted him.

# We Chose Alaska

The surprising discovery—he still had his anal plug! Not enough food had even been consumed to clean out his large intestine. Having just recently emerged from his winter den— his pelt was prime.

We loaded him onto the dingy and then onto the boat. That seemed so easy—it wasn't! He was a heavy, perfect-sized, medium black bear with an exceptional coat. I was VERY proud of my Marcia—as she was, of her success.

We returned to the village, skinned the bear and hung him in the water room to cure for a few days before butchering him. The hide was frozen for a later processing. I had a boat to build!

Now to move into the beginning of the 1971 school year. We had a houseful. Henry Jr. was with us again and my brother, Normand, had come to spend the fall with us. There was a lot of happiness around.

I started taking Henry Jr. on my trap line. We didn't go very far—just around the corner into Boulder Bay. I was setting some snare traps along a few of the worn animal paths that led onto the beach. They were quite visible and I thought they would provide a good chance at catching an otter.

# We Chose Alaska

Our routine, we made our usual approach—anchored the boat—took the dingy to shore and did our work. I headed to the edge of the beach and made several snare sites.

It was a great day; the weather was nice and the bay was calm. I spent a good amount of time setting the snares while Henry Jr. amused himself doing beach things.

When I figured it was about time to head back to the village—I couldn't find the dingy! I had asked Henry Jr. to bring it up toward the trees when we got out of it. I had been so preoccupied with getting my snares in place that I hadn't noticed just how far from the shore he had taken it. Evidently it wasn't enough! It was my fault. I should have been more alert.

There we were—in October—a few too many feet away from where I would have liked to have been—looking at our anchored boat, some fifty feet from shore! There was no solution but to just wait it out. Marcia would notify George about our 'no show' and he would come looking to see what had happened.

He did and landed his skiff up against the beach. Henry Jr. and I got in and George took us to our boat. We all headed back to the village.

# We Chose Alaska

George, Rusty and I went looking for the dingy, on George's seiner. We located it on his boat's radar, a good clip out from Boulder Bay. I was overwhelmingly happy. No dingy meant no access to the shore for a long period.

The next week, Henry Jr. and I went to check how well we had done with our snares. After having come ashore and pulling the dingy—out of harm—I went to check the snares. As usual, Henry Jr. amused himself on the beach.

We had been there for a short time when I came to the spot where one of my snares had been set. It wasn't there! I searched along the ground for any clue. Nothing—it had disappeared!

All of a sudden, I saw something to my left—a wolverine—snared by the neck hanging from a small tree—as if he'd been caught by a professional! I was stupefied by my own success. The setup worked amazingly well. I didn't touch a thing and hustled over to fetch Henry Jr. to help me look for my snare!

We came to where I had set it and asked, "Where could that snare have gone?" It took him a while—he saw it with a jolt! He had walked almost up to it before he raised his glance. There it was—a snared wolverine—big as life!

# We Chose Alaska

The wolverine is the largest species of the weasel family—more closely resembling a small bear. The wolverine is a ferocious solitary animal—able to kill other animals many times larger than itself.

We got back to the village just before dark and moored the boat. After having landed, I wanted to show George what we had trapped. I went over to his house and entered the Arctic entry—carrying my treasure—in my arms! I was about to knock on the house door when I saw that he had heard me and was coming to see what was going on. I waited and as he touched the doorknob—I sprung my 'friend' up in front of the door's twenty-four-inch square window!

George was caught by surprise—he jumped back! We both had a good laugh. He probably wanted to strangle me. He was very pleased at our success.

Since that seemed like a good trapping spot, I asked George if the next time he went deer hunting he'd save a hide for me. I was motivated by that random success—to change my trapping target. Wolverines are quite difficult and interesting to trap.

The new process yielded one more wolverine before the season was over. I had planted the deer hide in one of the small trees

## We Chose Alaska

near the beach; I placed a trap in a nearby location, under a large spruce tree. It was an appealing spot to place such a trap. It had a lot of protective cover—a rock ledge around it and the tree gave it a 'den like' appeal—the water flanked it to the right.

The following week, I came back to check if I had been successful. I knew exactly where to look—it could be seen from the beach as I landed. There, in the setting described above, was the wolverine!

I pulled the dingy up to the beach, and headed his way—rifle in hand. He saw me coming and his behavior became violently aggressive.

He had cleared an area the length of the chain, in the shape of a perfect half-moon! There was nothing living in that exposed area! I approached him, to place my shot where it wouldn't damage the pelt.

I quietly gave him a chance to calm down a bit; I shot and he dropped swiftly—a good shot!

# We Chose Alaska

Oh, yes, the school!

36.

## Tatitlek - 2$^{nd}$ Year pt-1

We started our second year with a genuine feeling of content with our new home. The State of Alaska had changed its management of the State Operated Schools. Regional Educational Attendance Areas (REAA) were created in 1971.

It shifted us from being an SOS (state operated school) to being governed by an independent, regional school board. As you

# We Chose Alaska

know Tatitlek is in Prince William Sound—some one hundred and forty-four miles to the south of Glennallen, AK!

Glennallen is the nearest town to Tatitlek that isn't a city. It was the regional district created by the state that was closest to Tatitlek. Valdez is only about 24 miles from Tattilek, by water, however it has its own city school system. I was now answering to my new boss, the Superintendent of Glennallen schools.

His name was Max Fancher—a very nice and friendly man with a good sense of how to run his schools. He tried to visit our school early on, but travel to the village during the winter months was at best—'a maybe situation'. He wanted to meet us and also get a feel for the village.

During our discussion when he came there, he asked what we had done and if there was anything needed to help me reach my objectives.

I saw that there was a great need to expose students to the mechanics of motors since it was a fishing community which has a drastic need of good running engines. I also wanted marine charts of their area of the Sound—and basic navigational plotting tools.

# We Chose Alaska

I also had some thoughts on showing them how to make down clothing for the winter. I asked Max if he could get me a few surplus military down sleeping bags from the military base in Anchorage for my project. I had picked up a way to make our own parkas when we first arrived in Anchorage in 1965. (My first job in 1956, after being discharged from the navy, was with Singer Sewing Machines. I had to learn how they worked if I was to be a successful salesman.)

A couple of weeks went by after Max had made his appearance. Much to my surprise, he had an old V-8 engine shipped out to us. We also received the charts, a few basic tools—and some used military sleeping bags! He impressed me with his prompt attention to my request.

We basically had each year's textbooks for all the curriculum levels, grades one through eight. We liked having grades one through four and five through eight in just two classrooms—with a teacher in each one. As far as efficiency, it was perfect.

All students were not on the same level. We could use any books we wanted if they covered the student's level. Another big plus was that it gave me the help of older students—to help the younger ones with their

# We Chose Alaska

work. This made it 'OUR' learning experience. The classrooms were never a problem.

The kids, in the morning, were at the front door of the school way ahead of time and very eager to learn.

We used the charts to plot and navigate between different landmarks that were familiar to them. The charting was a big success. Even the girls got with the program. It provided some fun experiences that everyone enjoyed. One of my fond memories of that particular program was that Rhonda Borodkin, one of my younger students, was good at it. It was a success!

The V-8 engine was also a hit. They were fascinated by the fact that they were going to tear into it—take it apart piece by piece—and find out all about its moving parts.

The down jackets were an independent program that could be done at home. I'm racking my brain to think of the number of students that participated—I think three boys and a girl (close to a third of the class).

They had a lot of fun and did a fantastic job. One of the other big events was the drying and the treating of the hides. This was my bear on the rear deck of the school.

## We Chose Alaska

Gus Vlasoff watched as I was tying the hide on a drying rack. I was glad that I was just starting the stretching process on the bear hide. If I weren't, it would be a very fine example of—what not to do! Gus was totally engrossed in the process. There were many very precious moments spent with the children on weekends.

As a winter project, I developed my sewing skills by taking on several REI hooded jacket

## We Chose Alaska

kits while in Anchorage. When I saw how simple the process was—I made the patterns from the actual material pieces in the kits—before sewing them into a garment. I then branched into making my own jackets for the family.

The picture is of one of the first jackets that I made. We were on an overnight camping trip to our 160 acres in the Matanuska Valley about 75 miles from Anchorage circa 1968.

When we couldn't drive any closer on our road—we had to backpack our supplies to where we would build our overnight shelter. We found a nice clear spot—fifty feet off the road. It would fill the bill. I chopped down some small spruce trees and made braces in the shape of a teepee. I cut off the branches that would be on the inside portion of the wall and made a floor mat with them. They were the 'subfloor' for our ensolite foam sleeping pads.

## We Chose Alaska

We had a small, light-weight Swedish stove made for backpacking. That supplied us with our hot meals and coffee water. The temperatures during the day were in the twenties—nighttime much colder by about fifteen or so degrees. We were prepared for a night of comfortable sleeping. We had REI down sleeping bags that would handle those temperatures easily.

We had packed a meal that just needed reheating for supper—we kept the menu simple. Our cooking plan for breakfast was oatmeal and toast.

Cooking the oatmeal wasn't a problem. Something was missing—we had to liven up the flavor. As we ate, we kept adding pieces of a candy bar to make it taste better. It was a comical situation. We tried to keep things pleasant! We enjoyed our 'roughing it' and camping episode.

The next time that we tried to camp out in the cold—was in our driveway! We slept in the van. The temperatures dropped to minus twenty-five degrees sometime during the night. When we started to notice the discomfort from the cold, we did a 'special ops' maneuver—we got back inside the warm house!

# We Chose Alaska

Oct. 1999—I'm very thankful that Marcia's letters to her mother were saved from our house fire in Glennallen!

> Sept. 2 - a.m.
>
> Dear Mother & Earl-
>
> Well, today will be our second day of school. I had only 7 kids yesterday, but the other 4 came in (in their boats) last evening. Henry will have 14 altogether - so we have enough for another year!
>
> We, naturally, have had some fairly decent weather since you've been gone. We picked and canned 24 jars of mushrooms. Really got the wild mushroom "bug", so we bought a good mushroom book—no more guessing. We canned orange delicious, puffballs and horse mushrooms. Plus we already have a case of commercially canned mushrooms—Guess we can eat them in everything this year. Henry pickled one jar of the orange delicious. Boy, were they good!

# We Chose Alaska

2.

I made some salmonberry jam. It didn't jell properly, but has a good flavor. The ladies here tell me that they are pretty watery. Suppose I should have used more Certo. We've used some on bread & toast. Would be good for pancakes or over ice cream.

Our car broke down when we were out moose hunting. Henry worked on it for about 6 hours — to no avail — so Herman came and got us. We bought over one hundred dollars worth of new parts. Still doesn't run. It's setting at the Gakona Lodge. The mechanic there will work on it and call Herman when it's ready. Don't know when we'll go to get it.

Henry II and I have picked and frozen around 30 cups of blueberries

3.

so far. They're really beautiful now — so big! I made a pie with some ~~yesterday~~ Tuesday — all fresh berries, not mixed with the canned pie filling. Delicious! Surely makes a difference.

Glad you had a good trip home. Hope you've recuperated by now from your vacation! We were so happy that you could come up.

This is a quickie — but have to make the bed, etc. Don't know when this will get out. Anne Jackson isn't here — so they won't bring our mail till she is here.

Love —
Marcia, Henry, Henry II

# We Chose Alaska

1.

Sept. 20, 1971.

Dear Mother & Earl,

So sorry to hear about Helen Thompson. I assume it must have been quite sudden and unexpected. How old are their children?

Had better answer all questions so I don't forget anything.
1. The kind of apples I don't want, are Delicious.
2. Would like you to send the pictures from Aunt Helen - but not the other things. What is the clarinet piece?
3. Still haven't heard that the car is fixed - don't think anyone has worked on it yet!
4. Saw Anne Jackson, Friday. Her finger still looks terrible. It's a bone infection. There's still a chance that she may

# We Chose Alaska

2.

lose it.
  5. Vera, the little gal with
  the bad tooth, lives in Cordova —
  H haven't seen her, but am
  sure she's fine.

The dentist was here last week —
nice guy. He had brought his
own food to cook — but he seemed
so lonely — we had him in
with us for the evening meals.
  Henry II was sick most of
the week. He really acted weird —
a week ago last Thursday and
Friday morning. Henry finally
sent him in to bed during Friday
morning recess. He went back to
school last Thursday. He complained
of ear aches and his glands were
swollen — but guess that was
caused by the mouth
infection. You should have seen

# We Chose Alaska

time. The dentist looked at his mouth and rattled off a name for the disease a mile long. His mouth was all swollen and inflamed – and covered (literally) with canker sores. He couldn't eat – and would barely drink anything – everything hurt him so. But the dentist said that once it started to heal – it healed fast – and thank goodness – it did. He's back to normal now.

Henry shot a black bear a couple of weeks ago – it's pretty fishy though. Tastes like a mild seal!

We went to Valdez over the weekend. Borrowed Maxine and Herman's car (Herman was out moose hunting) and went up the highway to pick cranberries and hunt for rabbits. We couldn't find our good berry-picking

4.

shot, so only got one 3-lb. coffee can full. Did get 12 rabbits and 2 grouse though.

Beans are finally growing on my bean plants! I have them in my classroom now. These kids are familiar with the canned variety, but have never seen them growing — much less tasted a raw one. Tomorrow, we're going to cut up and sample one bean.

Steve and Ellen put their crab pot in last week — so we've had crab meat — delicious!

Made my dress last weekend — with the red material that you sent me last year. It is the best job I've done. Finally figured out what I was doing wrong on the sleeves. Am really pleased with it — looks pretty professional!

Henry made Henry II a down

5.

jacket – like our blue ones. Boy – what a good job he did! Figure there are about $4. worth of material in it (the down came from an old sleeping bag) Henry II really struts around with it!

The nurse comes out this week – weather permitting. The superintendent was supposed to come last week – but didn't show up. Don't know what happened.

My parka came last Friday – with Anne. Had forgotten how huge it looks. Hope we get cold enough weather for me to wear it.

We still don't have all of our groceries – so have to whip a letter off to Ruthanne.

## We Chose Alaska

1.

October 3, 1971

Dear Mother & Earl —

Guess what — it's raining! My two Harrups, Geo. and Rusty Allen and Joe Kompkoff went out to Nidalgo to get some fish and, I think maybe, do a little seal hunting. So I get a chance to get a little work done around here — mainly to mop and wax.

Our superintendent still didn't make it out here. The last we heard, he and a large maintainance crew from Glennallen were coming the 2nd - yesterday. It was blowing and bad boating weather - so presume that's why they didn't make it. Sure will be glad when they do

425

# We Chose Alaska

2.

come, so that we can use our kitchen sink again. Did I tell you that the drain pipe came off completely? We have to do dishes, etc. in the ~~washing~~ laundry sink — a little hard on the back! Thank goodness we at least have that sink though.

Monday me. sure am short on news.

It really blew today. Our orange dinghy floated away — but somebody captured it and put it by the dock.

Sorry for such a short note — but at least you'll know we're okay!

Love,
Marcia, Henry, Henry II

P.S. Got a long, nice letter from Ronnie Spanton a few weeks ago!

# We Chose Alaska

37.

## Tatitlek - 2<sup>nd</sup> Year pt-2

There was a real feeling of belonging and accomplishment that we were experiencing. It made us certain that we had done the right thing in choosing to teach in the Bush. We felt loved and accepted by the families—young and old alike. The children enjoyed school and were doing very well academically. Simply said, "Tatitlek was great!"

Not only was our job a real pleasure, but we also were very involved with recreational events. If you get the feeling that we were happy to be in Tatitlek, you are absolutely correct. We have many precious memories of those days.

The pace and length of the days seemed to slacken quite a bit as winter rolled on. You could see a kind of 'closing in on you' due to the amount of daylight each day lost. The presence of cold and snow increased in its amount, frequency and severity.

# We Chose Alaska

It made you grow as an individual and as a family—either positively or negatively. Teaching in the Bush caused one of two things to happen. Either it gave you a sense of strength, which caused you to grow and enjoy life and overcome difficulties—OR it trounced you into the depths of anger, depression and cumulative misery. Teaching in the Bush was quite capable of doing both.

Basically, the choice was ours! You had to have a positive attitude and live accordingly. If you could master that little sentence—it may not stop a problem caused by someone else. Then again it just might!

I was short on events as winter came creeping in. The pace in winter really slowed. I was lucky to be able to use the skills that had I acquired. As Christmas gifts, I made mukluks, mittens, slippers and small couch pillows with my tanned sealskin hides. Marcia is modeling her mukluks in the picture.

I'm going to use Marcia's letters to help tell you some of our daily events. "Marcia, it's your turn."

# We Chose Alaska

"Please read below."

# We Chose Alaska

1.

Oct. 17, 1971

Dear Mother & Earl —

We didn't expect any mail (the plane, I mean) last Tuesday, or I would have scribbled off a little note to you. He's supposed to come once every two weeks now — you never can tell what will happen around here! Keeps things interesting.

Sounds as though our winter mail delivery - by boat - will be a bit shaky. Guess the guy who is taking the run, doesn't have the proper type of boat for the rough winter travel - and doesn't really know what he's getting himself in for. Think they had trouble getting anyone to take it at all.

2. We didn't have school Friday. A guy from Valley - but formerly from here died Tuesday - they buried him Friday. So they had all kinds of church services - starting at 9:00 a.m. We planned to have school as soon as church was over - but it went on and on and on - till we finally decided just not to have it at all.

Thank you for sending the apples - they didn't arrive yet - but we're surely looking forward to them.

Today we went to one of the islands out here in front of the village. Henry and Joe Kompkoff climbed - hunting for deer - no success - while Henry II and I picked blue-

## We Chose Alaska

3.
berries again. They're still good and we got two 3 lb. coffee cans full in no time. I had hoped to pick cranberries since Ellene Wolmoff told me that there were lots over there — but we didn't see any at all.

Have you had your pictures from your trip up here developed yet. If so, are they good? We got our slides back — there are several good ones — although the lighting could have been better.

Henry made mucklucks for Henry II — nearly finished.

I've been making place mats, papier mache do-dads and those aprons made with paper napkins.

Good night — will write more

tomorrow.

Monday eve.
9:40 P.M.

Just finished some ironing — was in the mood for doing it — which is very rare for me.

Mike (Jug) and Jenny Kompkoff have just recently moved out here to the village. Jug's dad owns the house next to George & Sylvia and that's where they're living. They're both real young — she's only 16 or 17. She came over today to find out about a correspondence course to finish high school. She's really cute. Said she was so pleased to know that there were other white people here — meaning Henry & me. She

# We Chose Alaska

said she's not ~~truly~~ the prejudice, obviously since she's married to an Aleut, but felt funny about being the only white person here.

Probably you've heard about the guy hijacking the plane from Anchorage. Can't believe it. He must be a nut!

We had a duck for supper tonight that Henry shot last Thursday. I roasted it - very tasty. Henry even liked it - not gamey tasting. Last night, we had clams - baked - good! Henry II is the clam digger. He thinks it's a ball - although I think he'd much rather dig them than have to eat them!

## We Chose Alaska

We finally got a letter from the Roods - last mail. We were surely pleased - hadn't heard from them in so long. Of course we hadn't written either. Hope we'll hear from Jackie soon.

Henry & I had stomach flu week before last - really was sick. He's in fine shape again though - thank goodness.

Guess that's it for now. Take care - Write

Love -

Marcia, Henry, Henry II

# We Chose Alaska

October 31, 1971

Dear Mother & Earl -

Happy Halloween! We had our Halloween party at school Friday. We thought it might be fun to have it tonight - but the kids voted this down. Guess they'd rather have a couple of hours off from school - than a whole evening of it! Anyway, it was really fun - with enough food for three times the number of people who were here. Henry II and John Borodkin, Jr. made ice cream. We also had cake, cookies, cupcakes, jello, pudding, juice, Kool-aid, candy and bubble gum. There is lots left over, as they'll finish it with their snacks during school this week.

Guess we'll be on our once-every-two-weeks mail run, by boat, now. Sure hope we get lots of mail this time!

We've been having king crab again lately. Steve Estenoff has had his crab pot out. My two Henrys went with him today, so I have a huge pot from the school kitchen on the stove now - getting the water hot. They got an octopus too - so we're

# We Chose Alaska

2.

going to have that for supper tonight. We've never had it, but understand that it's delicious. Am anxious to try it.

Sylvia finished Henry's sweater with the mountain goat on the back. Gee, it is pretty. She's working on mine now.

We're going to start the Friday evening movies in a couple of weeks. We're going to have to charge more since so few people are here (so many are in Valdez working for Winfeote). I sent a notice around today to see if they'd be willing to pay a $1.00 a person and all but one family agreed to it. Seems pretty high for little kids, but it's the only way we'd be able to show them at all.

Had better write to Henry's mother too — so will close for now.

Take care. Write.

Love —

Henry, Marcia, Henry II

# We Chose Alaska

Nov. 4 - 7:45 P.M.

Hi —
 Just a quickie. Don't think the mail boat came back through yet this morning, ~~so~~ will send this out.

The apples came Tuesday. The bottom layer was a bit bruised - and one really rotten - but boy do they ever taste good! We have been out of any fresh fruits or vegetables for quite a while now, so it makes them all the more delicious.

A quick reply to Christmas. We all need leather ski mittens - black. Henry II's

# We Chose Alaska

can be the same size as mine. That will be <u>plenty</u> plus (of course) the National Geographic, some plum pudding, and fruit cake.

We've had snow three different times now and it's been cold enough for me to wear my wolf parka.

Henry has nearly finished one of my mukluks – so pretty! He used skin from that dark seal that hung on the wall when you were here.

Better run. Take care. Write.

Love,
Marcia, Henry, Henryetta

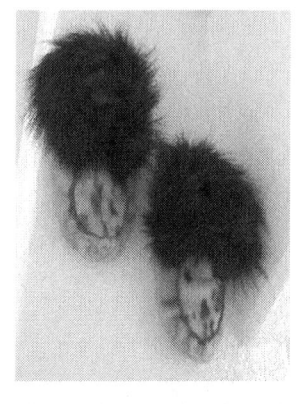

I found a picture of Marcia's mother's slippers which I made. It's a good example of how I occupied my time during the cold months. It was a lot of fun making things with hides that I harvested and tanned.

## 38.

## Tatitlek - 3rd year

In 1971, we were glad to return to our usual routine of being in school. It was a lot of fun when all the kids were so pleasant. Time certainly flew under those conditions. That year, however, we were having a 9th grade class. We weren't graduating anyone! We needed to maintain the necessary enrollment numbers for a two-teacher school. I was so

## We Chose Alaska

focused on 'the school year' that what had happened earlier was forgotten. I have to tell you about my herring story.

Sometime during the herring run, in May when they arrive in large schools to spawn their roe on kelp, I had picked up about a twenty-foot piece of herring net. We had developed a liking for herring starting way back in Angoon.

The usual catch method was with a fishing pole. The line had several triple hooks (about three or four) tied directly to it and a substantial lead weight at the end of the line.

The purpose was not to lure them in. When they were around, they were a very dense mass. You just dropped the line among them and started to jerk the pole upward to snag some. (In snagging, the fish don't bite—you try to hook them.) It was a very successful maneuver.

You could snag a five-gallon bucket full of them in a short time. We made pickled herring with the catch. I used the same method from our skiff. But I guess I wasn't satisfied—I liked to 'always build a better mouse trap'.

I had a net that only needed to be stretched out and anchored in the village's cove, by the pier. The tides are rather large in that part of the world. During the night as the tide rose,

# We Chose Alaska

the floats along the net top did their job. Up went the net—in swam the herring. They tried to force themselves through the mesh that was just big enough for their heads to come through. The effort allowed the net to hold them, just behind the head and gill section—basically trapped them.

I was really excited, in anticipation, about what my maneuver would produce. The next morning, when the tide had regressed sufficiently to expose that part of the beach—I headed down to see what I had caught. When I got to the beach—my eyes just about jumped out of my head! There laid the net stretched out where I had put it—amply filled with this gorgeous silver array of herring!

Suddenly, the stark reality of the situation hit me! "What in the hell am I going to do with all these herring?" I got to work, collected and placed some of my catch in my five-gallon bucket.

Thank God! It became a community project. I offered anyone who came around the same greeting, "Go get a bucket and join in!" Needless to say—it turned out to be a blessing.

Now, to get to work on the gutting and cleaning of the catch. The herring were placed in buckets in layers of salt and fish—then stored for the winter. When we'd want pickled

# We Chose Alaska

herring, we took out what we needed. They were sweetened (soaked in fresh water) until they were ready to be pickled.

During my third year in Tatitlek, I started thinking about the possibility of going into seal hunting as a full-time job! Seal skins were bringing a fairly good price. It had gotten into my blood.

I luckily decided to keep on teaching. It was probably just a touch of the crocodile hunting disease in 1965 that came back to haunt me!

Then the next year, this happened.
[The **Marine Mammal Protection Act** (MMPA) was enacted on October 21, 1972. The MMPA prohibits, with certain exceptions, the "take" of **marine mammals** in U.S. waters and by U.S. citizens on the high seas, and the importation of **marine mammals** and **marine mammal** products into the U.S.]

In all the seal hunting that I've ever done, there was only one seal that I ever regretted shooting. Marcia and I had gone seal hunting in Fidalgo Bay—at one of our favorite little spots. It was well protected and had a great beach for camping. There was a small, protected cove, where we could anchor the

# We Chose Alaska

boat safely—then use our dingy to shuttle twenty feet or so to the beach. We had our tent setup—with a fire pit. The large rocks around the small cove drew in the seals.

One day, I shot a seal (properly, in the back of the head) and took the dingy out to fetch it. When I got it up to the beach, I started to dress it out.

[Field **dressing** is the process of removing the internal organs of hunted game.me, It's a necessary step in preserving meat from **animals** harvested in the wild. Field **dressing** must be done as soon as possible to ensure rapid body heat loss and prevent bacteria from growing on the surface of the carcass.]

Basically, dressing out a seal, (and most animals) you open the abdomen from between the legs, forward of the genitals, up to the bones of the chest cavity. As I did that, I noticed that my seal was pregnant!

WHAT!!! UGH! Oh .... No!

I delivered' the pup, tied off the umbilical cord, and wrapped the pup in a towel—headed for home. The pup had a fluffy light coat of silvery grey hairs. It was magnificent! It was cute. I made a small spot for it near the laundry area.

Remember this was pre-internet days. Not that it would have made a difference. We were

# We Chose Alaska

very remote and would have lacked a proper signal. I had no way to find out exactly what I needed to feed the pup. If I had known, it probably would have lived longer than four days! We did use fish products. It probably just needed its mother's milk. DUH!

In the water—there is no way to tell if a seal is male or female. I would never have shot a pregnant seal. All you get to see of them is a head about the size of a large softball—sticking up out of the water.

Seals manifested a great part of our lives while teaching in State Operated Schools. That is mainly because the villages where we taught were coastal villages. In another part of Alaska, other food sources, such as moose, caribou etc. would have been dominant.

I know that all this killing will not please everyone. Remember where we were. Life was basic in the bush—it was also very beautiful! You're getting a true picture of it—in this book. It is—what it is! It's just a fine line that divides our behaviors.

Just imagine that you don't have any grocery stores where you live! You'd more than likely be trying to feed your family in a wilderness setting. You have to eat. There are only two provisions—either by hunting or by

# We Chose Alaska

paying someone to do your killing! No chasm here—just a fine line!

If I had become a professional seal hunter—my fate would have been sealed! The law provided for only natives to gather mammals—under special conditions. I, who used the 'whole' seal—would not be legal anymore! I felt as if it were a form of discrimination. I'm glad I had the good sense to not make that choice—before this law was imposed!

However, my desire was intense! We could have stayed in Tatitlek—with Marcia as the only teacher! We were leaving because the school enrollment dropped below the student limit for a two-teacher school.

We were looking at it as a brand-new adventure. There would be a lot of pluses for being in a school district situated on a major highway. It involves life 'in a faster lane', so to speak! Everything (Anchorage) had an easier access in order to meet our needs. The biggest factor was the guaranty of continuing employment with an excellent superintendent.

That closed the chapter on the insecure feeling of being unemployed in a few weeks! Glennallen seemed like the magic ring on the carousel!

We only had to 'GO FOR IT'!

It shows that a person doesn't really have total control over his life. Circumstances reign supreme! Divine Intervention pulls the strings!

# We Chose Alaska

Sunday - Nov. 14

Dear Mother & Earl -

We went in to Valdez yesterday morning - got back this afternoon around 4. It was nice to see the Kordaginis again - plus we were able to get some groceries. We had used our last onion Thursday, so we had to get in to town! The travelling weather was good except going in, it was pretty sloppy around Rocky Point.

The Kordaginis have invited us for Thanksgiving, but we're really thinking about going to Anchorage. Of course, the final decision will be the weatherman's! Henry called Bob and they had a long chat. I talked with him for a

# We Chose Alaska

few minutes. They have their duplex up for sale and are buying a house up "in the hill" - south of Anchorage. Or at least the bank is trying to figure out now whether or not to take the risk! They really do need more space - with three little ones - they're feeling very cramped!

Sylvia went (flew) to Seattle a week ago last Wednesday. George had gone down a couple of weeks before that with his boat - to have work done on it. Joe says they should be back next weekend. George wanted her to bring Jeff and leave Rusty and Parker here since they're in school - but she took them anyway.

## We Chose Alaska

3.

People here were so worried about that blast at Amchitka, and she was too, I think.

I sure have been having trouble thinking up things to write lately! Guess as long as you know we're okay – it's sufficient. Won't seal this one till the last minute (before the mail boat comes) – maybe I'll think of something else.

love
Marcia, Henry, Henry II

P.S. Nope.
If I don't get another letter off before Thanksgiving – have a happy one! What are you going to do – go to Mariani's? Richard's?

# We Chose Alaska

November 29, 1971

Dear Mother & Earl,

Well, we spent Thanksgiving here in the village. Uilly Ann was one nothing mess the whole time — from Wednesday afternoon right through to last evening. Didn't do much during our vacation — but it was fun anyway, and I cooked a big Thanksgiving dinner — we had roast chicken with bread stuffing, roast duck with hamburg & pork stuffing (Henry's mother's recipe), baked sweet potatoes, (baked white potato for Henry II), wild cranberry sauce, peas, two kinds of home made rolls, cabbage-gelatin salad, mincemeat and pumpkin pies. We ate by candle light (the little kerosene lamp), used some of those fancy napkins, and topped the meal off with a grasshopper made by the bartender in this family. Really a perfect day!

Yesterday, we had a real good snow storm — much to the delight of Henry II. Henry went out to the brain the black on the boat — and about half the time he was out there, I couldn't even see him — it was snowing so hard.

This morning, just before lunch, Anne Jackson came up to borrow a scale. She and Doria Kempkoff had just delivered a baby boy — which

451

# We Chose Alaska

2.

was supposedly due near the end of December. People have been tramping in and out of that house all day. Don't think that would be too good for a new born baby, but guess it went ok okay. Though he was over there. He says the baby weighs 6 pounds.

Sylvia made me another hat like the blue one — her popcorn stitch. This one is white. She's going to make a hat for Henry also.

Christmas is so near and I haven't even started cards yet! Don't know if I'll get around to making them this year or not.

I finished my shirt and each were to to school last Tuesday. Am very pleased with it. Have a green dress — also a camel colored one cut out — but have to wait for an order from Singer's with thread, zippers, etc. before I can sew them.

(My class had a big Thanksgiving dinner last Tuesday. They did all of the cooking, baking, etc. I had them make white bread, corn bread, cranberry sauce, pie crust and pumpkin pie, bread stuffing, baked potatoes, and stuffed roasted ducks (four of them) and popcorn. We also had juice and creamed corn. They used some of the white bread for cubes for the stuffing. Everything was really

452

# We Chose Alaska

3 delicious. I was a little worried a couple of times when, for instance:

① Phyllis was going to put 9 inches of grease in the pan for the corn bread. The recipe said, "Put grease in a 9-inch square pan."

② Chuckie nearly put ½ cup of ginger in the pumpkin pie filling. The recipe said, "½ teaspoon of ginger."

③ The pie crust makers added "a little bit of flour" by great flourishing handfuls.

We also did some sewing. Each boy sewed an Indian head band which he decorated with "magic markers". They used duck feathers. The girls made Pilgrim hats. They all used muslin for their head gear. There was lots of learning involved—how to thread a needle; how to tie a knot in the thread; how to sew like this ▭▭▭▭ or this ▭▭▭▭ — many of which looked like this: ▭▭▭▭; how long to leave the thread so that you would have room to tie a knot when you finish sewing; etc., etc. They really helped each other too. There was lots of finger pricking and comments of "boys shouldn't be sewing" as they stitched happily along. They were really proud of their accomplishments. Me, too! I

# We Chose Alaska

4. took lots of pictures - sure hope they come out. It was such a success that I think we'll do it again at Christmastime — but we have Henry's class cook too - and will make enough so the whole village can come and eat with us.

Buddy-bye time. Last time, I bualed around with your letter for so long that I missed the mail boat when it came through going to Valdez. Had to wait till it came back through. Will try to get this one over to the P.O. in time tomorrow. Take care. Write.

Love,
Marcia, Henry, Henry III

# We Chose Alaska

December 15, 1971

Dear Mother & Earl—

Boy is it ever snowing — beautiful! We surely will have a white Christmas. It snowed all night, I guess. It's 1:30 in the afternoon now and still at it. (My class is busy с??? writing — so I'm taking advantage of it.)

Got your letter yesterday — but not the Christmas package. We won't have another mail boat before Christmas, but somebody will probably be going in — and we'll pick up the village mail for us.

Am anxious to hear more about Doug. Isn't he in high school? We wouldn't be able to let him come since this school goes only to 8th grade. Do hope you will write what the problem is, what Richard and Dorothy had to say about it, etc.

Yesterday we had a nice day. The Coast Guard cutter "Sedge" invited us — with the school children and a few other adults

# We Chose Alaska

2.

to come out to their ship. They picked us up in a large dinghy - they made two trips from our docks to the ship to carry all of us. We toured the ship - guided and on our own - ; ate a meal with them, and watched a full length movie. The kids had a comedy about the Coast Guard and the adults saw "Cotton Comes to Harlem". Quite a film! - Good. Each child left with a bag filled with candy, cookies, an orange and an apple. Plus they sent three big boxes with Christmas cookies, cakes, fruit, etc. for us and the other villagers. They also brought 30 boxes of books for our library. The captain said that his men had decided that that is what they wanted to do as a being for their Christmas. It certainly was lovely. We went out about 12 noon and got back around 4 in the afternoon - after dark. The kids were really impressed too.

We received several Christmas cards. I

# We Chose Alaska

*3.*

*are sending yours and Richard's together — you'll see why when you get them. You might tell them — they may be late.*

*Want to let Henry II take this over to do so bye for now.*

*Merry Christmas.*
*Love —*
*Marcia, Henry, Henry II*

### 39.

## Tatitlek - The Goodbye

Our third year started as calmly as expected. Everyone was eager to resume village life after a summer of working in the fishing industry. Early fall was a time for many trips to town to get the supplies needed for the winter. This meant food, fuel for the homes (fuel oil) and fuel for the skiffs (gasoline). It was a time of very hard work for all.

## We Chose Alaska

When a boat came in with a load, many people came to help unload. There were always plenty of volunteers around to help each other. Luckily our needs were met by the state, except for our groceries. When we arrived with our shopping, we also were given a much-appreciated hand to help us get the supplies up to the school. Those young men in my 7$^{th}$, 8$^{th}$ and 9th grades were very capable—of happily doing some chores for us.

On the weekend of Oct. 15th, Marcia and I went camping in Fidalgo Bay where we hunted her black bear last year. You can see the location on the map below (2 markers in upper center). It was another gorgeous camping time, very sunny and warm. I shot a seal and we ate the liver for our supper—as usual.

Sunbathing was begging! So, we responded gladly. We were lying on towels to be more comfortable having something between the rock and us!

All of a sudden—we heard a small aircraft coming toward us. Needless to say—Marcia panicked—we were sunbathing! I said, "Don't worry relax. He probably won't spot us!" I think it fell on deaf ears.

# We Chose Alaska

She covered up and was pleased that she had! The plane did a thorough search of the area!

Later that week, we heard on the news that they were searching for U.S. Rep. Nick Begich—whose plane went missing. He and several others in a Cessna 310 had more than likely crashed! When I looked up the exact date so that I could be more specific with my facts,—I was confused.

We were on that rock island on the weekend of the 14th & 15th. His death is recorded as on Oct. 16, 1972. They were searching by plane on a Sunday, the 15$^{th}$. No way would we have been there on the 16th. That was a Monday. And Monday was a school day. The date of death must have been a selected date since nothing was ever found about the crash.

During the winter, a particular weather sequence brought a session of many heavy spells of snowy days. This was followed in late winter with some beautiful clear sunny days.

 One evening after dark—on a full moonlit evening—George and Sylvia and Marcia and I decided to go behind the village for a walk! The snow may have been several feet deep—but it could support our weights easily! Those warm sunny days—followed by cold nightly intervals had developed a super-strong crust of icy snow!

Going for a walk—on such a night, under an immensely bright full moon was really something special—for all four of us. It was as if the landscape were being illuminated by a giant bright light! It was! By the MOON!

Everything that was white (snow) had a bright glow. Then everything encircling that glow was the dark outline of the spruce tree forest that meandered up and down and all around ahead of us. That was one of my most cherished moments!

I don't like how I presented it; I just think that the words fail the immensity of it! I wish I could speak as my heart feels.

In early spring, Max Fancher, the superintendent, arrived and wanted to talk to us about our plans for the coming year! He knew that the school was dropping to a one teacher school and was wondering if we'd be interested in a position at the Glennallen School. He was mainly interested in Marcia—as usual—I went along to do whatever! He knew that my certification was for junior high on up through high school.

However—by then I would have had four years of teaching elementary grades. That is justifiably enough to be used as proof that I

# We Chose Alaska

could do the job proficiently. He was offering Marcia the first-grade class and I'd have the sixth grade class. Thus, the worry about what to do and where to go was no longer the case!

We were facing somewhat of a crisis. If we had chosen another location, we would then be thought of as 'flaky'—always changing schools. Remember that under the old State Operated Schools, they required you to change schools (villages) every three years.

Teaching for the new REAA districts, they would like you to stay forever. Hence, we would be considered as flakes. So going to Glennallen gave us a continuum which would be more favorable on our records.

Sometime in early spring, I had to go to Valdez and tend to business about our new teaching positions in Glennallen. I took our skiff in and had a good trip. After staying overnight at the Londagins—I conducted my business using their home phone.

When I had made my calls and eaten a late lunch, I headed out into Valdez Bay, which usually can be anything but calm. That day it wasn't bad at all. The Narrows also looked calm. The Narrows is, as the name implies, a narrow area of water, pictured below.

# We Chose Alaska

You know that if I'm writing about this—it's got to be quite a memorable time in my life! As I headed out of the Narrows into the Sound's influence the weather started to be a little more hectic.

The wind picked up and I started seeing some choppy water ahead! I continued to hug the coast as I passed the opening to Jack's Bay. About halfway across it—all of a sudden—everything erupted! I was surrounded by a very strong wind and increasing waves! My boat started going up and down the growing swells—the largest that I'd ever seen! I was very familiar with navigating through some

## We Chose Alaska

fairly good-sized ones—these were something entirely different. It was a—you shouldn't even be out in this—moment!

These were a bit more than my experience could handle! All of a sudden, I found myself at the top of a very large swell. The one minor detail that my years of running my own boat had neglected to have me experience— was how to safely steer through such a demon!

I started sailing down into the trench at a slower speed. Usually this allows you to safely go from swell to swell. Not this time! The reason I say it that way is because—I didn't give it a second chance.

I found myself in that trench with the boat leaning rather heavily sideways! I wasn't proceeding to the top as usual. I was in a very bad capsizing position and was being carried up to the top of the next swell.

I came so close. UGH! I quickly figured (thank God) that I had to enter the next downward slope with a more definite counteracting steering. As soon as I crested—I steered hard right, rather than holding it straight. It worked! As I headed into the trench, I was no longer sideways—but straight forward, up the back side of the swell! I was so relieved!

Thankfully—I continued to use that procedure for quite some time. Those

# We Chose Alaska

swells forced me to cut down on my speed. That left MORE time to ponder the situation!

The whole Sound was in an uproar! I could see the breakers hitting the reef that juts around the front of Rocky Point. They were shooting very high above the rocks—into the sky—that was a huge problem! "How do I get to safely go around Rocky Point?" My experience told me—YOU DON'T!

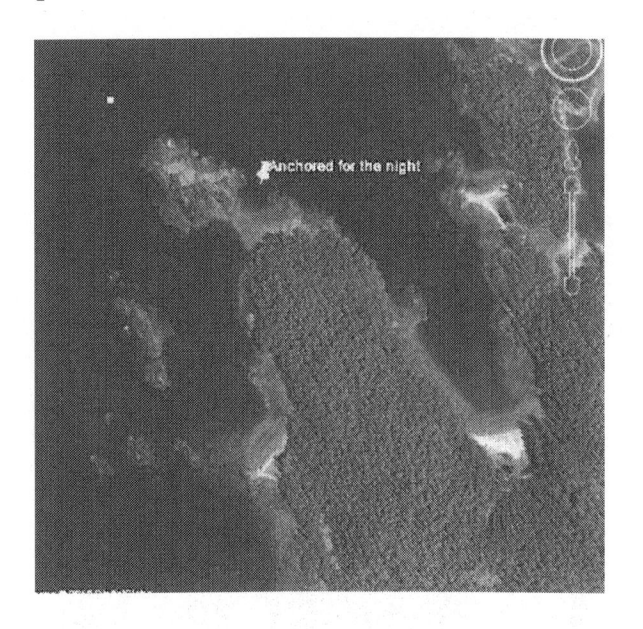

Anchored for the night

Slowly I made it all the way across the entrance to Galena Bay (fairly huge expanse). I found a nice little cove on the east side of Rocky Point that was well protected by the

# We Chose Alaska

shore (above). The waves were showing their anger! No Way—was I going to attempt to round that point! I had had enough of a workout coming the distance that I had. I was tired. (No, BUSHED!)—in no mood to push my luck.

There are times to be in it—and other times—you've got no business being there. If it looks like a no-win situation—don't push your luck—listen to your instinct! That little cove was a very welcomed haven. I was so close— YET so far! I was just minutes from being around the point and into Tatitlek Narrows!

The area to the northwest of my anchorage, is Rocky Point. I anchored to the left of the pin marker on the chart above. I set out my double anchor (a Danforth anchor with a mushroom anchor, tied six feet ahead of it—for extra drag). I really felt secure—it held nicely. It was my standard anchoring procedure when we 'stayed put' for the night.

I went to bed before dark and SLEPT—I truly did! When I woke up in the morning, I could see a small shallow spot—between the boat and Tatitlek Narrows on the back side of Rocky Point, (the narrow section on the chart) that might be passable! The area around Rocky Point was still mayhem! I started the engine—picked up the anchor—headed for

# We Chose Alaska

that spot. As I approached it—it got shallower. I was just creeping along—I could see that the low spot was quite narrow. I thought I'd give it a try! After all—it was an incoming tide and if I got stuck—ran aground—it would only be a temporary situation. I went a bit faster with a spurt of energy—idled the motor—raised the outdrive in order to minimize the boat's draft and held my breath. I felt the boat slide along the bottom, into deeper water—I made it!

I was thrilled when I saw that I had successfully made it through. It was as if I had won the lottery! I have no idea what that feels like—however I could guess. It felt surreal!

It was an easy trip from there, hugging the shore till home. As I looked back—the Sound was still in an uproar! I made it home in good time—to a relieved wife—and late for work! C'est la vie! And I still had mine!

The rest of the school year went smoothly. We cleared out our pantry and gave the food away. We hauled our personal gear into Valdez in our boat. The village was to undergo a huge change for the coming school year—fewer children—smaller enrollment and dropped down to one teacher school. The high school students had to attend school away

# We Chose Alaska

from the village. This meant a relocation for some of the families.

This story deals with the person who replaced us, Max Meeker. He was an excellent teacher and much loved. We went to visit George and Sylvia for a few days—the following year. While there, they invited Max and his family to have a meal with us.

We jumped in—as usual—to help. I served the beverages. These were in large water containers in the kitchen sink. I asked, "Who wants what?" I picked up the grape juice pitcher and poured it for our guest. I thought it was a grape drink of some sort.

There was also a bottle of wine on the counter—which I poured for the rest of us. (I didn't know that the so-called grape—was actually wine!)

As the meal progressed—I noticed that Max got a very perplexed appearance—after having put his glass to his lips! He was stunned! He thought that we were playing a joke on him! He wasn't laughing! When asked what was wrong, he said "This is wine!" Whoops!—I had really screwed up!

Well, as the story unfolded, he realized that I had—accidentally—given him the wine. I would never do that kind of joke to someone with very strong religious beliefs. My feelings

# We Chose Alaska

are—the more who abstain and say "no"—the more for me! ~ It's a win-win situation! ~

I know that our time teaching in Tatitlek was only three years long—however we would have done our entire careers there—if allowed.

We still feel very fortunate to have been able to spend those 'FANTASTIC' three years in Tatitlek! They are some of our fondest memories—a real treasure. We also have lifelong friends and acquaintances, as a result.

Our son Henry II, his wife and their four children moved to Tatitlek after he became a commercial fisherman and had his own boat. They also enjoyed their time and friends while there.

They were going to try and make it—by living on their boat! George—my compassionate friend, was staying in Cordova full time because his children attended school there. He had heard of Henry's intentions! He decided to let Henry Jr. and his wife and four kids move into his house which was unoccupied. They stayed there several years. George saved their butts with his generosity.

~ "Lookout Glennallen, we're heading your way!" ~

# We Chose Alaska

## Epilogue

I didn't have a clue—writing this book was all new to me. The story that I wanted to tell you, seemed to need extra coverage. At first, I was a bit concerned about the size of the project. When I originally started to put the book together, I knew that I had a lot of good stories, which encompassed our lives.

I've learned a lot on this voyage! I had to change the title, to a part one, to reflect the amount of material. I had fun doing this. The increase to another book—part two—is a welcomed task. We've had our problems in what you've seen in part one. I'd like to go on record and say, "You ain't seen nothing, yet!" I know that sentence would cause Shakespeare to flip in his grave! It may not be the only thing that grabs him wrong!

Our experiences in the move to Glennallen—surpassed our expectations. We had lived in Anchorage for four years, prior to working for the Alaska State Operated Schools. We hadn't a clue of what 'life' was going to be like—in temperatures of minus fifty to minus sixty degrees! It's another world.

You might say that some areas of Alaska 'play at winter'! I can tell you that winter in the Glennallen area, is definitely not a game. It can be a very beautiful area—really majestic and alluring. But all the factors you need to kill yourself—will be present during the cold of winter. It is a very wild and unforgiving land—for those ill- prepared.

The rest of the story deals with our experiences, not only with the temperatures—but also the Copper River—where we've lived. We are still living there—after forty-four years! There's got to be something—worthwhile for us to remain here—all those years!

I'm going to do my best to continue to bring life in the wilderness to you—by sharing our stories. Many of our friends have urged me to write our story. We had many tragic memories and have been pushed and jostled aggressively—by Mother Nature and her elements. We've always managed to survive and overcome whatever situation handed to us. As the saying goes, we were given lemons, however we always have managed—to make lemonade!

My Marcia has been with me through all that happened. She is a sweet loving person with an internal strength—to withstand tons of pressure. I have to admit—I sometimes push that to the limit! We rely heavily on each other for love and comfort—so necessary to survive.

We have hope that maintains us through all of our catastrophes—the many we've had. She is my love and my strength. The wonderful moments reign supreme! I'll do my best in presenting them to you—along with the 'not so wonderful' memories!

I've enjoyed writing this book immensely. It is my sincere hope that you can say the same about reading it.

I'm looking forward to working on We Chose Alaska volume 2. See you then.

**www.wechosealaska.com**

Made in the USA
Columbia, SC
27 October 2022